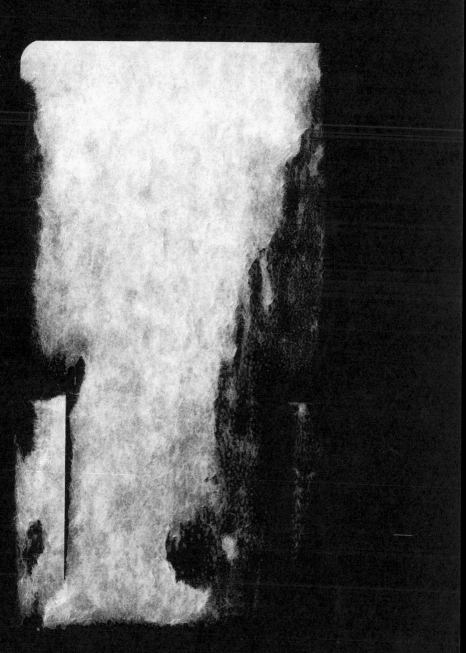

BRIAN JONES

BRIAN JONES

THE INSIDE STORY
OF THE ORIGINAL
ROLLING STONE

NICHOLAS FITZGERALD

G. P. PUTNAM'S SONS
New York

Acknowledgments

For their assistance in the preparation of this book, I am grateful to Bernard Toms, Ellis Amburn, Margaret Cook, and Seymour Harrison. Also, many thanks to my parents.

G. P. Putnam's Sons
Publishers Since 1838
200 Madison Avenue
New York, NY 10016

Library of Congress Cataloging in Publication Data

Fitzgerald, Nicholas.
Brian Jones : the inside story of the
original Rolling Stone.

1. Jones, Brian, d. 1969.   2. Rock musicians—England—
Biography.   I. Title.
ML420.J754F57   1985   784.5'4'00924 [B]   84-26609
ISBN 0-399-13061-6

Printed in the United States 'of America
1   2   3   4   5   6   7   8   9   10

In memory of Brian Jones,
a good friend and a fine musician

CHAPTER

1

J OHN LENNON ONCE TOLD BRIAN EPSTEIN, "The Rolling Stones will break up over Brian Jones' dead body." July 1969 delivered the body.

Brian's girlfriend Suki Potier, who had once gone with my cousin Tara Browne before the car crash that killed him, called me at 8:30 P.M., July 1, 1969, at my apartment in the Chelsea section of London. I was finishing dinner and having a glass of wine with Sara, the girl who lived with me.

Brian until recently had been having a passionate, often stormy affair with Suki, who remained deeply in love with him. There was a great deal of strain in Suki's voice as she said, "Nicholas, when did you last see Brian?"

"Last week. He was here in London. Why, Suki?"

"I'm very worried about him. Something's going on. He's called me three times. Thinks he's in some kind of danger. Says he's being watched. Followed even. What's wrong, Nicholas? D'you know anything?" This sounded like one of Brian's bouts of paranoia; I tried to calm Suki.

"When he called me this morning, he seemed quite cheerful."

"He's all right in the daytime," Suki said, "when Mrs. Hallett's there. It's in the evenings when she's gone that he calls."

"Come on, Suki. You know as well as anybody that he likes making mountains out of molehills. In town last week I thought he looked more relaxed than he's been for years."

"I'm still worried about him. I don't like the kind of people he's been hanging around with down there at the farmhouse. What d'you know about the girl who's moved in?"

With anybody else but Suki, I would have jumped to the obvious conclusion: green-eyed jealousy. But boys and girls involved in relationships with the Stones and the crowd that floated on their fringe were well aware of the limited rights of proprietorship that sex bestowed. Suki knew that loving Brian gave her no rights at all. This was the Swinging Sixties and these were the Rolling Stones, iconoclasts and rebels, beating the hell out of the end of a decade of sexual revolution.

I told Suki I had met Brian's girl only a few times and didn't know a lot about her. "At least," I added, "she can keep an eye on the hired help."

"I really am worried to death. Go to Cotchford Farm and see; don't tell him you're coming. Just see if everything's all right. Just to put my mind at rest. I can't go myself for obvious reasons. We'll just get back to square one, and that won't solve anything."

In the end I promised to think about it and call her back. I hung up, convinced that Suki Potier, normally a lively and lovely young girl with a relatively stable temperament, was allowing her affection for Brian to take over her senses.

I had been seeing Brian Jones for about four years and we had become intimate friends. Brian would call me on the telephone at all hours of the day and night from places as far apart as New York and Hong Kong to tell me his problems. When he was happy and feeling secure I might not hear from him for weeks. He was the only person I have ever known who could reduce me to tears on the telephone; he could sound so desperately sad and lonely.

He was also paranoid. It was not unusual for him to call from a booth and announce, "All my phones are being bugged."

I was astonished that a man in his position—a star, if not the star, of a group whose world fame was only matched by that of the

Beatles—could be in actual danger. Brian was six years my senior. As a member of the Guinness family, brewers of fine stout for centuries, I was a financially independent young man-about-town. I had nothing much to do and a whole lot of time to do it in, but I was ill-equipped to deal with the world of intrigue and in-fighting that surrounds rock stars.

Being Brian's friend was virtually a full-time job. You either loved Brian Jones or found him intolerable. He could be thoughtful or selfish, kind or cruel. His mood swings went from black to white with nothing in between. Nothing was ever simple. When he fell in love he agonized over every development in the relationship. He was a guilt-ridden soul, a condition which had been exacerbated by drugs and booze, although he was not now hitting these as hard as the press claimed.

Brian's paranoia had alienated him from many former friends like John Lennon, who during 1967 and 1968 avoided his phone calls because he knew they meant trouble. Brian couldn't seem to comprehend that other people had their own problems, and when they hinted as much he was hurt, assuming they didn't care about him. Perhaps it was just as well that he knew he could depend on me and his succession of girlfriends.

That night I tried to relax with my own girlfriend and forget about Suki's call, but every now and then Brian would spring to mind. At 11 P.M. I decided to dial his number. My girl went to bed, no doubt feeling neglected.

Normally someone at Brian's would snatch up the phone in seconds, but this time the phone rang interminably before it was picked up and promptly put aside without a word spoken. I called several times afterward, only to hear the busy signal.

Now *I* was worried. I decided to drive to Brian's farm the following morning. Suki, when I called her with the news—omitting to tell her about the odd incident that had made up my mind—was delighted.

At 10:30 A.M. I awoke to the sound of the phone. A rough voice growled, "Nicholas Fitzgerald? My name's Ralph Hampton. I live near Hartfield. Last night I bumped into Brian Jones outside the

Hay Waggon. He gave me a pound and asked me to call you, tell you to call him this morning and keep calling till you get him. It's very important. Got it?"

Before I could reply, he hung up. It would be useless to call Brian this time of day because he always slept late. I'd call from Hartfield.

At 11 A.M. Richard Cadbury turned up at my apartment. He was a nineteen-year-old student who did odd jobs for me, including chauffeuring. I asked him to drive me to Brian's farmhouse. With Richard along, I felt safer. I invited my girlfriend to come along, but she refused, sensing a crisis. At eleven-thirty we set off for Sussex.

On the journey I turned over in my mind the facts Brian had given me about the breakup of the Rolling Stones. It was only during the previous week, at my place in Cheyne Court, that Brian had poured out his heart. During the last weekend in May, Brian had received an unexpected visit at Cotchford from Mick Jagger, Keith Richard and Charlie Watts, who told him they wanted him to leave the group. This was because two drug cases had been brought against Brian, and U.S. Immigration would certainly turn down his work permit for the upcoming Stones' tour of the States, their sixth, and that it would be better if he left now rather than create a fuss in the press when he was refused entry.

Brian saw their point and reluctantly agreed to leave. He was understandably very bitter. He had founded the Rolling Stones, given the group its distinctive name and character, and promoted them to fame. If it had not been for Brian, there simply would never have been any Rolling Stones.

Before Mick, Keith, and Charlie went to Cotchford Farm, they consulted with Allen Klein, their manager in London, and agreed on an offer to be made to Brian. It sounded generous. As far as the press and the fans were concerned, Brian would resign primarily to allow the Stones to carry out the U.S. tour. It would be announced as a temporary absence to allow Brian to work on solo projects such as his *Jajouka* album. In addition to royalties from past Stones albums and singles, he would be paid approximately $250,000 per year for as long as the Stones stayed together. If he wanted to rejoin at some future date, they would be agreeable. They did not fire him. They were not legally able to do that, but Brian felt that this was going to be the end, that they were in the process of squeezing him out. To me he confided that behind it all he sensed the hand of Jagger, his rival for attention and adoration.

RICHARD CADBURY AND I arrived in Hartfield at 1:30 P.M. We decided to have lunch and a beer at the Hay Waggon, from where I could telephone Brian.

Shortly after we arrived in the old pub, Brian Jones walked in. He was with a young man who looked like a construction worker. I had never seen him before.

Brian seemed vexed at seeing me and snapped, "What are you doing here?"

"It's a nice day," I said airily. "D'you mind?"

His manner altered, and he smiled. The construction worker bought him a glass of wine.

There was still a lot of tension in the air, and I commented, "Didn't think you drank at lunchtime."

"Just came down to use the phone," Brian said. "Mustn't be away from the house long."

He took a look around the bar and greeted some of the locals, who seemed fond of him. Since moving to Cotchford, he played two distinct roles. In one he was the pop star jet-setter; in the other, a country squire sharing a drink with honest men of toil. He had even applied to join the local cricket club.

Cotchford seemed good for him. He'd managed to kick drugs (except for the Valium he took for his asthma), no mean accomplishment in view of his addictive nature.

As if sensing my thoughts, Brian said, leaning on the bar, "I'm a boozer again. I often bomb down here on my motorcycle and down a few beers with the boys. They're *real* people, Nicholas, not the junkies in London, ripping you off, pushing strychnine for coke."

I went to the john and, just as I was zipping up, Brian appeared at the next urinal.

"I've got to talk to you somewhere away from everyone," he said.

"What's the matter?"

"Not here," he said, peering over his shoulder at the door. "I'm being followed, watched. I've got to get rid of some of the gang. Christ, they're taking me over. It's as if I work for *them*. But there's someone behind them, telling them to watch me. There's got to be. Can you help me?" He looked vulnerable, wretched. I was furious that someone had worked him into this state.

"Who's the guy with you?" I asked.

"One of the bunch hanging out at the farm." Brian said that the Stones' management had employed a man to do a $25,000 renovation job on Cotchford Farm. This character had been hanging around there so long with his men that he seemed to have taken up residence. Brian was sure the office had hired them as henchmen as well.

He now proceeded to tell me, standing at the urinals in the Hay Waggon, about how he had sent a servant to buy furniture some weeks ago and afterward had discovered that the man had bought two sets of everything—keeping one of each for himself. Brian confronted him and was advised not to be so petty. Employed by the Rolling Stone office, he had been Keith Richard's chauffeur and bodyguard, using combat techniques learned in the army, but after they fell out over Keith's allegation that he was ripping him off, he took over the same duties for Brian Jones. He had been very much against Anna Wohlin moving into Cotchford, which struck me as suspicious. I asked Brian why he didn't fire this servant.

"I don't employ the bloody man, Nicholas. The office employs him like a jailer." He took hold of my arm, using real force. "Some days they hide my motorcycle. When I'm on the phone, the line will suddenly go dead. Then when I get the engineers in, they say there's nothing wrong. They're always leaping up to answer the phone and then they tell me it was a wrong number. I just can't trust anybody. I know you think I'm paranoid. Maybe I am, but not about this. I know they're up to something. They're treating me badly, and I know how much they're ripping me off *for*. Christ, Nicholas, it's like one of those bad movies, where everybody's trying to convince a guy he's bananas." He seemed to hear a noise then. He let my arm go and glanced around nervously, but no one was there.

I recalled my attempted telephone calls to Cotchford last night. It was seeping into my mind that Brian really was in some kind of danger. He looked terrible now, though stone-cold sober. He was haggard and drawn, and his eyes were like a hunted animal's.

"We'd better go back," Brian said. "But I want to talk some more at the house. Please stay with me tonight, Nicholas. Just to hold me."

When we got back to the bar, the workman who had come in with Brian was gone. My friend Richard, who had been reading a book, hadn't seen him go. His unfinished beer was on the bar. Brian looked panic-stricken.

"We'll have to get back quick. If they know I'm missing, there'll be hell to pay."

We left and took him in my custom-built Mini-Cooper to Cotchford.

Brian Jones had bought Cotchford Farm in 1968 for $75,000. In this sixteenth-century farmhouse—once reputedly occupied by William the Conqueror—A. A. Milne wrote *Winnie-the-Pooh*. Ironically, the gardens were maintained as a shrine to childhood with right of access in perpetuity to the Winnie-the-Pooh Society. A sundial with carved figures of Eeyore, Pooh and Piglet stood in the center of a manicured lawn. Marooned among clusters of roses stood a life-size statue of Christopher Robin.

The farmhouse lay well off the highway from Hartfield on the edge of Ashdown Forest, and was reached by a private road through the grounds, which extended to eleven acres. The house was built of red brick, and its roof tiles were weathered and mossed to a solid green. The inside had been renovated and modernized in opulent style. There were six big bedrooms and three magnificent bathrooms upstairs. At the side of the house was Brian's swimming pool. He would die in it that night.

Having been hounded and threatened and even physically assaulted, I have only now attained the necessary retreat from the rock world to tell exactly what happened on that tragic night.

As we approached Cotchford, I asked Brian whether he had received the $250,000 he had been promised for the first year. He said he hadn't and proceeded to tell me that he was almost broke, living on credit. This seemed ridiculous to me, and I told him so. He then went on to explain that all the money he had earned had been invested in the U.S., where he had spent a lot of time. It would be difficult to shake any of it loose.

On my last visit to Cotchford, when Brian had still been a member of the Rolling Stones, he had told me that he had between sixty and seventy-five thousand dollars hidden around the house as well as some fifteen thousand dollars in Swiss francs. He had not been under any pressure to pay bills; most of that was done by the Stones' management, who also paid the servants in cash. And all drugs he had ever bought had been paid for in cash. But when I asked Brian now what had become of the rest of the cash, he simply shrugged and said, "Gone. Ripped off."

As we turned off Maresfield Road into Brian's property, he said, "Park here. Don't go down the drive. I don't want the help to know you're here."

We got out of the car in silence and, instead of walking down the drive, the logical thing to do, we approached the house and the pool by passing through a copse. A couple of youths were fiddling with one of the two spotlights above the pool. They didn't appear to see us. It did not occur to me to ask at the time, as it would later, why spotlights should be stationed above a swimming pool.

Apart from a gardener who was working some way off, there was nobody else around. It was very peaceful and beautiful there that warm summer day, and I could understand why Brian loved the place and why, before that, A. A. Milne had found inspiration at

Cotchford Farm. The house blended harmoniously into very English scenery—trees, shrubbery, and rolling fields. Birds chirped
lazily and bees were buzzing among the flowers.

Yet, as we approached the house, I was overcome with foreboding. It might have been brought on by the sight of Brian, walking a
little ahead of us, still handsome but a nervous wreck, that stirred
this uneasiness in me. I knew he was in danger and that the peace
and beauty around him were a snare.

We went around to the other side of the house away from the
pool. Brian asked us to sit down on some garden furniture outside
while he went in to see who was there. After a while, when Brian
still hadn't returned, Richard Cadbury got up and strolled off into
the shrubbery. I was left to my own thoughts and misgivings.

Suddenly I felt an attack of asthma threatening to come on. The
pollen count was high, 124. On the previous day, it had soared to
its highest that summer—355. Asthma was one of the many things
that Brian and I had in common. We both carried Ventolin inhalers
and both took Valium—prescribed—to relieve the symptoms.

I had never seen Brian have a serious asthma attack, but then you
didn't have problems if you had an inhaler—and Brian used his a
lot. His father had told me that as a child Brian had been subject to
very severe attacks but seemed to "have grown out of the worst of
it."

I began to wonder where everyone had gone, especially the
servants and hangers-on. On my last visit there had been people
lounging about, helping themselves to Brian's involuntary hospitality, wandering around half-naked on the lawns or by the pool as
if they owned the place. Now there was no sign of any of them.

Eventually Brian emerged carrying a bottle of chilled wine, a box
of biscuits and some glasses. We settled down to chat and he
seemed more at ease. I decided it would be best not to inquire about
the rest of the household in case it might upset him again.

I asked if he intended going to the Stones' free concert in Hyde
Park on the following Saturday. He said cynically that Mick Jagger
had persuaded Keith, Charlie and one or two others to ask him to
attend.

"The bastard wouldn't ask me himself, though. He's worried about what the fans will think—about my dropping out. They'll think I've been conned. He doesn't think they can make it without me.

"D'you know what Keith suggested, Nicholas? Bloody cheek. He said maybe I could 'guest' on a few numbers with the group—just to show there's no hard feelings. Guest with my bloody own group, eh? I told them they could stuff it."

He had been slowly working himself into a state of anguish again, but now he sighed and took a sip of wine. "No, I told Keith I won't be rejoining the Stones. Not ever. They offered to keep my place open for me. Bloody big of them! But I don't want it. It would just hang over my head, an excuse not to do any work. No, I just want to get on with my own new band and it's going to be bigger than anything—*ever*."

"Bigger than the Stones?"

"Much bigger. We won't be turning out the kind of commercial crap they're into now. Give me a couple of months and we'll have the best band in the world." His even-featured face, as he sat back, relaxing at last, reminded me of Suki's. When the two of them had been together, playing childish games, dressing up in each other's clothes, they could have been twins. They were a beautiful pair.

And now here he was, this intelligent and attractive misfit/tortured rebel/musical genius, talking about starting again from scratch, having left the great money-making monster he had created to the less tender, less talented care of its other members. And yet at that moment, I believed in him, I believed he could do it.

In fact, I don't think there would have been anything to stop him now that—musically at least—he had found his individuality. Brian had been having long sessions both of talk and music with other gifted musicians such as Alexis Korner, John Mayall, Micky Waller and Mitch Mitchell, Denny Lane and Jimi Hendrix. They had all spent many hours with Brian at Cotchford.

Suddenly a window slammed shut somewhere in the house. Startled, I asked, "What was that?"

"It's probably Anna," Brian said, unconcerned. "Where's your friend Richard gone?"

"Just taking a little walk somewhere."

"I like to know where people are when they're on my property," ha said pompously. Then he seemed to catch himself and grinned, continuing his observations on music and his ambitions. He wanted to get back to the first kind of sounds that had moved him as a boy—the blues. He also felt inspired by Creedence Clearwater Revival.

A car engine revved nearby, but as Brian didn't appear perturbed, I ignored it. In retrospect, though, it was odd that he should have been nervous about Richard walking around his property while paying no attention to the engine.

We talked about the LP **Beggar's Banquet** He said the only track he liked was "Stray Cat Blues."

"The band I'm forming," he said, his eyes lighting up at the thought, "will play a combination of trad jazz, rhythm and blues, gospel and Moroccan music. A bit of a mixture. But it will work; I know it will. And I've learned the sax—soprano sax. Play it Sidney Bechet style. I'll play you some tapes later. You'll like it."

Brian looked up as two men came walking past. They were perhaps in their thirties, scruffily dressed and with longish hair. One was carrying a guitar case. They passed within a few yards of us without speaking to us or even acknowledging our existence.

Brian eyed them sullenly. "More of the help's henchmen," he growled. "What the hell are they up to now? If they have their girlfriends staying here tonight, I'll throw them all out tomorrow. It's only a small town. People will talk." He got up. "I'm going to see what's going on, Nicholas. Help yourself to more wine." He disappeared into the house.

The Valium I had swallowed that morning, combined with the wine and the warm summer air, began to make me drowsy, and after a while I stretched out on the grass and dozed off.

I was awakened by the noise of an engine—either a car or a truck. My watch indicated six o'clock. The sun was no longer shining on that part of the garden, now shadowed by the shrubbery. I felt cold. There was nobody in sight, but I heard music coming from the other side of the house. I got up and went around, discovering Richard and Brian looking at the two new spotlights that had just been fitted. The expression on Brian's face told me that his earlier calm had left him. He was puzzled and anxious.

Seeing me, he said, "I don't know why the servants think it's so important to have two spotlights. They've been tinkering about here all day with them. What do they want two spotlights for?"

Then he looked down into the pool and pointed out the new colors that had been painted on the floor and sides. This again seemed to calm him. He was more mercurial in his moods than ever that day.

"Look, Nicholas, at last I've managed to get the combination right. It's the color of the sea on the coast of Morocco. I fell in love with that color over there."

Nothing I could have said would have soothed the hurt that the memory of what had happened in Morocco must have been stirring in him. The memory of losing his gorgeous Anita Pallenberg to Keith Richard.

Anita Pallenberg had been the deepest and truest love of Brian's life, though he could no more have become monogamous for her than a child in a chocolate factory could confine himself to one candy. When she broke with him in favor of his best friend in the group, the effect was devastating. It probably did more than anything to plunge him into addiction and into a series of chaotic affairs with other women.

We retired to Brian's plush ground-floor studio and listened to his tapes. Around the wall and standing on the blue carpet was part of his collection of some fifty rare musical instruments. One sitar alone had cost him $15,000.

As I listened to a tape of Brian's rehearsals with other noted musicians, I saw a blond girl pass by the French windows. I barely had time to register that she had long hair, long legs and full breasts. And she wore shades over her eyes. I automatically assumed she was Anna Wohlin and that she would come in and join us. But she passed out of sight.

Brian hadn't noticed. He was listening intently, and the fading light from the windows caught his profile, emphasizing the lines of care on his face. In spite of what he said, it was clear that his past rejections—by his mother, by Anita, and finally by his own creation, the Stones—had hit him very hard. This picture of him is the one which, because of what happened later, will always remain in my mind: a helpless boy who had scarcely reached maturity and yet had experienced phenomenal success as well as unendurable despair. As I looked at him with his head tilted back as if in final defiance of a world that had showered him with wealth and yet left him so alone, I felt tears coming to my eyes, quickened by the pathos in the music.

It was while Richard was out of the room that Brian suddenly switched off the tape, turned anxiously to me and said, "Nicholas, I'm bloody scared. Scared out of my mind that they'll try to stop me." He darted over to the French windows and closed them. Then he perched on the side of my chair and put his arm on my shoulder.

"Who will try to stop you?" I asked.

He ignored this. "They know I'm in a position to start this new band. They know it could knock the Stones out of the charts. It's my name and the fans will know it's me. It'll be bigger than the Stones. I've done it once and I can do it again."

On the tapes he'd been playing, we had heard Brian and John Lennon, Brian and Jimi Hendrix. Since he'd left the Stones he'd been approached by many big names, asking him to play on their records or produce them.

But he was off on another track now. "Things keep disappearing around here. Last week I spent over twenty hours working on a tape and now I can't find it. Other things keep turning up missing. Even a bloody motorcycle. How d'you mislay a motorcycle? I'm not that bad, I know where I put things. People are trying to make out that I don't. I'm not mad, I know what I'm bloody doing."

"For Christ's sake, calm down," I told him. He was on the verge of hysteria. I stroked the back of his hand; on other occasions this had calmed him. "Take it easy. Listen, when you called me on Monday you said something about lights in the garden at night. What did you mean?"

"Yes," he said, his voice low, his eyes glazed. "I heard some sort of noise in the night. I got up. You know I don't draw the curtains. I looked out. There were two colored lights flashing on and off out in the trees."

"Were you stoned?"

"I'd had a few. I wasn't stoned, though."

Brian went off to answer the phone, and I tried to judge how much fact and how much fantasy were contained in his complaints. When I had first come to know Brian in 1965 he wouldn't go out of doors until after dark because he believed someone was out to harm him—someone in the U.S. and someone in London. He told me Bob Dylan had warned him that there was a contract out on his life. I didn't know what to make of that, but I do know that Dylan wrote "Ballad of a Thin Man" about his fears for Brian's safety. The famous line about something wrong going on and Mr. Jones not knowing what it is used to frighten Brian every time he heard it. He was always influenced by what Dylan said and regarded him as something of a guru.

Brian reappeared after a minute or so.

"It was a chick called Luciana. She's at Haywards Heath station. Wants picking up."

"Who?" I asked.

"Luciana Martinez Delarosa." He read this from a scrap of paper he was holding. "That's a lot of noise to go to bed with. She's come to stay for a couple of days. God knows what my girlfriend's going to say. Something pretty damn crude, I guess."

"Who the hell *is* she?"

"I guess I met her in London."

"You guess? Weren't you expecting her?"

"Well, not exactly. You know how it is. You have a few beers and meet a pretty chick. Ask 'em down. Most don't turn up, or get lost, or get turned away by the guards. I'd better call a cab for the kid."

Richard came in from somewhere and I volunteered to pick up the girl. "What does she look like?" I said.

He shrugged. "Sounds Spanish."

"Does she *look* Spanish? You do know what she looks like." He looked sheepish.

"She'll be in the lounge bar of the Hayworth Hotel. Ask at reception."

I was preparing to leave via the French doors when I saw two men again fiddling with the spotlights at the pool. I pointed them out to Brian and he came to the window and froze there, glaring at them.

"What the hell are they up to?" he said quietly. "They should have knocked off work at six. I'm fed up with this. I don't trust them. I'll have another go tomorrow to get the whole mob out of here. I want Spanish Tony instead. I want him here to look out for me."

"Spanish Tony" was Tony Sanchez. He was chauffeur and bodyguard to Keith Richard—and, much later, author of a bestseller entitled *Up and Down with the Rolling Stones*.

But Brian Jones was to die that night.

On July 24, 1965, I met and fell in love with Brian Jones. I was seventeen years old, living with my parents, and I had taken my girlfriend Marilyn to an elegant party in Royal Leamington Spa. In the middle of it Brian made his entrance.

The well-bred guests stood in shocked silence. This was the first time any of us had encountered one of the Rolling Stones—infamous, long-haired, South London yobs who urinated on garage walls and got taken to court for it. Brian was wearing a pink and blue blazer, yellow pants, and blue shoes. Under his arm he carried a stack of LP records. The hostess, Binky, introduced him as "Brian Jones from Cheltenham." Cheltenham is the embodiment of all that is genteel and respectable, home of the cucumber sandwich. One of the guests whispered to me, "Looks more like he'd come from some festering slum of a council estate to me."

My date, Marilyn, was gushing over Brian, telling him he was better-looking than his photographs. He thanked her with a grin. Conceited, I thought, though I was nonetheless impressed. Brian looked at me and said that my cousin Tara Browne was one of his closest friends. I was surprised by the refinement of his accent, not unlike my own public-school drawl—nothing like the ugly, patronizing whine of Mick Jagger.

Marilyn suddenly lost control and started squealing like a fan.

Sensing my anger, Brian said, "It's all right, I have that effect on women." He gave me a hot look, clearly implying, "and men, too." I started to look away but didn't. His steady, caressing gaze was arousing me. It was the kind of rush that, until then, I had associated only with desire for a woman's body. He looked almost exactly like Marianne Faithfull, whose pictures I had seen in newspapers, and it occurred to me now that she and Brian could be twins. It was the face of a beautiful woman; yet Brian was macho enough. Marianne was utterly feminine, Brian the masculine version of her blond, symmetrically featured type. I felt the unmistakable stirrings of an erection, quite a shock in those preliberation days, especially to a Roman Catholic boy.

Brian asked Binky if he could play the records he'd brought back from L.A. Most of the animosity had melted away by now, and everyone was watching Brian as he announced the numbers, chatting to the people near him while his music filled the room.

"What are *you* thinking?" Marilyn asked, looking at my erection. I cursed the mandarins of fashion who had decreed that trousers be tight that year.

Offering me a joint, Binky said, "Here—maybe this will calm you down." Crossing the room to get another drink, Brian accidentally collided with a dancing couple. The guy turned aggressive and snapped a nasty remark. I didn't hear exactly what was said, but there was some reference to the pissing incident. Brian stopped dead in his tracks and stared the man full in the face. Everyone in the room fell silent, and there was an air of expectant tension as the two faced one another, the girl behind her man. The music continued to beat out, but nobody was listening now.

Everyone must have been expecting Brian to act tough, to use gutter language and put his knee in the guy's groin. I know I was. Instead he muttered a polite apology, turned and walked out of the room. The guy appeared relieved and surprised, then quite proud of himself, until his girl snarled something at him and led him to a couch. Brian's polite behavior was wholly at odds with the public image of street toughs.

Half an hour later, as I bemoaned his apparent departure for

London, Brian came back, bringing with him, from somewhere, an opened bottle of brandy, the sight of which made me feel drunker than I already was. He went and stood in Binky's crowd. His manner was changed. My first impression had been of a very confident—even arrogant—young man. Now he looked as if he'd been crying, yet another refutation of the Rolling Stones' reputation. Brian seemed unsure of himself, morose and self-conscious. His smile, as he tried to regain the mood of the party, was false and forced. He reminded me of an injured animal.

Binky came flapping over and apologized for the rudeness of her guest, who had left by now, fighting with his girl. I drifted closer and heard Brian saying he was used to people trying to provoke him. "It's one of the hazards of the job. Please let's forget it now, eh?"

Binky looked at the brandy bottle and asked where he had gotten it, obviously assuming he had brought it with him from some exotic place.

"I found it in the hall," he said. "I hope you don't mind?"

"Oh, no, of course not," Binky said. "No, it was just that I didn't know we had any and I thought you had . . ." Her voice trailed off as their eyes met. This poised and confident young lady who, though sloppily dressed, had managed the party like an experienced hostess, turned to jelly as that knowing, glowing light rekindled in Brian's eyes.

Stifling a laugh, I collapsed in a chair, forgot my date, and instantly passed out. The room was empty and dark when I awoke at 3:30A.M. Suddenly Brian appeared in front of me, offering a blanket. I noticed we were alone as I wrapped the blanket around my shoulders. Brian handed me some champagne.

"What happened to Marilyn and Binky?" I asked.

"Gone to their beds," he said. He flashed a flirtatious grin. "Gone where all the good little girlies should be at this time of night."

"What, together?" I asked.

"I don't know," he said, flopping into the next chair. "Why? Is Marilyn into that scene?"

Shocked, I retorted, "Of course not."

"Do they call you Nicholas or Nick?"

"I don't mind."

"I'll call you Nicholas. I'm glad to be able to talk to you. I meet a lot of interesting people. Rarely get a chance to talk to them properly. Tara's connected with the Guinness family, so you are as well, I assume. Poor little rich boy?"

"Oh no. I'm quite happy. Except when they nag me about what I'm going to do with my life."

"I know the feeling. My parents used to lecture me too. But I guess they had cause. I put a girl up the stick in Cheltenham."

Again I felt shocked. "Made her pregnant, you mean?"

"That's right, and I'm not proud of it."

"That was before the Stones?"

"Yes, I was broke then. It made it all the more sordid. She wanted to settle in an apartment and have diapers hanging around. Christ! It all sorted itself out in the end."

We talked for a while about music and about how he formed the group and in the early days had pointed it in the direction he had wanted it to go.

"Can anyone still relate to you as a person, or are you totally consumed by your fame as a Rolling Stone?"

I'd hurt him. He gulped his brandy and said, without looking at me, "It is very difficult." Again I thought, for all the Stones' reputation as punks, Brian was sensitive, even touchy.

"What brought you here?" I asked.

"I had to get away from the Stones for a while. That stupid pissing business in the papers got me down. Andrew Oldham, our manager, he thought it was great—no such thing as bad publicity. I think there is. What about our families and friends? What the hell do they make of it all? It's just not necessary."

"So Tara sent you here?" I persisted.

"I called Tara yesterday and said take me away from all this. We went to Cheltenham. I wanted to make amends somehow for the stories in the papers. Drink tea and eat cucumber sandwiches on the lawn; prove I was not a lout. Then he had business in Birmingham so he rang Binky and got me invited."

"How about making number one in America?" I said, hoping to cheer him up. "Satisfaction" was a sensational hit in the U.S.

He completely ignored my question and went on to talk about a house he had bought in Los Angeles. "I'd like to spend more time there," he sighed, dreamily.

There was a silence and I thought he was drifting into sleep. I could easily have done the same thing. The side of my head was against the back of the armchair; my eyelids were heavy.

And then, with no preamble, he sat up straight and said, "We were supported by the Byrds at a concert in Long Beach. And Paul Revere and the Raiders. I love the Byrds. They're coming over in a couple of weeks and, boy, they'll really wow the British."

"Bob Dylan wrote their 'Mr. Tambourine Man,' didn't he?"

Brian's face lit up. "Yes. Now, *there's* a man I admire. The way he seems to be able to put a song together without any effort, hardly."

"Do you write any songs, Brian?"

"Yes, but they're not the right songs, apparently. Not commercial, more bluesy. Bill and I are both writing at the moment but it's hard to write popular stuff, like Mick and Keith. Everything has to be so damn commercial. Sod the music; all Andrew wants is the money. If the music suffers, along with people's characters, well, fucking hard luck."

"But you've got everything going for you. How can you be so unhappy?"

"Sometimes, Nicholas, I've got so many ideas inside my head I just don't know where to begin. I'd like to record my own songs myself. I've got a good enough voice to do folk-type stuff. I could never sing like Mick—but then I wouldn't really want to. I mean, he's out on his own, isn't he?"

"You obviously enjoy being a musician, though."

"It's my whole life. There's never been anything else. But I've got my own ideas and I don't much like the direction the group has taken. I'm sure my way is right for the Stones. After all, it was my own group to begin with. They'd be nowhere without me. But now they won't listen. Andrew, Keith and Mick have got their tails up now and they're trying to gallop ahead without knowing the best way to go. It's like setting off for Glasgow in a fast car and ending up in Cardiff because the road is easier."

"Or going to hell because all you have to do is slide."

"D'you read the Bible?"

"No."

"Oh. I do. Haven't made up my mind about all that yet. Anyway, Eric and Bill listen to me and I think they know what I'm getting at. But of course they're not driving the bloody car. Andrew is, with Mick and Keith cheering him on. They won't listen to me, the back-seat driver." Eric was Eric Easton, the Stone's co-manager.

Drinking, we watched the skies lighten outside. Brian told me how the Stones' tour of Australia, New Zealand and Singapore had been marred for him by the press coverage, with fabricated stories of all-night parties and orgies in hotel rooms, all designed to enrage parents, while boosting the Stones' popularity with the kids.

By five in the morning I had somehow slumped to the floor and had my head against the cushion of the chair. I was ready for sleep, but Brian, having disposed of half the contents of his brandy bottle, was wide awake.

"I like talking to you," he said. "We've been talking all night and you haven't once called me paranoid."

"What's that?" I asked blankly. It was the first time I'd heard this buzzword of the Sixties.

"Having a persecution complex."

"Why should I call you paranoid?"

"The others do. Andrew, Mick; when I make waves, try to put them back on the right road, and shout at them when they won't listen. That's me being paranoid, according to them."

"Where are you going to sleep?" I said, feeling that I was slowly but surely passing out.

"The bedrooms are full so I'll crash out in one of those sleeping bags." There was a pile of sleeping bags and blankets in a corner. He stood up, quite steadily to my surprise. "What about you?" he said.

"I'm all right here." I thought about something that had been nagging at the back of my addled brain. "Hey," I said, as the point came clear, "how d'you know the bedrooms are full?"

"I was up there, man. Then I came down to see if you were all right. It was very interesting up there. I'm going for a wee-wee." He went out.

It's difficult to work oneself into a jealous frenzy while fighting off a narcotic stupor, but at least a section of my mind was asking how many of the girls upstairs Brian had laid that night—and had my date been among them?

This led to other amorous thoughts, including a fantasy of Brian lying naked on my girl as I watched. This in turn led to another erection, which meant a postponement of sleep. I wanted to go to the john too. But Brian was there. If I happened to pick the same john he was in, he would no doubt think I was making a pass at him.

For a while I was back at my old boarding school, where in the dorm two boys would play with each other's naked bodies, ending with mutual masturbation, while the rest of us pretended not to notice. The fact that I had noticed and, in spite of myself, found the sight of the hairless bodies quite beautiful had aggravated my Catholic guilt complex.

Then Brian came back and, before I had fully gained my feet, stripped naked. I hurried out. When I came back, Brian was in the bag on the floor and appeared to be asleep. Relieved, I settled in my chair, put the blanket over me and, with a long weary sigh, settled down and shut my eyes.

"It's a pity we don't have a double bed," Brian said, and his voice told me he was still wide awake. "I don't like sleeping on my own."

I felt—cautious. I grunted, pretending to be asleep.

There was a scrambling noise and a sound of padding feet; then his voice came directly in front of me. "Come back to London with me. Stay a few days. Okay?"

"What?" I opened one eye and saw him standing over me. He had put on some shorts.

"Come back with me. My girl's in Paris, so you can stay with me. I've got most of the week off. We could have fun, what d'you say?"

I moaned and shut my eyes. "I can't just get up and go to London. Go to sleep."

"Why can't you?"

"I'm at college. We don't break until Tuesday. Marilyn and I are going on vacation then. Going to London for ten days on Wednesday. We'll come see you."

"You don't like me, do you?"

When I opened my eyes again I found he was kneeling beside the chair and his face was no more than two inches from mine. I moved back. "Of course I like you, don't be stupid. Go back to bed and we'll talk later."

He just stared at me, like a little boy deprived of a special treat. He looked hurt and lost, and I couldn't help feeling attracted to him, though my confusion was short-circuiting my responses. Was it just his resemblance to Marianne? I was in no state to try to work it out.

Gently I laid my hand on his head. His wild hair was soft to the touch. "Go to sleep, Brian. We'll talk about it later. Okay?"

He dropped his gaze, got up slowly and went away.

Binky woke me with tea. She was still in the same scruffy clothes. I looked around and found that Brian had gone. Binky said Brian had seen Marilyn and told her I was going with him to Great Yarmouth. Marilyn had then gone off in a huff. I felt too ill to be annoyed.

A few minutes later Brian came in looking as fresh as a daisy. He tossed a copy of *The Sunday Times* onto my lap. He had another copy.

"I've just had an unnerving experience," he said. "Some great gallumping woman leapt out at me in the hall and almost devoured me whole. Said she'd missed seeing me last night as she was being seduced in somebody's bedroom. Luckily Binky seems to have some control over her. She shooed her away."

"What's this nonsense about Great Yarmouth?" I said, trying to sound annoyed.

"Oh, didn't I tell you? We've got two concerts there tonight. Then directly after the second one you and I can go to London. Marilyn won't be coming. She's gone off home." He seemed pleased about this, and I was to find out later that he was the type that believed in two being company, three a crowd. "Okay?" he said.

"No, it's not all right. What would my parents say? And I want to see Marilyn too—"

"Call them," he said. "Your parents, I mean."

"There's college tomorrow. Even if it is the last day, the head will feel obliged to tell my parents if I'm not there. Anyway, what did you say to Marilyn?"

He shrugged. He was sulking. "You don't want to come, that's all." He mooched off to the other end of the room and sat down to read his paper.

"If I was going to London I'd need more clothes, for one thing."

"Plenty of shops in London. *You* can't be short of a few bob."

I realized Brian had no sense of responsibility and began to understand how the Rolling Stones could be exasperated by his behavior and his moods. I decided to put my foot down and be firm with him. In retrospect, it was the best thing I could have done; one of the anchors of our friendship was the fact that I refused to pander to him. Because he was so famous and adored, most people would give him anything his impulsive nature demanded.

"I'm going home this morning and I'm going to college tomorrow. Marilyn and I will be coming to London on Wednesday—unless you've destroyed our relationship."

He rustled the paper and held it in front of his face.

Binky came in with toast and coffee for us, and announced that Marilyn was back. I heard Brian grunt.

Marilyn strode in, ignored Brian and gave me a big smile. "You're not really going to Great Yarmouth, are you, Nicholas?"

"Of course not."

"Good. Shall we go riding?"

I had to let her down on this. Riding a horse in my condition would be fatal.

Suddenly Brian emerged from the paper, bright as a button now. "Hey, let's all drive out to some nice country pub for lunch."

Marilyn glared at him. Binky discreetly left the room. And then, putting an end to any doubt, Caroline, a one-girl Mardi Gras who had been at the party, arrived and bawled out the news that she knew of a country pub where a jazz band played on Sunday mornings and that we were all going.

Three pubs later, after Brian's chauffeur-driven car had led a convoy of lesser vehicles through lanes navigated by Caroline, we had found no jazz band, so we settled for lunch after all.

Marilyn kept me away from Brian most of the time, but when the time came for him to set off for Yarmouth he steered me out with him to the car. Marilyn had gone to the bathroom.

Out of earshot of everyone except the chauffeur, he said, "So you're trying to prove you're hetero, eh?"

I started to go red. "Nothing of the sort."

"All right, so you're hetero. I don't care. I like you. Like your company. Please ring me." He dropped a card, with his telephone number in Chelsea, into my pocket. The car drove off and I waved, but he never looked back.

As I boarded the train to go home, I wondered what I'd say when my mother asked, as she would, "Now sit down and tell me exactly what happened."

At midday on Saturday, July 31, 1965, I was in a phone booth in London, having told Marilyn that I was just popping out for a newspaper. Brian answered. He knew exactly who I was. All my anxieties dissolved at the sound of his voice.

"I was wondering what had become of you," he said. "Why don't we meet for a drink?"

"Where and when?" I said, no longer trying to hide my enthusiasm.

"Ten minutes," he said. "At reception in the London Hilton." Then without another word he hung up.

Once again I was in a mess. What about Marilyn? Already she had begun to ask why I kept disappearing from the house. Today she wanted me to go shopping with her around the West End. In spite of all that, I found myself hailing a cab and heading off to the Hilton. Not for very long, I told myself, lying.

At the Hilton, the top-hatted, green-uniformed head doorman

opened the car door and gave me a respectful "good morning," and it was only then that I discovered, to my horror, that I hadn't enough cash with me to pay off the cabbie. I asked him to wait while I went into the lobby, where I hoped I might find Brian. The driver exchanged suspicious glances with the doorman before reluctantly agreeing. Brian wasn't there. With rising panic I went to reception. Then just as I was about to ask for Brian he tapped me on the shoulder.

He was grinning. He was wearing white trousers, white shoes and a sweatshirt with RUDOLF RASMUSSEN SPORT loudly printed on it.

I told him my problem, and he turned and led the way out, cheerful and reassuring. At the taxi, instead of settling the fare, he climbed in and signaled for me to do the same, which I did in a kind of daze.

"Where are we going?" I said, thinking guiltily of Marilyn.

"You want a drink, don't you?"

"Yes."

"Right." To the driver, he said, "Flanagan's Bar, off Kensington High Street, please."

As we swung into Park Lane, he said, "It's a nice little Irish place that sells your family brew, Draught Guinness."

I felt quite flattered.

Getting out of the cab at Flanagan's Bar, Brian felt in his pockets, smiled and said, "Funny, you not having any money. Neither have I." He looked at the driver's face, which was growing angrier by the second, laughed, and told me to wait with him. "I'll get some," he said, and crossed the pavement into the bar. In less than a minute he was back, bearing a five-pound note.

The bar was dimly lit. We sat on high-backed stools at the counter and were treated with great respect by two bartenders in Edwardian dress and gray top hats. A collection of stuffed-animal trophies—lions, bears, foxes, deer—gazed down at us with glass eyes from the walls. I noticed that the plaques beneath them claimed frivolously that they had been shot by such celebrities as Harold Wilson, Barbara Castle and Adolf Hitler.

Brian ordered a double whisky and coke for himself, rendering his remark about Draught Guinness superfluous.

Unaccustomed to midday drinking, *I* ordered a bottle of the family brew. Neither of us paid, but this didn't seem to worry the two guys in fancy dress. I assumed Brian had some arrangement with them, although it is illegal for drinks to be served over the counter on a credit basis. Since it's illegal for a seventeen-year-old to be served on any basis, I asked no questions and enjoyed the Guinness and the company of Brian Jones enormously.

I had him almost to myself. Apart from the barmen there was just a man and woman having an intimate conversation at a corner table. They obviously didn't know who Brian was. Above the animal heads at the bar was pinned one of last year's election slogans, LET'S GO WITH LABOUR. (In October Harold Wilson had led the Labour party to victory after thirteen years in opposition.)

Brian didn't seem eager to talk yet. He was savoring his drink as if he had really needed it. Idly looking around the place, I wondered what was Irish about it apart from the name.

After Brian had finished his drink and ordered another, insisting I should too, he took off his dark glasses and gave me a friendly grin.

"I'm glad you called me at last," he said. "I needed someone to talk to. Someone uncomplicated, someone who hasn't got an angle or a claim on me. How are you, Nicholas?"

"I've tried about a dozen times to ring you. Always no reply, except once. That was on Friday. Someone called Dave answered and said you were out. Who's Dave?"

To my astonishment, Brian began to blush. "You mean Dave Thomson?"

"If he answers your telephone, yes."

"Oh, he's a Scottish student, a friend of mine. He's been staying with me at the mews." The mews was Brian's converted stable—it was then very fashionable to live in one. He went on, "Funny he didn't tell me you called." Then his embarrassment melted away and was replaced by puzzlement.

"Tell me straight, Nicholas. Do I seem like the kind of guy who imagines things, who is halfway to being a certifiable nut?"

It was an awkward question to be asked on so short an acquaintance. It would have been awkward coming from someone I'd known all my life. Yet it was not rhetorical. The earnest expression on his face told me he desperately wanted an answer.

"Well," I said, trying to sound wise for my age, "you obviously drink too much and you're obviously high-strung and emotional. But that doesn't make you mad. Is somebody trying to tell you you are?"

"Keith and Mick worry me. Especially Mick. He wants the Rolling Stones to be about him. He wants to put me down in the shadows along with Bill Wyman and Charlie Watts. You know how the cameras almost ignore those two and concentrate on Mick, Keith and me?"

"Yes, I've noticed."

"And most of the time it's Mick they pick up."

"That's only natural. He's the vocalist."

"I'll go along with that. But at the beginning Andrew used to encourage Keith and me to sparkle—sort of flirt with the audience, project the image. And I can do it. When I'm in the mood I can switch on the sort of sex thing that gets the girls wetting their knickers, knee-trembling."

"I know you can," I said, conscious of the effect he'd had on both Marilyn and me at Leamington.

"Right. Well, a few weeks back I was doing it, and the camera was on me and the kids started to scream—and then I felt Mick looking at me. And he was looking at me with such a menacing, threatening glint in his eyes that it completely threw me. Nicholas, you'll find it hard to believe this, but it was like he was saying, 'Back off, boy, pull your head in, this is my show.' I was scared. Really scared by the message that was coming across from him."

"You shouldn't let him scare you. It's not so surprising, is it? A bit of professional jealousy. They say actors do it all the time—try to upstage one another."

"Yes, of course, of course," he said, impatient with me. He finished off his second drink but held the empty glass in his hand. "It's much more than that. All the time now, offstage, he and Keith and even Andrew avoid me as much as they can, and when I turn up unexpectedly there's always an awkward silence. They watch me out of the corners of their eyes. Not Bill and Charlie, they're okay—easygoing and quite happy to be the minor characters of the outfit. It's pretty plain to me that if I was to knuckle down and be like those two, everything would be just the way they want it. But why the hell should I, Nicholas? Who went through all the poverty and the hardship to get the show on the road in the first place? And now they look at me as if they'd like me to fall under a bus."

"You must have had arguments with them. Are you always disagreeing with them?"

"Quite a lot," Brian admitted. "They probably find me a bit of a nuisance when I object to the way they're organizing things, arranging the music. I can understand their getting annoyed with me over that, but with Mick it's more than annoyance. He really hates my guts."

Brian ordered another drink, and when the top-hatted barman had served him—I had refused more—he waved him away to the far end of the bar, saying we were talking business. The barman seemed not to mind. Brian spoke quietly now, leaning towards me, confidentially. "You know our last single, 'The Last Time'? Keith and Mick wrote that. Last week we were playing it, and I started to flirt with the audience. I caught his eye again. Mick. He had come to the lines about warning someone that they're going to have to pay a price. He sang them—snarled them almost—directly at me, as if saying he'd told me once and now he's telling me again that there's some price I'm going to have to pay. He wrote those words for me. And I don't mind admitting I was really intimidated. It was hot, but I felt the sweat on my back turning cold. Now do you think I'm nuts?"

I shook my head, not really in reply but in wonderment. Then I said, "I don't know enough about you or the other Stones to form a judgment, Brian. You don't sound mad to me."

"Right," he said, finishing his drink and sliding from the stool. "We'll have to see that you get to know me and the others better. We'll go to my place now."

*   *   *

Outside in the bustling street he said, "We'll take the car," and went to a weird-looking compact parked across the road. "If I leave it there much longer, the police will tow it away."

As we literally climbed over the side of it to get in, I asked what it was.

"It's a Mini Moke." He started it up. "It's been here a couple of days now. Last time I came to Flanagan's I was too drunk to drive it home."

The engine roared, the hood virtually leaped into the air and soon the Moke was jerking and jumping through the traffic like a demented kangaroo. It might have seemed to Brian that he was a good driver, because on the two or three occasions when fatal impact looked inevitable he managed with a flick of the wrist to avert it, but to me it was more like divine intervention. When we pulled into the mews, behind the ABC Cinema on Fulham Road, I sent up a silent prayer of thanks and a promise: *Never again.*

It was a cobblestoned cul-de-sac surrounded by converted stables. The conversions had been tastefully done; these kinds of places were fashionable now. Whereas once they had housed the horses and the stableboys of the rich, they now housed the rich themselves, while the big townhouses to which they were attached had been either torn down or converted into studios for office typists.

In retrospect, it seems to me that there could have been worse fates for a young man in the Sixties than running around London with a rock star. It felt sexy, and I am glad that the romance of the moment was not lost on me then—or now.

As we pulled up at one of the brightly painted doors, about half a dozen young mini-skirted girls appeared from nowhere and stood around the car, pens and autograph books at the ready. Classic Sixties birds. There were a few delighted squeals as Brian got out, but there weren't enough of them for mass hysteria that was common those days wherever the Stones appeared.

Once we were inside, I said to Brian, "Do you always have fans waiting?"

"Usually a few. It's amazing how some of them always seem to find out where you're living. I think they must bribe real estate brokers or something."

So this was where Brian Jones lived. Brian took me into the living room. I surveyed the mess—lived-in, to say the least. Junk was strewn all over the place. "You'll have to excuse the mess," he said. "My cleaning woman's ill."

The room, I saw now, was a combined living and dining room. Apart from the mess it was tastefully furnished in Regency style, with long velvet curtains at the windows. The dinner table looked elegant in itself but was stacked with dirty dishes. The rest of the furniture was littered with letters, magazines, clothes, suitcases, the remains of take-out meals, record sleeves and unidentifiable substances.

Brian somehow found a place to sit, while I stood awkwardly with my feet in two of the empty spaces of unoccupied carpet. He began to fiddle with the controls of the record player.

"Yes", he said, "it's odd how they find you. I've never solved the mystery of how three fan letters were waiting here for me on the day I moved in."

I remember asking Brian whether he rented or owned the place.

"I rent. Eric Easton found it for me about four months ago."

There was no place for me to sit, so I just stood there as Brian fiddled around nervously. He went on, oblivious to my awkwardness. "Eric's been very good to me. I don't know what I'm going to do without him. He understood me, he was always on my side. That's why *they* want to replace him. That's the reason, the only reason. The excuses they make don't fool me." He stared at me, searching my eyes, looking to see if I would be an ally. *An ally in the fight against what?* I wondered.

Rock was not my world, my society—I had no idea who Eric Easton was. I tentatively ventured a guess: "Is Eric Easton one of your managers?"

"Eric? Well, he's our comanager with Andrew but now *they* don't feel that they need him."

"Who do you mean by *they*?"

"Andrew, Mick and Keith."

"Andrew *Oldham*, Mick *Jagger* and Keith *Richard*, you mean?" Then, more sympathetically, I added, "It's a bit of a mess, isn't it?"

Brian thought I was referring to the mess his place was in. "Yes," he said. "I told you, the cleaning woman is ill. I've been staying in a hotel most of the time." He got up. "Come on, I'll give you a guided tour of the stately home."

The cottage consisted of five small rooms in all—each one, it seemed to me, untidier than the last. There were two bedrooms, a double and a single. In the larger one was a double bed. I sat down on it, recalling what Brian had said about not liking to sleep alone. All his clothes were scattered or draped over the furniture, while a large wardrobe stood with its door open, empty.

Looking into the spare room, I noticed this was crammed with clothes also, but whether they were Brian's or not I couldn't make out. I wondered about his Scottish student friend Dave. Did he sleep here? Or did he, when Brian's girlfriend was away, have to share the double bed? I had to ask.

"Is this where Dave sleeps?"

"Sometimes." Brian turned that mischievous, slightly seductive look on me again. "Why?"

Feeling embarrassed, I tried to shrug it off.

"The sleeping arrangements," Brian went on, "depend largely on who's here. You'll have to take up my offer to stay sometime; then you'll find out for yourself." Deliberately trying to catch my eye, he added, "Won't you?"

"Yes, I suppose so," I grumbled, following Brian down the stairs.

When we reached the bottom, Brian suddenly turned around and looked me in the eyes. He said, "Mind you, Nicholas, I rarely end up sleeping *alone.*"

Now he had gone too far. Even as a naive seventeen-year-old I had my limits to how much of this coy manner of his I could take. Was he doing this to live up to his reputation for being outrageous? Or was he propositioning me? I was too screwed up and callow to take the initiative myself, and that left us exactly nowhere, a not uncommon predicament for complicated bisexual males, then or now.

"While we're on the subject of sex," he added, "where's Marilyn?"

"Marilyn?" Nearly an hour and a half had gone by since I'd stepped out of the house for a paper. That I had hardly thought about her was in itself a revelation to me. What was happening to me? I wondered helplessly. Before any reply presented itself, the phone rang.

This had an astonishing effect on Brian. He was like some furtive intruder about to be discovered on someone else's property. His ever kaleidoscopically changing humors and attitudes were truly amazing. At the time I remember thinking, *He's raving mad.*

"I can't answer the phone," he said, panic in his eyes. "You answer it, Nicholas. If it's anyone for me say I'm not in."

I tried to calm him down. "Let me see who it is first, okay?"

He nodded and I picked up the receiver. The woman at the other end sounded French. She spoke shattered English.

"Hello. Brian, is that you?"

I covered the mouthpiece and told him, "It's a French girl for you."

He gave a heaving sigh of relief, as if he had been expecting a posse of policemen, and took the receiver. "It must be Zou Zou," he said before launching into a long, involved conversation. His French was worse than her English.

I decided to make a start on clearing up the mess and then make some tea. As I shifted some of the stuff that was lying around, I noticed that the only mirrors in the mews were either above your head or at your feet. Odd, I thought.

Going into the kitchen, I attacked the dirty dishes. It looked as if Brian had been billeting a small regiment for a month. Yet if he had been staying in a hotel for a few days, as he'd told me, it must have been Dave who had made this mess. I tore into it and soon had it down below eye level. I glanced out of the steamy window and beheld a billy goat tethered to a pole, quietly munching at a wilderness of weeds that had once been a lawn.

I stuck my head into the living room. Brian was off the phone and sitting back in a chair, listening to a Bob Dylan record.

"D'you know there's a goat outside the window?" I said.

"What? Oh yes, That's Billy G. There's this little patch of garden that goes with the house, so I got him to tidy it up. I've got a Manx kitten, too, and a poodle called Pip, but they're not here at the moment. Can you make tea?"

"Of course I can make tea."

"Well, somewhere out there you'll find a silver teapot and some bone china. I like it made and served like that. If you wouldn't mind, of course."

"No. Do you drink much tea, then?"

"Oh, gallons of the stuff." He turned his head. "I do—honestly—and especially served like that."

"The Cheltenham way," I observed.

Carrying in a tray of tea and biscuits half an hour later, I nearly had a disaster in the middle of the living room over an overflowing sack of mail which I had been unable to find a home for earlier.

"Can't you find somewhere to keep this bloody sack?" I yelled. "I nearly had the tea all over the place."

Idly draped in his chair, eyes half-closed, listening intently to Bob Dylan's LP *Bringing It All Back Home*, he said, "It's fan mail. I'm going to start answering some of them this evening."

"Well, it doesn't have to be in the middle of the room, does it?" Balancing on one leg with the tray in my hands, I gave the bag a hefty kick and felt a bit better. "You can still answer the letters without endangering life and limb by sticking them in the bloody way. True?" I set down the tray and sat in another armchair that I had unearthed.

"You remind me of Dylan," he said, smiling at me, amused. "You've got the same mop of wild hair. Bob's a good friend of mine. He's the most unusual person I've ever met in the music business. Not unlike John Lennon. He's out on his own."

I picked up the LP cover and studied the photograph on the front. It showed Dylan crouching in the foreground and holding a cat, while in the background a girl in a red dress reclined with a cigarette between her fingers.

"I wish I could write songs like that," Brian said soulfully. "Did you know that before he was twenty Bob had lived in Gallup, New

Mexico; Sioux Falls, South Dakota; Phillipsburg, Kansas; Hibbing, Minnesota; and in Minneapolis? During which time he met all sorts—all races—of people, listened to what they had to say, and then turned their words first into poetry and then into songs. And that's what I've tried to do, Nicholas. D'you know, I write down anything relevant that people say to me."

I decided that henceforth I'd do the same. "Did you travel much when you were in your teens?" I asked.

"No," he said, sadly. "I went to Scandinavia once, but apart from that it was just bloody Cheltenham. Studying. Though what the hell for, I don't really know. Waste of time. To think that all that time I wasted in school I could have been out on the road like Bob Dylan—listening to ordinary people, finding out what makes them worry, what makes them fearful, what gets them mad, and then setting it all down so beautifully that the better-off people of the world have to stop and listen." Brian pointed out that Dylan's real name was Zimmerman. "He took Dylan from Dylan Thomas. He told me that. He said in his lyrics he was inspired by Dylan Thomas. In his singing it was Woody Guthrie who influenced him. But Bob likes to be thought of more as a poet than anything else. Have you read any of Dylan Thomas' poetry?"

"Yes," I said. "I like most of his stuff, especially when he speaks it himself."

"Yes. Performs it almost. Bob Dylan loves that, too. First thing Bob ever said to me was, 'Is Jones your real name?' When I said yes he asked if I was Welsh, I guess because Thomas was Welsh. He was so pleased when I told him my father was; he could hardly stop talking about Dylan Thomas."

Both Brian and I had Welsh fathers. His had come from Pencoed, near Bridgend; mine was from Abergavenny, Monmouthshire, not far from the English border.

We found that we could be comfortable with each other in total silence. I had only experienced that with steady girlfriends such as Marilyn.

When the LP finally clicked off, Brian sighed and said, "I could listen to Dylan all day and all night. Some of his songs are like a word-picture of Charlie Chaplin—the little man in the street going around corners on one leg. The words are flowing nicely and then there's a sudden, funny kick up the ass. Some people say he's too sentimental. They don't understand. They're not really listening. He's completely unsentimental, often cynical, but always truthful."

It seemed to me that with Brian's commitment and sensitivity he should be able to write songs and lyrics to rival those of anybody else in the business—profound and beautiful songs that could electrify the pop-music world.

Brian's favorite Dylan song was "With God on Our Side." But, while the song's lyrics are bitterly ironic, Brian was truly a man in search of a faith.

He seemed to know everything about Dylan and was almost besotted by the man. He told me, for instance, that Dylan ran away from home seven times before he was twelve, that John Lennon was a fervent devotee, and that a lot more successful people envied Dylan's sincerity and were quite jealous of him.

Later, we talked about Brian's relationship with girls. I asked if Zou Zou was his current girlfriend. He smiled rougishly and said she was.

"But she's not the one I've read about in the papers," I said. "The one who's trying to get a paternity order against you."

"Oh no. That's Linda." And then, to my horror, Brian gave a sudden sob and burst into tears.

In the mid-1960's, to a person brought up in an English public school, there was nothing more alarming than masculine tears. You were taught to suppress all emotion except patriotism and sportive jubilation. You simply did not show sadness or distress any more than love or hatred (though contempt was acceptable).

Part of me wanted to go to Brian, put my arms around him and comfort him. But I was too uptight, a creation of our homophobic world. Instead, I did what my mother always did when people were upset. I went to the kitchen and got him a strong drink of whisky. I handed him the half-pint glass first and poured the stuff in, but my hand was so shaky I sloshed out at least three full shots. To remedy this I went to the kitchen again and got a can of coke to dilute it, but by the time I got back Brian had drunk the whole quarter-pint straight. He was drying his eyes.

"I'm sorry," I said, sitting down again. "I didn't mean to upset you."

"Oh, I'm just being stupid. It's not really Linda's fault. It's her family who are putting her up to applying for this paternity thing. But I feel so terrible about it all."

"Well, I'm sorry to have brought the subject up. It's none of my business anyway."

"No, don't say that; really, I'd like to talk about it. Only to you." He reached out and put on another record. He settled back, composed again, as Bob Dylan's voice filled the room. "I don't often meet people I can relax with. Most quote me to the press."

"You're safe with me, Brian. But hey, I don't want to hear anything you might regret telling me later on. Perhaps we'd better change the subject."

He went on, though he was obviously irritated at my man-of-the-world attitude. "No, I'll tell you. You're seventeen, aren't you?" He said. "When I first met Linda in 1962—it was at the Ricky Tick Club in Windsor—everything was great between us. I didn't have a lot of money then, but we always managed to have a good time. She told me she loved me and I *think* I loved her."

Brian sensed that this discussion was making me uncomfortable. Love was not a word widely employed where I came from. "Go on," I said.

"Later, when I met her parents, they were very good to me. When I had nowhere to live, after I'd fallen out with my own parents, they invited me to stay at their place in Windsor. They were amazing, really; so easy-going. They turned a blind eye to our sleeping together, and even tolerated it when I smoked pot." He fell silent for a while, smiling.

"So what went wrong?" I said.

"I'm not quite sure. She got pregnant. I got successful. Maybe it was a combination of the two that split us up. Maybe that's the price of success. I don't know."

"What did her parents say about your getting her pregnant?"

"At first they took it so well I couldn't believe it. Perhaps they were looking forward to having a rich pop star as a son-in-law. But then they started on about getting married. Things came to a head about Christmastime last year. Her father asked me point-blank when I was going to marry her; I told him I didn't feel in a position to handle the responsibility of marriage just then. It was then that he turned nasty and said I had abused their hospitality. They threw me out; Linda's brother kept my car to compensate for unpaid rent."

"D'you still see Linda?"

"Occasionally. She fetches the baby round here sometimes. The thing is, now, her life is quite simple, where mine is so bloody complicated. I mean, she still thinks we can get together and pretend nothing has happened. The whole situation is ridiculous." He poured himself another giant measure of Scotch.

"Drinking won't help," I pronounced with all the piousness of youth.

He smiled. "No, Father," he said, and then he changed the subject. "D'you know I've got a ghost in this cottage? It opens and closes doors; calls my name in a female voice."

"Do you really believe in ghosts?"

"In a way." His eyes were very thoughtful. "I think they're real but only as products of the mind."

"You mean people imagine them?"

"Oh no. They do exist, but only because people want them to exist. It's a bit like wishing hard enough and your wish is granted. If the atmosphere is right—say that it's a pitch-black night in a howling gale—and you and I look out into the darkness, you might not see a ghost but I might. But just because you don't see it doesn't mean it isn't there. It's there for me.

"I've read a lot about the supernatural. It's a very deep subject. There are certain people who attract spirits. They have some sort of warmth about them that's felt by spirits. Some people say that the ghosts of the morning can be seen on the skyline if you concentrate hard enough."

"D'you think you attract spirits?"

"I don't know. I must if I have a ghost here, I suppose. I can't say I've ever seen it, but I do hear it."

He got up abruptly, saying he was going for a bath and shampoo. He told me to make myself at home and disappeared upstairs.

Later, Brian came downstairs wearing only a pair of cream corduroy trousers, his shoulder-length wet hair falling over his tanned shoulders. The erotic nature of the man bowled me over and my confused mind started desperately trying to conceal the fact.

"Do you like it?" I said, pointing to the record player. Donovan was singing.

He shrugged. "He's not Dylan."

"No."

"But he's not bad. You seen the hairdryer about the place?"

"No. Did you hear a door bang just now?"

He smiled and didn't answer—went on turning over cushions and searching for the dryer.

"What about your girlfriend?" he said. "Won't she be missing you?"

I took this as a possible hint that I had outstayed my welcome. "Yes, I suppose I'd better get back. Can I use the phone? I'd better tell her I'm on the way."

"Give me the number and I'll dial it for you," he said.

The number was written on a piece of paper in my wallet. I handed it to him and he dialed. Then he put the phone down. "Busy," he said, "I'll call a taxi for you." He dialed again.

It was a bit humiliating, I thought. He was obviously eager to get rid of me.

When the taxi came, he gave me some money for the fare and then escorted me to the door, still only half-dressed.

"By the way," he said, "I always keep the bathroom door open."

"Yes?" I said blankly.

"So it wasn't the bathroom door that slammed. Think about it, Nicholas. Maybe we'll meet again before you go back home to Birmingham."

CHAPTER

4

*B*ACK AT HANS CRESCENT I was greeted, not with a bang over the head, but by a warm, passionate and inviting kiss on the mouth that immediately channeled my mind and body in one direction. But then Marilyn pulled back and fussed with her hair in front of a mirror.

I was about to seek an explanation, but she said, "Before you say anything, Brian has explained it all."

"Brian?" I said blankly, sitting down on the bed.

"Yes, Brian Jones called not long ago and explained everything. He was very charming and I forgive you."

"Oh, thanks," I said. But instead of being relieved I felt put out. What the hell was Brian doing calling my girl? What had he said to put her into this strange, elated mood? And where the hell did she think she was going, dressed to kill?

She wore tight, red, bell-bottom slacks and a white lace shirt. I was always attracted to that body of hers and never more than at that moment. She stood at the mirror, bending slightly from the waist, so that her neat, tight, round rear was at it's most tantalizing. The long blond hair shimmered and rippled over her shoulders and back and framed her symmetrical features as they reflected back at me. Then those light blue, rather mocking eyes caught mine and twinkled at me in that mysterious knowing way she had, and I knew very well that she was all too aware of what was passing through my mind.

"Do you mind telling me what the occasion is?" I said. "Are you going somewhere? Are *we* going somewhere?"

"I thought you'd never ask." She came to me then, bubbling over with excitement, and it all came tumbling out: "Brian Jones has asked us out. He and his girlfriend and you and me, we're all going to a reception for Sonny and Cher at the Hilton, and then on to a nightclub for dinner. Isn't it *marvelous?*"

"Great," I said, though still with reservations about the way Brian went about things. Why hadn't he asked me at the mews instead of practically throwing me out in that offhand way? It could be that he liked doing things dramatically. Or maybe, after I'd gone, he had had another sudden change of mood and just thought of the idea in an optimistic flash.

She was crouching before me with her forearms resting on my parted thighs, and the view down the cleavage under that white lace was sufficient to distract a monk from his devotions.

"Aren't you excited?" she said.

"Very excited." I put my hand slowly inside the top of her shirt and managed to burst open another button. I slipped my hand in over silky flesh until I felt the gradual rising of the mound, Marilyn's gorgeous tit . . . and then she stopped me. She did it very gently, looking into my eyes with a touch of sadness and removing my groping hand tenderly with the two of hers.

"Not just now, Nicholas," she crooned. "Not here. The time will come, you know."

Well, failed again, I thought, but things did at least seem promising.

I did not know very much about the management of the Rolling Stones beyond the fact that it was shared by Eric Easton and Andrew Loog Oldham. I had seen Andrew, who had formerly managed Marianne Faithfull on the TV show "Ready, Steady, Go"

As we entered the reception we were greeted by a smart young lady in a blue two-piece suit, who asked who we were representing.

At the same time a waiter presented a tray of champagne and we took a glass each. I told the young lady we had been invited by Brian Jones, and this seemed to throw her for a moment. "Oh, really", she said sarcastically, and walked away toward a group not far off. In this group I recognized Andrew Loog Oldham. He was speaking to someone who was later identified as Larry Page, the manager of the Kinks.

When the girl interrupted Andrew and went into a huddle with him, I saw him look over at us with undisguised hostility. He was an odd-looking character and I was startled to see that he was wearing makeup. He was twenty-one then and had sandy hair, which was longer than was normal at the time. He wore dark glasses. His manner struck me as rather camp. Vaguely, with my limited experience of sexual matters, I wondered if he was homosexual, but then thought he couldn't be because I recalled reading an article about him that said his wife had given birth to a baby in May. Strangely, I even remembered the child's name; it was Sean Loog.

He came striding over to us and said, quite tersely, "I understand you say Brian Jones invited you?"

I said, "Yes?"

"Well, as far as I'm aware, Brian Jones hasn't been invited himself." His glance landed on Marilyn's face and his manner softened a little. He still looked peculiar to me, though, and I was at a loss to explain why he wore makeup.

To play for time I introduced Marilyn, and when I mentioned her father's connection with CBS Records he was won over and made us feel welcome. He and Marilyn chatted, and I studied him more closely.

Andrew Loog Oldham could have passed for a pop singer rather than the management figure he was. In fact, he had earlier fancied himself as a pop star, hounding every agent in London to take him on, even though he couldn't sing a note or play any instrument. When he finally saw the futility of this he got various unlikely jobs from waiter to PR man in order to keep himself in the eye of the rich and famous. He was obviously fanatically ambitious. He gave that impression now, talking earnestly to Marilyn about her father's American connections. He was telling her how he was thinking of forming his own record company. Marilyn appeared to be enjoying his attention, but I didn't see this rather effeminate creature as any threat—and it wasn't because of that fact that I took a strong dislike to Oldham.

There was just something about him that I couldn't put my finger on. Maybe that he was the first man, in my experience, to wear makeup had something to do with it. Anyway, from the way he occasionally glanced at me with deep distrust, the dislike was mutual.

Sonny and Cher had arrived. They were hustled in by a phalanx of admirers, friends, musicians and photographers. If I had thought Brian's dress outrageous at Leamington, their appearance was, to my conventional taste, almost beyond belief.

Sonny, who I noticed was being followed closely by an irate-looking hotel employee, was wearing a red sweater, a leopardskin vest, trousers with a huge buckle, from which the leather belt tapered down into shredded ends, and Alaskan fur boots. He was like something from another civilization, if not from another planet.

Cher was in an abbreviated pants suit that was bright yellow and left a bare, slim midriff on display. The pants were bell-bottoms and the whole outfit was trimmed with white *broderie anglaise*. Half-Indian, she had magnificent hair—long, black and lustrous.

There were gasps of astonishment as this colorful pair and their far-out entourage swept in; it was like the opening of a musical spectacle onstage. Marilyn was spellbound, with her fingers held limply to her open mouth, and her eyes glowing like those of a little girl seeing her first Punch and Judy show.

Brian came up to us and planted a kiss on Marilyn's cheek. I was surprised to see Andrew Oldham glare at Brian and then without a word stalk off to greet Sonny and Cher.

Brian appeared not to notice the snub. He was gazing at the two new arrivals. "Aren't they wild?" he said. "The people downstairs almost freaked when they saw them come in."

But I was thinking about Andrew. Why had he looked like that at Brian? It had been a look of distrust and dislike.

More champagne came around. Brian, Marilyn and I stood near a table with a scarlet cloth on it that was laden with sandwich triangles, biscuits, cheese cubes, cheese straws, vol-au-vents and crackers—a fine spread, as they say. The record companies could well afford it. It was the Sixties, the youngsters had the money and surrendered unprecedented millions of dollars for the thrill of hearing their idols sing to them.

Brian was telling us of his first encounter with Sonny at Los Angeles International Airport the previous June—1964. Even then, when Sonny was just a PR man for London Records, the Stones' American company, Sonny dressed in far-out gear—candy-striped trousers, colorful scarves and bangles around his neck as well as his arms.

"I'd never seen anything like it," Brian said. He himself tonight was in a relatively quiet suit, brown with red pinstripes. "And to top that," he went on, obviously full of admiration for Sonny, "when he opened the trunk of his car it was *full* of records—I mean, *thousands* of them. Well, in England, at that time, you never saw records like that—actually on their way to the stores. He's a crazy man."

Through a champagne haze I realized Brian was introducing us to Sonny and Cher's managers. They were Brian Stone, who looked lean and hungry, and Charlie Greene, who everyone said looked like one of the Ivy League (an English group). Both of them wore gold chokers with dollar signs on them. Neither wore makeup, thank God, and they were very witty and obviously enjoyed a lot of fun. And of course I remember Sonny himself mooching over to join us. His hair was as long as Brian's and he made some comment on the fact.

Brian grinned and said, "But you had it long before I did."

"Yeah, true. I had this hair before the Beatles. First time I saw their picture—in *Time* magazine—I thought, hell, they're gonna outdate me. But they didn't, eh, Brian?" It was Brian Stone he was talking to, and he slapped him on the back. Both the managers fell about laughing. Everybody was quite drunk.

"People came up to me with photos of The Beatles and they'd say, 'Hey, Sonny, they got hair like yours.' I'd say, 'Hell, man, how d'you figure they got their ideas?'"

When Sonny was laughing or smiling his whole face lit up with humor, yet when he was serious, his eyes had a kind of sad, lost look; the same kind of look that I had seen in Brian's eyes sometimes. He was a heavier, more stocky man close up than he had seemed at a distance.

Sometime later, Cher came and stood with us. By now nobody was bothering with formal introductions, but she and Marilyn were soon chatting away as if they were long-lost sisters. Marilyn was in her element, surrounded by fellow Americans. It was hard to make out whether it was their nationality or their fame that made her sparkle. Perhaps it was just the champagne. Maybe all three. Whatever it was, she and Cher looked really lovely together—the one dark and sleek, the other blond and with peaches-and-cream coloring. If at that moment, by some unlikely miracle, I had been asked to make a choice between taking one or other of them to bed, I should have to have asked—demanded even—to take both.

"I had trouble with the way they speak," Marilyn said, talking about the British. "I'm okay now."

"Well now, I've been learning real English, especially for this visit," Cher said, giggling. "Now I can say 'Big Ben' and 'Tower Bridge' and 'loo' for the ladies' room and, er . . . oh yes, 'Hello, Rodney.' How's that?"

They both laughed. I stood and watched them, enjoying their beauty. Brian, too, seemed quite content to say nothing and just drink in the little pool of feminity they represented, until Cher asked him if Scott Walker had arrived yet. The Walker Brothers had been booked to support the Stones the following evening at the London Palladium. It was to be the Stones' first concert there. Marilyn and I had tickets.

Brian said to Cher, "No, he's *not* here. In fact, Cher, the Walker Brothers have pulled out of our concert tomorrow."

Cher gave a disappointed "Aw!" and turned away from Brian, probably because she had seen that teasing look in his eye, which meant that he was going into his outrageous flirt mode. Turning to Marilyn and me, Cher said, "I used to know the Walker Brothers back home. They had their sister as lead vocalist then. Imagine having to pull out of the Palladium. Gosh, play the Palladium and you're a world star already."

Marilyn said yearningly, "Are *you* going tomorrow night, Cher?"

Cher's face dropped a little. "No, we're booked in Birmingham for a TV taping."

"That's bad management," Brian said, and the two managers joined in the laughter. But Brian wasn't laughing. He wasn't even smiling.

It was unfortunate that Cher's young sister Georgianne—as fair and pretty as Cher was dark and beautiful—should have come at that moment to say Andrew Oldham wanted Cher to go over and talk to him. It was obvious even to me that Oldham was deliberately avoiding any group that contained Brian Jones that night.

Brian snapped, "Tell him if he wants to speak to Cher he should come over here. Who the hell does he think he is?" Brian's face was white with rage.

We all fell silent. Georgianne looked uncertainly from Brian to Cher and back again. At last Cher smiled and said, "It's all right. I'll go." She took off, followed by her sister.

Brian watched them go, and I could see tears forming in his eyes. Quickly, and as cheerfully as I could, I said, "Hey, Brian, how about that nightclub?"

He slowly turned to me and stared for a moment, as if coming out of a trance. Then he put a handkerchief to his face, beckoned and went out of the room. Marilyn and I followed. In the elevator he pretended to blow his nose. Then he took out a Ventolin inhaler and placed it in his mouth. Hoping to bring him out of the sulk, I produced mine and said, "Snap." And by the time we reached the ground floor he was grinning.

The Cromwellian is located in a three-story Georgian house on Cromwell Road in a row of similar buildings, most of them going to seed or being refurbished as apartments and "bed-sitters," or studios. It was, and is, quite exclusive, and most of its clientele is drawn from the world of entertainment. Practically anybody who was anybody in the pop scene was a member, and it was the kind of place where a star could go and not be hounded by newsmen and autograph-hunters.

It was elegant and comfortable, with a long bar and good, solid furniture. Downstairs was a discotheque, upstairs there were gambling rooms. We chose the bar, which was known to all as Harry's Bar. Brian bought more drinks. It was late and there were quite a few people in the room. Marilyn was beginning to wilt after the excitement of the evening, but all the same kept looking around her in the hope of seeing yet more famous people. "Isn't that Herman of the Hermits over there?" she said.

But I was listening to Brian as he launched into a bitter catalog of complaint and recrimination about Andrew Loog Oldham, interspersed with small eulogies on the subject of Eric Easton. He spoke in a low, confidential tone and reminded me of a child confiding his complaints and hurts to an understanding parent.

"It all began with me and Eric," he said. "I mean—I formed the group, Eric got it off the ground. But the guy who got Easton interested was Oldham. I've got to give him that. He came down to see us at the Crawdaddy Club in Richmond—the back of the Station Hotel in Kew Road. He was a young go-getter. He was only about nineteen then, and he'd heard that the Beatles had been down to see us and were so impressed they gave us free tickets for their first big concert—at the Albert Hall."

"I remember," I said, proud to be a walking encyclopedia of pop. "The Beatles Albert Hall concert was on the fifteenth of April, 1963."

"Take your word for it," Brian said, completely unimpressed. "Anyway, Oldham picked a bad night to come. The fellow who ran the club, Giorgio Gomelsky, happened to be away that night, and we were just playing some old blues numbers. We weren't even onstage. Just sitting on bar stools. Anyway, he looked us over and said he thought we had a lot of sex appeal; said he'd like to take us on if he could find a backer." Brian sighed. "I don't know, he seemed somehow as if he cared about our music. I spoke for the group then. It was my group.

"Well, I said yes, find a backer and we're with you. He tried Brian Epstein, but he said no. He had his hands full with the Beatles. Then he tried Eric Easton. Eric was an old hand at show biz. He handled sort of popular middle-of-the-road artists. Bert Weedon, Julie Grant, the pub pianist Mrs. Mills, the disk jockey Brian Matthew—people like that, successful but not sensational. He came down to see us. It was a normal night and the kids were lining up to get in. We belted it out—wild rhythm 'n' blues—and they lapped it up. I don't think Eric really liked the sound, but he could see the kids were crazy for it and that was what mattered. It all took off from there."

"Eric backed you?" I asked. "What about Andrew Oldham?"

"Well, he sort of acted as agent, mostly under Eric's control—at first. Now the bastard's trying to squeeze Eric out."

It was about this time that Marilyn became restless and wanted to go home to bed. She said she'd had a wonderful evening and that if I wanted to stay on she didn't mind. I called a taxi, put her in it and paid the driver. I was feeling pretty tired myself, but Brian had made it obvious that he needed to talk to me; though why me I still couldn't say. It was dawning on me gradually that Brian was relying on me as his special confidant, the trusted one. Brian managed to get a final drink from Harry, and we returned to our table.

"D'you know, Nicholas," Brian went on, "from the moment I met Eric Easton I knew he was straight and I could talk to him. He's a bit like a father figure; much more mature than Oldham—and more substantial in every way. Look at his build to start with. He's got flesh on his bones, he's balding and he wears glasses. You'd buy a car off him! When you look at Oldham you think, 'There's a man who's out only for himself.'"

I nodded, having thought something of the sort earlier on.

"That first meeting, in Eric's office in Argyll Street, I took Mick along. There was him and Andrew, me and Eric. Mick went out at one stage, and while he was away Eric said he thought Mick ought to be dropped in favor of a vocalist who could really sing. Don't forget Mick Jagger was nothing then. I wasn't all that hooked on his voice and I said I'd try to get a chap called Paul Pond. You heard of Paul Pond?"

I admitted I hadn't.

"He was at Oxford and used to sing with a group called Thunder Odin's Big Secret. I sat in with the group a few times and I really thought he was right for my Rolling Stones. Well, I tried to get him. I didn't mind dropping Mick, but Paul was determined to go on with his studies and wouldn't join. In the end he changed his name to Jones and joined Manfred Mann. All through the conversation I noticed that Oldham said nothing but sat listening with a foxy look on his face. Mick came back and then Andrew took us to a coffee place and hinted that he might be able to get us a recording contract because he had a contact at Decca Records. Not boring you, am I?"

"No," I said, though I was feeling quite tired—and quite seventeen years old.

"Well, Eric Easton soon got things drawn up legally. It was a three-year exclusive management agreement with Eric Easton and Andrew Loog Oldham, as well as a three-year agreement with Easton making him the sole agent to the Rolling Stones. But only I signed it, Nicholas, remember that. I signed as leader of the group, and I was recognized as leader by a clause giving me fifteen dollars per week more than the others. Now can you see what's happening?"

I shook my head vaguely. "Not really."

"It's obvious. They are trying to get me out, so first they get rid of Eric, then they get rid of me. Then the Stones become the property of Mr. Bloody Oldham!"

At the Rolling Stones concert at the London Palladium the following evening, policemen were struggling with teenage girls and trying to put them into orderly rows along the pavement. Once inside, the girls began chanting "We want the Stones," "We want Mick" and "We want Brian."

In one of the baroque, gilt-fronted boxes opposite ours, I saw the large, lugubrious features of Lionel Bart, a neighbor of Brian's, looking down at the front orchestra seats. Next to him was Noel Harrison, son of Rex Harrison.

At last, just after eight, the musicians in the orchestra pit struck up very loudly and drowned out the noise of the fans. The curtains parted, the fire screen was pulled up and the concert got underway. It was a star cast and it kept the girls' hysteria down to a heavy simmer, except when each act came to an end, and then the chanting broke out anew—"We want Mick," "We want Brian."

The preliminary acts included the Moody Blues, the Fourmost, Julie Grant, the Quiet Five, Sugar Pie Desanta—the American blues and gospel singer—and Steampacket, featuring Long John Baldry, Brian Auger, Rod Stewart and Julie Driscoll. All the artists seemed at their best, and it was obvious to everyone in the audience that it was turning out to be a gala night.

And then the penultimate act came to an end. The secondary curtain came down—and all hell let loose. The girls in the orchestra seats and in the galleries began to chant. Then the screaming started. A line of security men appeared immediately and lined up behind the footlights. Another line came to the pit.

But then a short second intermission was announced and a rush began, not as usual to the bars but to the ladies' lavatories. I found the orchestra bar not too crowded. I saw Eric Easton standing alone to one side. I recognized him from photographs I'd seen in the music papers. He was a bit overweight, in his forties, and smoking a large cigar. He was, as Brian had said, a comfortable, reassuring sort of figure, wearing glasses and balding.

I went up to him, cheekily perhaps, and said, "Excuse me, I believe you're Eric Easton."

He regarded me with understandable caution. "Yes, I am. You are—"

"Nicholas Fitzgerald. Brian said I could go backstage after the—"

"Oh yes." His soft voice was friendly now. "Brian was telling me about you. I'm afraid it won't be possible for you, or anyone, to go back tonight. The police want them straight out of the building—before these kids get a chance to get outside."

I nodded. "I'm not surprised. Haven't seen anything like it since the Beatles' first concert."

Eric Easton smiled. "The snootier papers say it's all organized by the groups' managers. It's not, you know. Well, not directly. We give the boys their image and if it's the right one the kids will come and go crazy without any prompting from us."

The frenzy of screaming and chanting was beginning again, building steadily to a crazy pitch.

Talking over the noise, Eric asked me where I was from, and we discussed my family for a while.

Then Easton said, "Brian seems to have taken quite a big liking to you, especially considering your brief acquaintance. He's a nice guy, and I think he needs all the friends he can get."

He looked a little sad. Obviously he wanted to convey more to me than he was saying. I didn't pry.

The house orchestra struck up then. Eric Easton put out a hand and patted my shoulder, and we parted. I went back to Marilyn in our box—one of the six on that side of the theater—and took a seat. By now you couldn't hear the orchestra for the screaming. Marilyn put her hands over her ears as the houselights dimmed.

Ray Cameron, the emcee, yelled into his microphone, "Ladies and gentlemen, the Rolling Stones." The decibels within that old lady of a theater must have passed any level of tolerance to the human ear.

The curtains parted and my eyes went to Brian immediately, by far the most attractive character on the stage. For the first two numbers, most of his time was spent with his head down watching his fingers moving on the guitar, and on the magic occasions when he did look up he seemed surprised to discover where he was—in front of a huge mass of people. Then he would simper a little and bow his head back to his instrument. For my money, Mick Jagger didn't stand a chance beside the cherubic figure of Brian Jones.

As the Stones thundered into their first number, girls were flinging themselves at the stage. While being unceremoniously repelled by the security men, the girls revealed that they were wearing nothing under their miniskirts, which hardly covered their behinds when they were right side up. It was one way of coping with the summer heat, but I recall it fondly as a bonus on a memorable night.

Despite all the commotion, Bill Wyman and Charlie Watts remained stoically impassive and poker-faced in the background. Bill chewed gum like a contented cow and held his bass almost vertically. Charlie sat at his drum kit with his mouth open and seemed to be in another world.

Keith Richard staggered around in front of his amplifier and twanged his guitar without apparent effort, looking as if he'd just been dragged out of his bed after a heavy night. Mick Jagger, too, seemed to have made a great effort to appear unkempt. He seemed totally wrapped up in his efforts at performing new dance steps, which included turning his back to the audience and waggling his unattractive seat at them like a trousered baboon.

The intense, brash beat of the Stones' music erupted for the first time in this hallowed hall, and the theater, as if in shock, trembled and vibrated to the sound of the Sixties, rebellious and raucous, screaming defiance at the Establishment and warning the old world that another age had dawned. I looked at Brian, hoping that he, not just a rock guitarist but a serious and ambitious musician, would become the sane link between the old world and the new. With his charisma, anything seemed possible for Brian, or so I felt that night, watching him rock the Palladium. He was very noticeably a true musician.

During the third number, a very odd change came over Brian. The song was "The Last Time," which was a Jagger and Richard joint composition.

Brian started to play to the audience. He began to give sudden flicks of his soft, flaxen hair, teasing girls into hysteria, winking and thrusting out his loins, playing out his newfound role of "jean-creaming demigod" for all it was worth. It appeared to be a deliberate attempt to upstage Jagger with his snaking hips.

And then I noticed what Jagger was doing—and Brian's reaction to that—and I thought, *My God, it's all true.* What Brian had told me in Flanagan's Bar the previous day, and which I had dismissed as paranoia, was actually happening in front of my eyes.

As Jagger, in his broken-bottle voice, sang the threatening lines about somebody's having to pay the price, he glared at Brian, who shrank back from him as if Mick had a gun pointing at his head.

Was it a gimmick? It looked too real to me, though nobody else seemed to notice.

As the Stones concluded their concert with "Satisfaction," I found there was a man bending down and speaking into my ear. "Sorry, Mr. Fitzgerald," he said. "I did knock but you couldn't have heard. I'm Mike Dorsey. I'm a road manager with the Stones. Brian would like you and Marilyn to meet him at the Lotus House after the show. You know it?"

I nodded.

"You'll be there?"

I tried to say yes but couldn't compete with the music, so I nodded again.

Dorsey was a tall, thin man with craggy features and dark hair combed back and held together with oil. He looked quite tough and unfriendly to me, but later I found he was a loyal friend to Brian, and had a lot on his mind that night.

As the song was coming to a climax, I glanced to the back of the orchestra seats and saw him again. He was standing next to Eric Easton and the two of them looked to be worried men.

The Lotus House was at 61 Edgeware Road. It was a very high-class Chinese restaurant. I had been there once or twice before but wasn't recognized.

The head waiter, a distinguished little man, approached us as we stood inside the door looking for Brian. There was no sign of him.

"Can I help you, sir?"

"I'm meeting someone. I don't think he's here yet."

"You have a reservation?"

"Er, no, I haven't. But he might have."

"His name?"

"Mr. Jones."

The old man looked puzzled and took a small book from his pocket, opened it, and ran a finger over the page. "No. No Mr. Jones. I am sorry, sir, but there are no free tables this evening. I am sorry."

Feeling very embarrassed, I turned to go; and then the door burst open and Brian was standing there, beaming at us.

"Ah," said the head waiter. "Mr. Blian. You come this way please."

As we walked between the tables following "Mr. Blian," we came under the shocked and disapproving scrutiny of some of the upper-middle-class diners, who couldn't understand why this long-haired freak in denim trousers, yellow shirt, scarlet tie and yellow shoes hadn't been kicked out on his ear.

We ate a meal, selected by Brian, which contained a lot of seaweed. He ordered three bottles of Mateus Rosé, polishing one off by himself before he'd eaten the main course. I was impressed with the class Brian was showing. In a carefree and ebullient mood, Brian was totally oblivious to the well-bred sneers of the other diners.

His talk was mainly of the concert, but when Marilyn excused herself to go to the ladies' room, Brian said, "You two sleeping together?"

It was a surprise question, and if it had been anyone else I would have said, "Mind your own business." Because it was Brian, I said, "No. But I'm living in hope."

"Won't she let you?"

"It's not really a question of that. It's more a lack of opportunity."

"Use my pad. Fetch her round sometime. I can always go out. Unless you want me to watch."

My face was getting hot. "No thanks."

"No thanks to what? You don't want to use my pad or you don't want me to watch?"

I couldn't think of an answer to that which wouldn't sound stupid. Miserable, I sat there blushing—hoisted on a petard of confused teenage bisexuality.

He laughed and patted me on the shoulder. "I know, we'll have a threesome. I like you both."

It was a bit of a relief to me when Marilyn came back. I thought the subject would have to change. She came across the room with a freshened face and freshly brushed hair, her white cotton miniskirt revealing more than half her bronze thighs, looking as pretty as I'd ever seen her look.

"She's got some gorgeous pins on her," Brian said, and he ordered brandies for us all.

She sat down and smiled at me and then at Brian. He leered back at her with all that mischief that he'd had in Leamington. She dropped her gaze but then let it wander back to his face. Normally she wouldn't have looked back at a man leering. At first I blinded myself to what was going on and chose to believe that my girl was just feeling the effects of her drinks.

The brandy came then and Brian shoved Marilyn's across the table. "That's right," he said. "Forget those inhibitions. Your hair is down, now let's have the defenses down. And then—"

He looked at me. I was taking a long, long pull at the brandy, afraid of what he was going to say. Quite suddenly and inexplicably I found myself saying, "And then we'll have your panties down."

"Nicholas!" she said, reddening a little, but Marilyn's smile—bestowed like a knighthood—told me she was feeling a little thrill.

Brian laughed uproariously. The stuffed shirts glared at him.

"We were discussing a little party at my place," he said to Marilyn. "Just the three of us. We all climb into bed naked. I demand to be in the middle." He turned to me again. I drank more brandy as I felt Marilyn's quizzical glance.

Then he was leaning across the table towards her. "You would look nicer with just one more button undone, Marilyn."

She held his hand as he reached out for the button. She held it but allowed him to undo it all the same. The tart, I thought. She smiled sexily at him as he removed his hand. He was excited. He looked at his watch.

"You on?" he said to her. "Three in a bed?"

"Don't be silly," Marilyn said, but the thoughtful smile was still there.

"I'll go and ring Dave Thompson and tell him to clear out for the night." He got up and went to the phone booth.

"You can go on your own," I said, as if it didn't matter to me. I was seething with jealousy.

"Don't be stupid," she snapped, probably angry with herself. "We'd better go home." She picked up her handbag.

"What for?" I said, knowing I sounded like a schoolboy. "If you fancy him, clear off with him. Take *all* your damn clothes off for him."

"You're so prudish," she said. "Just because he undid a button."

"Oh, well, I'll stop being prudish immediately. We'll do whatever Brian says. Three to a bed. Okay, definitely not prudish, right? If that's what you want, Marilyn, let's *do* it."

"I'm going home," she announced, but she didn't move, obviously expecting me to beg her to stay. When I didn't, Marilyn said, "I'm going to get a taxi. *You* go with Brian. You seem to like him more than you like me. Sounds as if you've been to bed together already anyway."

Just as we were getting into high gear for a violent row, Brian came back. He was a changed man. His face was pale.

"I've got to go," he said, remaining standing. "It's Marianne. She collapsed after a show in Morecombe. Dave thinks she's in the hospital. How the hell can I get up there?"

I had heard rumors that Brian was having an affair with Marianne Faithfull, although she'd just got married to John Dunbar. "What's the matter with Marianne?" I asked.

"I don't bloody know. Somebody called and told Dave she's in the *hospital*." He started making for the door.

We followed. Outside, I managed to talk him into waiting until morning when he could get a train. Brian's sudden outburst of concern for Marianne, sincere and understandable as it was, made for an anticlimactic epilogue to that evening's sexual innuendo.

The next day, I put him in a cab for the station. Just as the cab was about to drive off, Brian opened the door and spoke emphatically to me, very clear and lucid now.

"Meet me on Friday at the Rediffusion Studios, can you? The Byrds and Sonny and Cher are going out live on 'Ready, Steady, Go'. It's the show's second anniversary. Come and see them with me. Oh, and say a prayer for Marianne, Nicholas. Ciao."

CHAPTER

5

"T HE WEEKEND STARTS HERE" was the slogan of the greatest
and most successful "beat show" of the Swinging Sixties,
"Ready, Steady, Go." It began in 1963, with Keith Fordyce as
presenter or emcee. The Rolling Stones made their second-ever
television appearance on this show on August 16, 1963, and from
that time, whatever else they were doing, they were more than
willing to drop everything in order to reappear on "Ready, Steady,
Go." They weren't the only ones to realize the value of the show as
a vehicle. The American equivalent in star-making clout was Dick
Clark's "American Bandstand."

Back in 1963, Francis Hitching, the gifted and far-seeing producer of "Ready, Steady, Go" who then lived near the Crawdaddy
Club in Richmond, hadn't failed to observe the enthusiasm of the
fans whenever the Stones appeared, even before they had made a
record. In much the same way, he had spotted Manfred Mann, the
Animals, the Kinks and the Dave Clark Five, all of whom made
their television debuts on "Ready, Steady, Go."

The first appearance of the Rolling Stones on the show had
coincided with that of Cathy McGowan, who co-emceed it with
Keith Fordyce. Cathy, a teenager herself, was very nervous that
night, but she went on to become a cult figure with British teenagers and to be voted Top Girl TV Personality in 1964 in the music

trade. She had previously met the Stones at The 51 Club on Great Newport Street, London, where, between shows, they would join the dancers on the floor.

Brian loved the filming of that first show, especially since it was done in London. He hated travelling to Birmingham—a "foreign excursion," he called it—in order to record a spot on "Thank Your Lucky Stars," another popular and influential British TV show.

For their first appearance on "Ready, Steady, Go" the Stones performed their single "Come On." In 1963 the system was that the record was played and the stars lip-synched it in front of the cameras. Cathy had found the Stones very confident but not conceited. She said that Brian was more like the classic conception of a pop idol than any of the others; he seemed to glow in front of the stage lights. When they started to play that first night, all the girls in the studio audience went completely berserk.

When the Stones became regular guests, the show really took off, becoming a phenomenal success, far outstripping any other pop program in terms of viewership.

"Ready, Steady, Go" went on at eight minutes past six on Friday evenings, when the week's work was done and teenagers were preparing to go out on the town. The show's appeal was that the audience of young people was not confined to sitting in stiff rows in an auditorium. They were free to dance, wander around and mix with groups like the Beatles or the Rolling Stones in a completely informal setting in the studio. It was like a party, and competition for tickets was fierce.

By 1965, "Ready, Steady, Go" had become "Ready, Steady, Goes Live" and lip-synching had been abandoned in favor of more exciting live performances. On Friday, August 6, after a few days in Paris with Marilyn's father, she and I stepped from a taxi at the Wembley TV studios. Brian greeted us warmly and took us into a small reception room, where a girl with long black hair, a pale face and huge eyes was standing with a glass in her hand. He introduced us; her name was Marie and she was apparently French.

She gave us both a continental kiss on either cheek. She seemed very sad and upset. Marilyn spoke French quite well, and the two of them went into a conversation in which it looked to me like Marie was pouring out her troubles and Marilyn was consoling.

Brian said to me, "She's moaning about my taking Linda on holiday. I promised Linda I'd take her to Tangier. It's going to be a kind of thank you for her dropping the paternity suit."

"You think you and Linda will get back together?" I asked innocently.

"Hell, no," he said. He handed me a glass of white wine. "I don't want to be tied down, especially now we've started to get big. Women are all so damned possessive. Like her." He indicated Marie, who now seemed on the point of tears, while Marilyn kept glancing over at him almost accusingly.

"Who's going to look after the child?" I said.

"What? Oh, him. Her parents, I suppose. We're not going to drag the little beanhead across Tangier, that's for sure. Where have you been all week? I wanted to call you, but I have lost your number."

I told him we'd been in France. I avoided the subject of the telephone number.

Just before six Brian led us all into the studio, where last-minute arrangements were being made for the live TV transmission of "Ready, Steady, Go."

Brian was immediately surrounded by the young people who were going to dance. Congratulations were flung at him about the Stones' new single, "Satisfaction," having reached number one in the States. It surprised me to see that Brian really loved this. My earlier impression of him was that he was rather timid. Now, even if he was basically a shy man, it was obvious he relished being the center of attention.

The show fired off with the pulsating sound of "5–4–3–2–1" by Manfred Mann blaring from the studio's speakers. Brian Jones was sitting next to me.

Not far away from us up on the rostrum was Cathy McGowan, now the show's only emcee, looking pretty, vivacious and fresh, with her long, sleek dark hair falling over her shoulders and breasts. She was introducing the "fabulous Byrds."

The Byrds were being touted as the biggest thing ever to come out of the States and as "America's answer to the Beatles." Busloads of British girls had greeted their arrival at London's Heathrow Airport and created problems for the airport police, who probably didn't know the Byrds from the fishes. Teenage fanaticisms at that time were running fast ahead of the adult awareness.

The Byrds had supported the Stones on their last U.S. tour in May, and Brian had been very impressed by them. They opened with "I'll Feel a Whole Lot Better." But something seemed to be wrong. To me the sound came across as technically poor, something that was unusual for "RSG," which employed the best sound engineers in the business. And the vocals were almost unintelligible. Whether it was the fault of the performers or the technicians wasn't certain, but halfway through Brian and I exchanged glances, and he shrugged and made a face as if to say it wasn't up to standard.

After their number ended, Brian said he was going to make a phone call. At the same time Cathy McGowan announced the Who, a new group from London. As they launched into their number called "Anyway, Anyhow, Anywhere" Brian, who had just gotten up, sat down and listened as if spellbound.

They presented a complete contrast to the Byrds as well as to the Beatles and the Stones. Their sound and their songs were peculiarly their own. They were a London group, from around Shepherd's Bush and Acton, the products of lower-middle-class upbringing and art school influence. And their music was all written by the various members right from the start. It seemed almost totally unrelated to anything that had gone before.

To a certain extent it could be said that both the Stones and the Beatles had, consciously or unconsciously, based their music on what had earlier come across the Atlantic and then been forgotten, only to be revived by the British bands and re-exported to the delight of a later generation of Americans. But the Who were wholly original.

Tonight they proved to be shock treatment to the "RSG" studio right from the start. They pervaded the ears of the audience—who were predominantly Mods—with the wildest and perhaps the loudest act the show had yet experienced. They had devised some way of utilizing amplification so as to provide a kind of feedback that created chaos and confusion as well as almost hysterical frenzy in the audience, which at the end of that galvanic performance simply screamed for more. Brian sat shaking his head in disbelief. Then he began pointing out to me various mannerisms and tricky pieces of fingerwork.

Pete Townshend, the twenty-year-old guitarist, was a quiet, sensitive art student, and Roger Daltrey—twenty-one and their vocalist—was a leather Rocker at heart. Actually, they were all a good deal older than the average Mod.

The Mods were epitomized by the suburban London teenager who spent most of his money on clothes and rode a zippy, much adorned scooter with a girl with a cotton dress or skirt on the pillion.

Rockers were mainly leather-clad, dirty, with greasy hair and rode big, loud motorcycles. Their girls, also in leather, showed more leg on the pillion seats, with their skintight miniskirts hitched up to their hips.

The two groups used to meet in hordes at seaside resorts at holiday times and knock hell out of each other while terrorizing ordinary people.

On the whole it was the Mods who influenced, and were influenced by, such musical groups as the Stones, the Who, and the Beatles. Mods used to swallow vast amounts of pills in order to see them through their hectic weekends that began with "Ready, Steady, Go" on Friday nights, and continued through the long hours at "in" clubs and cafes, like the Two 1's Coffee Bar and the Flamingo Club. Saturday mornings would be spent in Soho, on Carnaby Street, and along the King's Road in Chelsea.

Only one act could have followed the Who on that spectacular evening. It was Sonny and Cher. They sang that moving little song composed by Sonny, "I've Got You, Babe." The secret of their appeal was in the instant rapport they established with the audience, clearly demonstrated that night by the fact that most of the

audience was composed of the "RSG" dancers who, instead of dancing, gathered around the rostrum as if drawn by the magic of this
very unusual, attractive and unspoiled pair of singers. It was their
first British TV appearance, and their performance established them
firmly in the hearts of pop fans throughout the country.

The show was rounded off by two more numbers from the Byrds,
including Bob Dylan's "All I Really Want to Do." Again, in spite of
their excellent material, they seemed to lack coordination, and the
sound didn't come across as it should have; it also looked as if the
group had adopted a couldn't-care-less attitude.

Brian and I and the two girls left in a hired limousine with one of
the Byrds, Dave Crosby, whom Brian appeared to know quite well,
and headed for the 32 Club in Harlesden where the Byrds appeared
at nine o'clock.

After that it was back in the limo and through the endless streets
of London in the gathering dusk into Soho and to Wardour Street.
We pulled up outside the Flamingo Club. As we all piled out and
crossed the pavement, some startled tourists, daring to explore this
seedy part of the West End, gaped at Dave Crosby in his bright
green cape trimmed with dark brown suede.

The Flamingo was one of the few cellar jazz clubs licensed to
serve alcohol. The crowded, dimly lit room had about a dozen
tables, a small dance floor, a bar and a stage where a modern jazz
trio was performing. The Byrds were booked to play later. The
crowd grew as all the "RSG" team, together with the other Byrds
and the Who, arrived in our wake. A big pool of people were
gathered around the bar. Dusty Springfield sat at a table talking to
Vicki Wickham, the assistant producer of "RSG."

Brian started to talk to John Entwistle, the Who's bass guitarist,
who was complaining that no reporter had ever interviewed him or
asked him anything about the Who. Brian told him that the same
thing applied to Bill Wyman, the Stones' bass player.

"Maybe they got something against bass guitarists," John Entwistle said. "Now, Pete Townshend, they only gotta see him coming
and they jump on him."

"Yes," Brian said. "They do the same to Mick. But you'll have to keep your end up, John. There's always one in a group who wants to get on top and overshadow everyone else."

"You're damn right," said John. It seemed he was feeling some of Brian's bitterness, and I wondered if this sort of thing went on in every group.

A reporter later approached Dave Crosby, who was still in his green cape. I wasn't close enough to hear what was said, but Dave suddenly put his arms in the air, holding the sides of the cape, then sank to the ground and covered himself with it. The reporter, looking put out, was left standing over a green mound on the floor.

Just before the Byrds were due to play, Beatle George Harrison strolled in with his girlfriend Pattie Boyd, and there was a rustle of excitement. Palming off a few reporters, they retired modestly to a corner to listen to the music. After it was over, George and Pattie were joined by Dave Crosby, who appeared to keep them vastly entertained throughout most of the evening.

Brian, Marie, Marilyn, and I—by now quite tipsy—were standing at the bar when I noticed hazily that I could see two Brian Joneses. Then, pulling myself together, I realized that Brian had been joined by Mike Clarke—his "look-alike"—the blue-eyed, blond drummer for the Byrds. The resemblance between them was amazing, and in my present state of intoxication, I felt again the sexual rush I'd experienced when I'd first met Brian. This time, I immediately admitted the sexual nature and the attraction—to both Mike and Brian.

The next day, I knew, it would be upsetting.

I turned to Marilyn, after staring at Brian and Mike in conversation for at least five minutes, to remark on their similarity; but when I saw the look on her face I knew she had come to realize there was something gay going on in my head. I decided to say nothing, and she turned away, saddled with an uncomfortable truth. But I was feeling a rebellious elation and didn't much care anymore what she thought. I moved nearer to Brian.

Mike Clarke was saying, "I figured Mick Jagger might be here tonight."

Brian shrugged his shoulders.

From behind us came a quiet, cultivated voice. "Mick's not coming. He doesn't think he can face another argument with Brian."

We all turned and saw what to me and many others was the most beautiful woman in the world—Marianne Faithfull. Hers was a beauty totally unmarred by attitude; she had a disarming way of looking at you, as if not certain whether you'd like her.

Everyone, including Brian, greeted Marianne warmly, though I was expecting Brian to say something sarcastic or vitriolic about Mick. I wondered vaguely how Marianne had known Mick wasn't coming. She was married to the Cambridge academic John Dunbar and just that morning the *New Musical Express* had reported she was expecting a baby. I knew she had met all the Stones as a result of going to a party on Good Friday 1964, where she had also met Andrew Oldham, who had then and there got her a recording contract with Decca.

It says a lot for Marianne's magnetism—that mingling of virginal innocence with repressed passion—that almost every eye in the place was on her. Not because of her fame; most of the people there were as famous. Not really because of her beauty; there were girls as pretty. It was because of that special and extra, indefinable quality that drew men and women to worship her.

She said to Brian, "I see you've got your double with you," and she smiled at Mike Clarke.

Brian feigned surprise, giving Mike the once-over, "You think we look alike?"

Marianne laughed. It was a throaty but girlish laugh. "Good Lord, you mean you haven't noticed? Hasn't anyone remarked on it?"

Brian looked around for confirmation or denial; his eyes lit on me. "Nicholas, do you think I look like Mike here?"

It was my great moment. Marianne, the girl of my wet dreams, was gazing at me, waiting for me to speak.

I opened my mouth and to my horror all that came out was a croaking, "Yes."

Then Marianne's lovely eyes softened in sympathy with my gaucherie, and I was suddenly emboldened. "I was amazed by it myself," I said firmly now. "But there's something else I've noticed, too. The three of you could be identical triplets."

The result of this remark did my ego a power of good. Marianne opened her mouth, raised her eyebrows and put a hand to her chest in a gesture of amused surprise, as both Brian and Mike threw back their heads and laughed.

Marianne moved closer to me and touched my arm, sending delicious shock waves through my body. "You naughty boy—Nicholas, is it? Well, Nicholas, just for your nerve you can buy me a drink. I'll have a Bacardi and Coke, please."

Now a noble knight on an errand for my fair maid, I fought like a tiger to get through the pressing mob for her drink. Emerging dishevelled from the fray, I couldn't find Marianne. Finally, I spotted her sitting with John Entwistle and Cathy McGowan. She already had a drink in front of her. Champagne.

Depressed, I went back to the bar, taking the drink with me. Then I saw Marilyn. She was totally alone in the milling throng and her face was like thunder. I went up to her and, hoping to pacify her, handed her the Bacardi and Coke.

"Thanks," she said. "That's big of you." She then took unsteady aim and chucked the contents out of the glass.

The aim was not good. Some complete stranger, a burly, middle-aged guy who had been propping up the bar ever since we had arrived, was at first surprised and then extremely irked at receiving free liquor by way of his right ear.

As Marilyn flounced off and as Brian, to my left, began to laugh, the burly man slowly raised himself from the bar, turned and grabbed me by the lapels. He cursed me in some kind of Scottish dialect and shook me until I felt like a rat in the mouth of a terrier. People moved away to form a kind of circle around us. Brian came and tried to restrain the man but he was shoved back into the crowd with one swift movement of the brute's elbow. I could faintly hear the trio on the stage still playing.

Just as I was contemplating death from disintegration, a smartly dressed, stocky man wearing a dinner jacket stepped into the circle and shouted, "Sandy." Instantly, he released me.

"What's going on?" the man in the dinner jacket said.

"Sorry, Mr. Kruger," Sandy growled. "He threw a drink at me. Or someone did."

Brian intervened. "It wasn't him, Mr. Kruger. It was his girl. She's gone now. No harm done."

Sandy mopped his ear with a dirty handkerchief. My savior was J. S. Kruger, the club's owner. He said, "Okay, but don't forget you're here to sort out trouble, not to start it," and went away.

Brian and I settled down for a quiet chat. He said he was sorry Marilyn had been upset and hoped it wasn't anything to do with him. I said I didn't think so and that I was not feeling very serious about her lately. In fact for most of the holiday she had been rather a burden, something of a jailer. That, at least, was how I was feeling on that heady night.

"Well," Brian said cheerfully, "you're staying in the same house, so you should be able to kiss and make up later on. You want me to ring her?"

"Good God, no," I said, alarmed.

He chuckled. Then he said, "I don't know when I'll see you again after tonight. We've got a few days off next week, and I'm taking Linda to Tangier."

"Yes, you said. What's happened to Marie?" It had only now occurred to me that I hadn't seen her for ages.

Brian said, "Same as happened to your Marilyn, but a little less dramatic. She stormed off earlier. Very temperamental, these females. The male of the species is far less deadly." He was giving me the roguish eye again. "Why can't a woman be more like a man, as the song says?"

"Different shape," I said. "I like it. I don't know how any man could be gay when Marianne is around."

Brian looked over at her and his eyes twinkled. "She certainly has got something. Do you want to talk to her?"

I shook my head sadly. "She just thinks of me as a schoolboy. She won't take me seriously."

"How d'you like my double, Mike Clarke?"

"Haven't had a chance to talk to him yet."

Mike had gone off with the other Byrds to sit down in a group.

"Well, did you want to talk to him?" Brian said, and I could sense some ominous mood coming on him.

"I wouldn't mind. It's nice to meet new people."

"You find him attractive?" There was no smile now.

"I think he's interesting to look at. Like you."

"I'll call him over, shall I? Then you and he can have a nice, long chat." Now he was being bitchy and jealous.

"He looks quite comfortable where he is," I said.

"Well, Nicholas," he said, standing up to his full short height, and trying to sound nonchalant, "you mustn't let our friendship inhibit you. Don't think that just because I've introduced you to the great cutthroat world of pop that you have to stay tied to my apron strings. You don't owe me anything."

"Brian," I said, quite hurt and a little angry at his patronizing air, "you are drunk and I'm drunk. Let's not talk about things like that now."

"Okay, okay," he said, and he put his head on the bar, sobbed and fell asleep.

I left about four in the morning. The dawn seemed to sober me and instead of going home, I wandered down to Trafalgar Square and on then to the embankment, where I stared out across the silent river. So much had happened, so many strange urges and desires had been aroused in me. Was I gay? Bisexual? Society said either one was bad; what was I going to do about myself? Brian was always coming on to me, and yet there were always his girls. Perhaps if I had been older, more experienced and capable of taking the lead, Brian and I would have been in a deep love affair by now. Brian was flirting indiscriminately with everyone, and everyone was losing—often the dilemma of bisexuals.

Was Brian mad? He seemed so, or was he really being per-secuted? Did Mick hate him? What was my duty to Brian as a friend? How could I advise him unless I knew whether his fears were real or imagined? Oh, so many questions came, but no answers. They always said the young don't know the answers. But the Sixties kids thought they were going to change all that. Well, what were the answers now? Certainly not rising out of the leaden flames.

Wearily, I went off to Mrs. FitzRoy's house, where we were staying. A note had been put under my bedroom door.

> Nicholas, please don't be at breakfast. I am leaving shortly afterwards. I am sure there is something wrong with you and you should seek help. Meantime thanks for the lovely week and please do not ever contact me again.

It was signed, Marilyn.

*I*T WAS SUMMER VACATION. At home in Edgbaston, there was nothing to do but play cricket, quite a comedown from running around with superstars in London. It took Brian, I realized, to get my ass in gear, and when he called, I was glad. On Thursday, August 27, he phoned me at my parents' home. "Come to London for the weekend," he said. "I need to talk to you." I told him I would be along, and then he said, "It would be inconvenient for you to stay at the apartment. I suggest you book into the London Hilton." He made no mention of who would foot the bill. Though a Guinness heir, I was on a strict allowance in my teens. Sensing my hesitation, Brian added as an enticement, "You'll meet the other Rolling Stones."

That did it; I took the early morning train from Birmingham the next day.

What would the other Stones be like?

It had surprised me that Brian spent so little time socially with the other members of the group. I began to wonder if they were avoiding him rather than the other way around. This weekend, I'd find out.

On the previous Friday, the Stones' much-hyped single, "(I Can't Get No) Satisfaction," had been released in the U.K., three months after its release in the USA. However, unlike Brian Jones' most cherished Stones number, "Little Red Rooster," it crashed into the British charts only at number three, whereas "Little Red Rooster" came straight in at number one—the only time the Stones ever achieved this distinction. Above "Satisfaction" was "I Got You Babe" at number two and "Help" at number one.

In London I checked into a room on the twenty-second floor of the Hilton. After showering, I went to the bar downstairs. Brian had arranged to meet me there between twelve and two. The bar was filling up with lunch-time drinkers. I ordered a Scotch and Coke—bizarre teenage drink—and looked idly about the room.

There was a man wearing a patchwork jacket of wild colors, bending over a sketch pad on his knee, drawing a statue near him. It was Keith Richard. Nobody was taking any notice of him.

Taking up my drink, I strolled nearer to him and sat down. He shot a frigid glance at me, then turned back to his sketch. His face was as blank and stony as that of the sculpture beside him. The glance had for the moment unnerved me; the eyes had been so dead and there had been a corpselike pallor about the face. With his jet-black hair all awry and a cigarette dangling from his lips, Keith was an electrifying sight. He was tense and looked a little nervous. Yet that jacket was so frivolous it seemed to intrude on his solemnity like a garland at a wake.

On impulse I walked up to him and said, "Are you sketching the statue?"

"No, I'm not," he said. The voice was firm but not exactly hostile.

"Oh, what is it you're sketching?"

"The barman." He looked up, puckered his lips and crossed his eyes. He was grotesque.

"You weren't expecting me to say that, were you?" he said, letting his face return to normal.

"Er—no."

His eyes creased into twinkling slits and he directed a broad friendly grin at me, making me at ease. He handed me the pad.

"See what you think," he said.

It was a good likeness of the barman, and the standard of drawing was surprisingly professional.

"It's very good," I said. "A man of many talents. You are Keith Richard, aren't you?"

"So I'm told." Then I saw his eyes cloud over as they fixed on something behind me. "Oh God, here's trouble."

He stood up and took the pad from me.

I turned and followed his gaze to the door. It was Brian. He stood looking around the room. When he saw me, he smiled and started over. The smile turned to a scowl when he saw I was with Keith.

Keith said, "See you," and set off toward the door, leaving the rest of his drink. They passed each other without exchanging a word or even a sign of recognition.

Brian snarled, "What were you talking about with him?" He was waving his newspapers towards the door.

I was indignant at his tone of voice. "Why?" I said.

"I want to know. What were you talking to Keith about? What was he saying about me?"

"We were talking about the barman; I don't see what that's got to do with you." Even though I was annoyed at his aggressiveness, I found myself marveling at that expressive face. It was strained now, and the nostrils were flared and the cheekbones stood out. The chin jutted. In temper he displayed the characteristics of Welsh atavistic savagery. He even stood with his legs apart as if to guard against physical assault.

"Don't be funny with me. Let's get one thing straight, Nicholas, I'm no fool. You were obviously talking about me or he wouldn't have shot out like that. Now, what the hell was he saying?"

People were pricking up their ears and staring at us. Brian wasn't exactly raising his voice, but his anger was plain.

I tried to calm him. "I met Keith Richard for the first time just a few minutes ago. He doesn't know me from Adam; thinks I'm any one of a million fans just wanting the thrill of talking to a Stone. Why should he connect me with you? He'd have no idea I know you. He doesn't even know my name, Brian."

"Come on. You'd have told Keith we're friends, Nicholas."

"Sure I might have—if we'd had a conversation. We'd just passed a couple of sentences when you came in."

Brian grunted, his anger subsiding. "Well, don't discuss me with any of them, okay?"

"If that's the way you want it. But I don't like taking orders from my friends."

"All right." He set his newspapers down on the table. "You want another drink?" He spoke gruffily now, like a little boy making the first shy move towards reconciliation after a fight.

Brian went to the bar and I thumbed through the *News* and the *Standard*. I knew that if Brian was saving the papers, they must have stories about him. What I found, though, was considerably more than I had expected.

There was a large two-column story in each of them, and the first surprise was that the Rolling Stones had appointed a new agent. He was Tito Burns, who was the British representative of Bob Dylan. Secondly, an American accountant named Allen Klein had been appointed to replace Eric Easton, and he would now be comanager of the group with Andrew Loog Oldham. Thirdly, the Stones had landed a big new contract with Decca, their record company, to finance five films to be made over the next three years. The budget was to be about three million dollars. There was a suggestion in the *News* that Dylan might star in one of the films. The *Standard* stated that Sir Edward Lewis, Decca's chairman, had sent a personal letter to each of the Stones.

"Hey what about all this?" I said to Brian when he came back with the drinks. "This contract. It's fantastic."

He looked worried and suspicious. "I don't know," he said, slumping into a chair. "That's why I wanted someone to talk to. I don't know what to think. There I am on holiday in Tangier—with Linda—and I get an anonymous phone call, telling me someone's planning my removal. And you know how they get rid of people in the States. You can take out a contract on most people for about ten thousand dollars."

The subject switched back to Allen Klein. I asked, "What's he like?"

"He doesn't seem a bad sort of a guy. He's over here now. He seems to talk sense. He says we might be famous but we haven't made much money. He told me he can make me a dollar millionaire in five years. That can't be bad, can it?"

"No, and it doesn't sound as if he wants to get rid of you either. Does it?"

He sighed, "I don't know what to think. As I said, I wanted to talk to you before the meeting. I don't know what I ought to do."

"Why d'you think they all met first without you?"

"Afraid I might throw a monkey wrench in the works, maybe. I don't agree with a lot of their ideas. You know they went to the Shea Stadium concert in New York?"

"Yes. I read about it." The Beatles had given a concert at Shea Stadium. It had been a bit of a bomb as far as the fans were concerned. They had paid five dollars or more each to see their idols so far off they needed binoculars.

"Well, Brian Epstein had invited us all to that. Mick and Keith said they weren't going, so I didn't bother either. Then they went after all. And they had that meeting with Klein. I still haven't been told about it officially."

"Who d'you think made the anonymous call?"

"I don't know." He looked about him; then, with an air of conspiracy, said, "I think it could have been someone from the *New Musical Express*. Maybe one of their reporters covering the Shea concert. I don't know. Didn't recognize the voice. The hotel in Tangier told me it had come in from New York."

"Well," I said, thinking the solution was quite simple, "you can put it to them tonight, can't you? Let them know you're annoyed about it."

He smiled ironically at this. "That won't endear me to them exactly. They already say I'm a one-man opposition to anything they agree on. Maybe I am, but it's my group and I want to chart the course it's going to take. That's why I think they'll want to get me out of it, if not now, eventually. Don't worry, I'll let them know I'm annoyed but I don't like the idea of having them all ganging up on me."

"You make it sound like a war, or politics," I said.

"But of course it is. Whenever a group like this shows any sign of getting into the big loot there's always intrigue, politics, even all-out bloody war involved. In come the big exploiters, out goes anything even slightly uncommercial. You'll find the same battles behind the scenes with the Beatles soon, if it's not already—" He had noticed someone approaching us, he sat up in his chair and looked positively shifty. "Shh," he said. "It's Allen Klein."

Klein came up to us unsmiling. He was a tough stock character with a lantern jaw, a flat, blunt nose, large dark eyes and black hair swept back over his head. In his mid-thirties, he wore a red T-shirt, lightweight trousers and basketball shoes. Under the shirt I saw that he carried quite a lot of weight, especially around his pectoral muscles, which any fourteen-year-old girl might have been proud of. Altogether he did not make a good first impression on me. He was certainly a total contrast to Eric Easton.

Klein ignored me completely and said to Brian, briskly, "Everybody's here, if you're ready. You know where to go. It's on the twenty-seventh floor. Don't be long please, Brian." He gave a quick and dismissive look at me before he strode back across the room.

Brian got up nervously. "Hey, come to the 'RSG' studios tonight," he said. It was as if he were making a clandestine tryst behind the headmaster's back. "Five o'clock," he said, going off after Klein. "Don't be late. We're on tonight."

I watched him go, feeling as if I were sending a younger brother off to face some new hurdle for which life hadn't prepared him.

It was just after five when I found Brian again in the canteen of the "RSG" studios in Wembley. He was hunched up disconsolately over a cup of tea. Bill Wyman, who sat at the same table, was being interviewed by a dark-haired young man who was introduced as Keith Altham, a reporter for the *New Musical Express*.

I got my tea, and Brian and I moved to another table to avoid disrupting the interview.

"How did it go?" I asked.

Brian was glum. "Oh, all right," he said, "but I don't like all these changes. They've sacked Eric Easton and Mike Dorsey has resigned."

"I met Mike Dorsey at the Palladium."

"Yes, one of my few allies amongst the lot of them."

"They couldn't actually sack Eric Easton, could they? You said they were trying to get rid of him, but he had a contract."

"He's gone isn't he? They've squeezed him out, and Mike went with him. They were good friends. They told me Mike had resigned for personal reasons, but I reckon he was sacked. They say he's in New York, but I don't know. I don't seem to be told what's going to happen next anymore. They've kept Stew. But then he's on their side, not mine."

It did not seem the proper time to ask who Stew was. All this talk of sides reminded me of Brian's earlier remarks about intrigue, politics and all-out war. Brian had signed a contract with Easton as leader of the Stones two years ago, but now he was being left out of negotiations altogether. I thought it all very unfair.

"It could be me next," Brian said, sitting up and stretching himself as if in resignation.

Heads turned as Andrew Loog Oldham came sweeping in, accompanied by two pretty youths of about my own age. He came to our table, took a look at me as if wondering where we'd met before, then turned to Brian, quite amicably it seemed, and asked if he had been told the time of the flight to Los Angeles on the Sunday after next (September 5). Brian said he had, and Andrew nodded and went off to join the young director, Michael Lindsay-Hogg, who was talking to Francis Hitching.

Brian watched him contemptuously.

I asked, "Why are you off to the States?"

For the first time that evening, he smiled, and some of the old horniness was back in his eyes. It didn't embarrass me this time. I was too relieved to see him come out from under that cloud of sullenness.

"Two more recording sessions at RCA in Hollywood." He was cheerful now, obviously looking forward to the trip. "We've got to do a follow-up to 'Satisfaction' for the U.S. market. It was quite a marathon session when we did 'Satisfaction.' Began at ten on Wednesday morning May twelfth and ended at two-thirty on the following morning. After a catnap, Dave Hassinger, our engineer, and Oldham returned to mix down the tracks. At 1 P.M. we joined them for another nine-hour session."

"Do you always record in the States now?" I asked.

"Yes. They get things *done* over there. We can record right through from six at night to six in the morning without so much as a tea break."

Keith Richard came in with two other men who, armed with notepads and pens, were evidently reporters. Charlie Watts followed, looking bored, and when one of the reporters said something to him he just gave a one-word answer and looked away. The reporter said something else to him, and Charlie glared back, pursed his lips and said something like "piss off." Charlie was the lethargic, laconic type, obviously, and appeared indifferent to the spurious adulation that being a member of the Stones bestowed upon him. Compared with Brian, he was surprisingly normal. He wore a white turtleneck sweater, quite inappropriate, I thought, for the heat of a TV studio, and a dark suit.

Brian excused himself and went to the next table to talk to Keith Altham, the reporter from *New Musical Express,* and I was left alone to study the various characters gathering in the canteen. Keith Richard, Bill Wyman and Charlie Watts were sitting together, while Andrew Oldham flitted about from one table to another and answered telephones and loudspeaker calls. I was fascinated that these famous and important figures, including stars and press people, were sloppily dressed, picked their noses, used four-letter words and farted. Though the TV spectaculars they produced were incredibly glamorous, behind the scenes they were like anyone else at work.

Other celebrities were sitting about the room. Laurence Harvey was there with his tempting girlfriend. And then Mick Jagger entered and everyone—except Brian—focused on him. Mick was wearing a long-sleeved gray sweatshirt and trousers which made him look unexpectedly drab, but there was no denying, in spite of that, he had tremendous charisma. Of course the most noticeable feature was his mouth; those wide, fat, blubbery lips. He was quite slim and wiry at that time. His hair was untidy and reached to the bottom of his neck. He wore a thick gold ring on the little finger of his left hand. Some people described him as ugly. That was not my impression, but if "ugly" is the right word, then he was attractively ugly; certainly not repulsive.

He ambled over in my direction, followed by a train of acolytes, and when he reached me he stopped and slowly ran his eyes over me. Feeling nervous and embarrassed, I looked at Brian at the next table. Brian was glaring angrily at Mick.

Mick said to me, "Hello. You look cute. What's your name then?"

Like a flash Brian was out of his seat and standing beside me. "This is a friend of mine," he said belligerently. "Nicholas Fitzgerald. So don't start any of your antics with him."

Mick regarded him derisively and said, "Nicholas, eh? That's very interesting, isn't it, Brian?" Then he turned on his heel and went over to join Andrew Oldham. I noticed that Andrew was staring over at our table and looking puzzled, obviously having witnessed this odd incident.

I watched Mick settle down at their table, making no attempt to conceal my fascination. His bedroom eyes had stripped me bare and I felt the same as millions of young girls—and boys—who contemplated his brooding face on their boudoir walls all over the world.

Brian deliberately stepped in front of me, blocking my view of Mick. I looked up at Brian and saw he was angry. "What are you thinking?" he said, accusingly.

"I was thinking how different you all are," I lied, and gave him a big friendly smile to pacify him.

The loudspeaker system crackled and drowned out conversation. "Would the Rolling Stones please come to the studio for a sound check?" the announcer said.

Brian was about to leave when Mick came bounding over and said to me, "Will you be around after the show, Nicholas?"

Brian tensed and I thought he was going to lash out at Mick, but then Mick darted off. Brian gave me a quick, threatening look, then followed Mick out of the room. I was in that heady state of elation that comes over you when two attractive people are vying for you.

The only one of the Stones left in the room was Bill Wyman, the bass guitarist. He wasn't needed for the sound test. Sitting alone reading one of a pile of daily papers on his table, he was chewing gum, looking bored. It was pretty obvious that success hadn't gone to his head.

While I was gazing at Bill, I became aware that someone had joined me at my table. I looked across and saw a young, blue-eyed, blond man with a notebook and a pen in his hand. He introduced himself as a freelance reporter.

He said, "I heard them say your name was Fitzgerald. Are you connected with the Guinness family at all?"

Feeling panicky, I nevertheless contrived a smile and said, "I should be so lucky."

"Oh, you're not then." He looked disappointed. He was probably very inexperienced at his job and was as green as I was. "That's my luck. It would have made a good story. GUINNESS HEIR AT STONES TV PERFORMANCE."

"Well, there are plenty of others here worth writing about. Is Allen Klein, their new manager, here yet?"

"No, but I've done him earlier at the Hilton. D'you know much about him?"

"No. There hasn't been much in the papers yet."

"He's Jewish, you know."

"Is he really?"

"Yes, but he doesn't advertise the fact."

This rather odd young man then flicked through his notepad and read out. "He's thirty-three, was born in Newark, New Jersey. High-flying business man and accountant, first met Andrew Loog Oldham two months ago in the Scotch of St. James. That's a nightclub. Oldham says he has every confidence in him."

Andrew Oldham was chatting nearby with reporters and various studio hands. I was disturbed that people were assuming I was homosexual. Did I look gay? Mick and maybe even Brian seemed to think so. Or did homosexuals check out every good-looking man?

Mick Jagger came back. This time he ignored me and went to sit with the reporters at Andrew's table. Sitting nearby, I heard someone ask Mick about the first of the films to be made by Decca.

"I want it to say something," Mick said. "I don't want it to be a slapstick thing where they make out we're all clowns." He paused as Brian came and joined me and snorted at Mick's remark. Then Mick went on. "I want people to come out feeling they've seen something new."

Brian muttered to me, "He wants, he wants. He talks as if the whole bloody outfit revolves around him. If Eric Easton had had his way, he wouldn't even be in it."

That night the show really lived up to its reputation. The Stones performed three numbers, concluding with a wild version of "Satisfaction," during which Brian took a diving header over about six people as he was pulled into the crowd. Bill Wyman deserved a medal for the way he kept playing while two girls hung onto his black leather vest, and Keith at one stage completely disappeared in a flurry of arms and legs. Miniskirts rose above female bottoms as the frenzied girls rolled around on the stage. The security men had their toughest night yet.

"Fantastic!" Andrew exclaimed at the end.

Afterward Brian and I sat in the club upstairs. By now the "RSG" studios had become the place to go in the early evening on Friday. The place was noisy and packed that night with other celebrities such as Kenny Lynch and the Welsh singer Tom Jones.

Brian looked at Tom Jones. "He's a great performer but he doesn't seem a part of the Mod scene. He was on the 'Ed Sullivan Show' with us in May. He's very macho. He couldn't stand the dancers who were on with him, and they hated him. But he's got things going for him. His voice is great and he gets terrific songs written for him."

I studied Tom, standing in the center of a group of mostly small people—admirers and reporters—and he really did look a hefty brute and quite out of place among the Mod set. His tight shirt seemed to bother him. He had undone the collar and loosened his tie. "It is easy to imagine him stripped to the waist and working down a mine," Brian observed. And down a mine is where Tom

Jones might easily have ended up but for his determination to exploit his powerful voice.

Brian said, "Now you've met all the Stones, what d'you think of them? All as wild and nasty as Oldham tries to paint us?"

I looked around the room at each of the Rolling Stones before I answered. "Keith, I suppose, is the nearest to the older people's idea of a Stone. Does he ever comb his hair?"

Brian looked at him distastefully for a moment and shook his head. "I doubt if a comb would go through it. It must be filthy. And they all sneer at me for washing mine every day. They call me Mr. Shampoo."

I smiled at this and looked at his soft, shiny mop of hair. He certainly didn't suit the sociopathic image that Oldham tried so hard to disseminate, though when necessary Brian could put on a hostile antisocial face for the camera.

"What about Mick?" he said. "D'you fancy him?"

I was shocked.

Brian laughed amid the hubbub that was going on all around. "Your face! You look like a spinster who's just been touched up. Come on, then, what d'you think about Mick?"

"He strikes me as odd. I don't like the way he speaks. That sort of cockney whine."

"He puts a lot of that on. He's affected. He can put on any sort of accent, so I don't know why he chooses that one. I think it's horrible, too. Does he look like the public's conception of a Rolling Stone?"

Mick was quite close by, with Vicki Wickham, Andrew, Francis Hitching, Michael Lindsay-Hogg and a crowd of reporters, who all seemed to be hanging on his every word, while completely ignoring Brian.

"No," I said, "Not at the moment. He looks too clean. He looks more like a college boy. It must be the way he behaves onstage that gives the impression that he's a rebel."

"Right," said Brian, looking quite pleased with me, like a teacher getting the right answer from a pupil. "That's what it is. He's always been a bit like that, but Oldham got him to emphasize it."

"That leaves Bill Wyman and Charlie Watts," I said. "It seems to me they're both steady types but they work hard at being tearaways."

"Yeah," Brian said. "They're both nice guys. I get on well with them. Good, steady musicians. Charlie's always been the most reliable one of the lot. I remember in the old days—when Keith, Mick and I lived in a slum apartment at Edith Grove—Charlie was the only one among us who could be relied upon to buy a round of drinks and without going broke. As a drummer, he's marvelous. Holds the whole band together with that steady, perfect beat. Everybody thinks drumming is easy. Not the way Charlie does it."

Cathy McGowan stopped at our table to say hello to Brian. "You and the group were absolutely fab this evening," she said. Cathy looked quite pretty.

"Thanks," Brian said, but without a smile. He introduced me. Cathy exchanged a few remarks before joining Jagger's group.

"Mick has got the hots for her," Brian said. "I'm sure he'd like to have it off with her, given half the chance."

Later we had a long discussion over Brian's belief that most people are bisexual.

"They're just too uptight to admit it or practice it," Brian said. "A lot of people in rock are ambidextrous as far as sex is concerned."

I looked at Keith and his girl, who resembled him so much I thought she could be his sister, yet the way she was looking at him was anything but sisterly.

"That's his girlfriend, Linda Keith," Brian said, as if reading my thoughts. "Nice, isn't she? Excuse me a moment." He got up and approached Keith. When Brian kissed Linda on the cheek, I saw the smile fade from Keith's face. Keith and his friends became rigid and hostile. Brian just smiled and went on to the men's room.

I sat drinking in the scene. Nobody was taking special notice of me, but they didn't treat me as an intruder either. I could relax; I was now one of them. The moment was an epiphany. From the age of ten I had yearned to belong to the world of pop music. And now I had Brian Jones to thank for providing high-level entry. I was basking in excitement when the blond reporter accosted me again.

"I knew them before they had an arse to their trousers," he said. "I suppose you're Brian's."

End of peak experience.

"Brian's *what?*"

"His boy. His friend."

"I like to think I'm a friend of his. Why?"

"Did I hear him talking about Edith Grove?"

"Yes. He mentioned it."

"That's when I knew them."

"What's your name?"

"They used to call me Phelge. That's because they couldn't be bothered to remember my name."

I wished Brian would return, but there was no sign of him.

"I lived with them for a while—Keith, Brian, and Mick," said Phelge. "There was only one bed between the four of us. Most of the time I slept on the floor. It was Brian's apartment, really, but Mick and Keith joined him because they were in the middle of forming the band and didn't want the trouble and expense of traveling up and down. Sometimes the poor devils didn't have enough money for a meal, poor souls. Keith's mother used to send him some, and Mick had a grant from the London School of Economics, but Brian had nothing and was too proud to ask his parents. Had to do odd jobs in the daytime."

"Yes," I said. "I know all about that."

"Not *all* about it?" he said coyly.

I was getting impatient with his insinuations and started looking around the room. An unlikely character was leaning on Mick Jagger's shoulder and talking quite earnestly to him, even though Mick didn't seem interested. He was a tough-looking fellow with the kind of face usually found in places like Glasgow or Liverpool, with eyebrows that met in the middle above a nose that looked as if it had taken more than a few knocks.

"You don't know about him, for instance, do you?" Phelge said, and now I decided that perhaps he might be worth listening to after all. Obviously Brian had been waylaid somewhere on the way back.

"That's Stew," he went on. "Ian Stewart is his real name but they call him Stew. He's one of the road managers. Ugly-looking bloke, isn't he? Wouldn't like to find him in my bed, would you, ducky?"

"Don't call me ducky," I said tersely. "Where did they find him?"

"Brian advertised, way back in '62, when he was living at Edith Grove. Advertised in *Jazz News* for someone like himself, interested in rhythm 'n' blues, to join a new outfit. Stew applied and Brian liked the way he played piano, so they got together with a few others. This was before Mick, Keith and the others came on the scene."

"He's a pianist?" The man looked as if he had as much music in his soul as an engine tuner.

"Oh yes, he's good at his own kind of stuff. You know, jazz, that sort of thing. But when Andrew took over he found Stew was too straight and he was 'musically unnecessary,' according to Andrew. Luckily Dick Hattrell, the road manager, left when the group's schedule started getting too hectic, so Andrew offered Stew the job. Stew wasn't too pleased but he took it. You sure you're busy tonight?"

"I told you, it's not my scene."

"Oh, all right then."

"Is he still friendly with Brian?" I asked, as I watched Ian Stewart, who still seemed to be pestering Mick about something.

"Oh, bless you now, duck. Oh—sorry. No, he blamed Brian for some reason for getting him out of the group. I can't think why. It was Andrew's idea."

I turned back to Phelge and studied his effeminate face. "How do you know so much about it, anyway?"

"I told you. I lived with them for a while. We were all down and out. Two old ladies in the apartment below used to throw us scraps. It was all good fun."

"And you're some sort of journalist now?"

"Well, yes. At least I pretend to be. It helps me to get into parties like this."

Brian looked angry when he returned from the john. Stew stopped talking to Mick and glared at Brian. Brian glared back, then turned the glare on Phelge. At the same time I saw Mick look over his shoulder with an expression of wicked fun on his face.

Brian stopped a few feet away from us all and looked at each of us. Anger was mixed with fear now, as if he were sure we had all been talking and laughing about him behind his back. Then, ignoring Mick and Stew, he came up to me and pointed to Phelge, who cringed in intimidation.

Brian said to me, "What are you talking to him for?"

I felt the whole room looking at us, but actually only those immediately next to us were aware of Brian's vituperative attitude. My reaction was to be rude back. I didn't enjoy being spoken to like that, especially in front of strangers.

"Is there some house rule," I said, "that stipulates who I can talk to and who I can't?"

For a moment Brian looked as if he would explode into tears. He was trembling and his face turned a deathly pale. "You please your bloody self, Fitzgerald. I'm off." Brian stalked out, roughly nudging people out of his way as he went.

"My, my," said Phelge, relaxing again. "What a tantrum."

I found myself looking into the smiling eyes of Mick Jagger. He gave a slow shrug of his shoulders and I did the same in response, ignoring the unfriendly stare of Ian Stewart.

Mick called out, "Nicholas, you must come down on the second of September. My guest. You'll enjoy it. We're taking over the whole show that night. Will you come?"

Still smarting at Brian's rudeness, I said, "Thanks, I'd love to."

"Me too, ducky," said Phelge, but nobody else noticed him.

CHAPTER
7

THERE WAS A NOTE on the hall table that Brian Jones had called an hour ago. He'd left a London number and asked that I call back as soon as I arrived in Birmingham. Returning home, I'd assumed I'd never renew my friendship with Brian. I was depressed—I'd lost Marilyn, given up on Brian, and I had not joined Mick after his cordial invitation, unable to believe that Mick Jagger could have any reason to take an interest in me beyond wanting to stir up Brian.

Strangely, Brian's reaching out to me now did not elate me, though for a second or two my heart began to leap. Then I came down to earth with a jolt. I was home, and my outlook on life had started to slot back into the trammels of respectability, convention and dutiful routine.

Thoughtfully, I carried the note up to my bedroom and set it down on my desk. The postcard that Brian had sent me from Tangier a week or so ago was still there, with two bemused-looking camels staring up from it. I turned it over and noticed it was stamped from the El Minzah Hotel. The message read that he was staying there with some friends, Robert, Donald and Deborah— names that meant nothing to me—as well, of course, as Linda Lawrence.

For a long while I stayed at the desk lost in thought. One of the many things that crossed my mind was the anonymous phone call Brian had said he'd had from someone in New York. Surely Brian had been fantasizing about the possibility of someone taking out a contract on his life. It was absurd. Who did he imagine would organize such a thing? Klein? Keith Richard or Mick Jagger? No, surely Brian was just paranoid. I liked him, I had to admit. I had even felt some sexual attraction toward him, but surely it was time now to put his feckless world behind me and settle down, as my parents kept pleading and insisting I should, to my academic studies.

Besides, Brian was too complicated for me, and too moody for anyone to tolerate as a permanent friend. Of course I had had fun with him, had enjoyed his company; but at seventeen, with my fifty-dollar-a-week income, I was totally out of my element among these rock stars. I was also increasingly ambivalent about my possible drift into homosexual relationships.

No, I would not call Brian back. I took out a box of matches from the drawer of the desk and held up the postcard and my mother's telephone message about Brian's call.

I hesitated, thinking of Brian in the mews cottage, with his wet golden hair flowing over his bare shoulders. I thought guiltily of Mick. And I thought of the euphoric atmosphere of the "RSG" studio. Then I thought of Brian again, in his underpants at the Leamington Spa party. A wave of apprehension over my slide into homosexuality overcame me, and I struck the match. The camels and the note with Brian's number shriveled into black ash in the ashtray. And that, I thought, was that. My flirtation with the Rolling Stones, my glimpse into the sordid politics and bitchiness behind the scenes, was over. That night, instead of spending a cozy evening at dinner with my parents, I went out and got drunk before crashing alone in my bed.

My mother woke me the next morning to say irritably that a Mr. Jones was on the phone again and was demanding the return of his cigarette lighter. She said he had also rung again twice last night while I was out drinking. Now he was on a pay phone in Aston—a suburb of Birmingham.

Blearily, I raised myself on one elbow. "Lighter?" I said. "What lighter?"

"I don't know what lighter. You'd better come and speak to him."

Even in my present semi-conscious state I knew I should not speak to him now. He would manage to get around me and talk me into joining him wherever he was. The clock on the bedside table showed eleven-thirty. I asked my mother if she would mind telling him I had gone to church. This was the worst thing I could have said to my mother. She became even more annoyed and said that I should have been at Mass with her and my father at nine o'clock and not lying in bed with a hangover. She did not intend to commit a sin by lying for me. I had better get downstairs and settle the matter myself, and I had better not let her catch me smoking.

Downstairs I saw that my father had hung up the phone but within fifteen minutes Mr. Brian Jones was on the phone to my mother again, demanding the return of his lighter. This time she was tight-lipped and furious.

"He said he put it in your pocket after you had both smoked a *joint*, was it?"

"It's ridiculous," I said. "I never smoked anything with him and I know nothing about any lighter."

"Who is this Brian Jones, anyway? And what's a joint?"

She was going through my clothes where I'd thrown them last night. To my horror she held up a gold Dunhill lighter. It wouldn't have been more surprising if she had produced a white rabbit. I had never seen the lighter in my life before and couldn't recall having smoked even an ordinary cigarette with Brian that night.

"And what is this?" my mother demanded.

My father was to drive me to the Alpha Studios at Aston Cross—where the Rolling Stones were taping ABC-TV's "Lucky Stars—Summer Spin"—for me to return the lighter in person. My parents were horrified at the notion that I might be in possession of someone else's property.

My father told me that Brian Jones had wanted me to go alone in a taxi to the studios, but my mother had objected, saying that

Aston was a seedy part of town and that TV studios were well-known dens of iniquity.

Mother said, "He wanted to come *here*. He's a member of one of those scruffy rock bands, isn't he? One of the scruffiest of the lot, I gather."

"Brian Jones is just as respectable as we are, Mother. He was born in Cheltenham and went to a private school like Dad."

"Well, it's a great pity he didn't *stay* in Cheltenham."

"He's a friend of Tara's," I pointed out.

"All I can say is Tara should learn how to pick his friends more carefully."

It was useless to argue, though I had to smile at the memory of an article I had read in the William Hickey column of the *Daily Express* the previous November, which said, "There is no harm these days in knowing a Rolling Stone . . . And pop people do not seem to mind who they mix with. Some of their best friends, in fact, are fledglings from the upper classes."

My father and I set off in his new Sunbeam Alpine to drive from elegant Edgbaston to rather sordid Aston. My hand clasped the mysterious lighter in my pocket.

The parent show, "Thank Your Lucky Stars," had by now—after four years—become one of the institutions of pop music and was eagerly switched on by teenagers as well as older people on the ABC network around 5:50 P.M. on Saturday evenings. The regular show was emceed by deejay Brian Matthew, while the spin-off which sometimes replaced it was hosted by Jim Dale. The Beatles had made their first fully networked TV appearance on "Thank Your Lucky Stars" in January 1963 and so had the Dave Clark Five that April. And on June 8, 1963, the day after the release of their first single, "Come On," The Rolling Stones first appeared on national television on the same program.

I had seen them on that show and, having earlier read about them, wondered why there was all the fuss about the group, because they had appeared tidily dressed in uniform—check jackets with velvet collars and dark ties and trousers. Later I was to find out from Brian that the producers of "TYLS" had refused to allow them on the show in their ordinary scruffy clothes. However, after that first appearance there were no further sartorial stipulations and they had often appeared—at their fans' request—in all their usual gear.

The studios were surrounded by a mob of fans attacking a van carrying Herman of the Hermits, who peered warily out of a rear window.

Inside, Brian, dressed in a long-sleeved shirt that looked like a soccer jersey, greeted us.

Tara Browne, my twenty-year-old cousin, followed behind Brian. If I was amazed to see Tara, my father could hardly believe his eyes. "Tara," he said, "you here with this crowd?"

Tara, flaxen-haired, handsome, well-dressed and very wealthy, said, "How are you, sir? Yes, I like hanging about with these outfits. It's quite a lively scene."

"But are you *working* in this business, Tara?"

"Oh, no," said Tara, who still retained some of his Irish accent. "I'm learning to be an automobile mechanic."

My father shook his head briskly at this as if he thought there was some defect in his hearing. "A grease monkey? A man in your position?"

"I'm hoping to work on racing cars." Tara smiled. It was an Irish smile, mostly in the eyes. "Motor racing's quite respectable these days, you know." Later, Tara would perish in a car crash.

Father grunted noncommitally and asked about Tara's wife Nicky, whom he'd married in 1963, and about their two children, Dorian and Julian.

All the time Brian stood respectfully to one side with his hands behind his back. But at last Father's attention fell on him and I introduced him. Brian held out his hand and said, "A pleasure to meet you, sir."

The "sir" did a lot of good and so did the accent, and I noticed Father did not just touch Brian's hand and then withdraw, as he was wont to do if he disliked someone on sight. He gave Brian's hand a quick but firm shake. So far, so good, I thought.

Then Father said, not too gruffly, "Now, what's all this about the lighter?"

"I'm afraid I have a confession to make about that. You see I wanted Nicholas to come and see this taping, and as we'd had a bit of an argument last time we met, I dropped it in his pocket so I'd have an excuse to ask him over. It was—"

What Father made of this confession of romantic intrigue I'll never know. Before he could say anything, the fans beyond the glass doors spotted Brian and all hell broke loose. The police frantically waved us out of sight. The captain whisked us into the elevator and up to the canteen.

When Brian, my father and Tara got inside the canteen, the Rolling Stones were assembled there with about thirty other people. The Stones were looking very nervous.

Even Charlie and Bill, normally bored and implacable, seemed to be on edge. They were sitting together at one table. At another table, actually two tables pulled together, were Mick and Keith, with eight or nine reporters and studio technicians.

Father churlishly accepted Tara's offer of a cup of tea and went to a window overlooking the fairly busy main street below. He tossed his head irritably as he caught sight of some of the fans running back and forth across the road. Like a dutiful son, I went and stood beside him, though I nodded at Brian, who had preceded us in the elevator and was now seated with a group of four. When Tara brought the tray of tea, though, father agreed to my suggestion that we sit at the table next to Brian's.

Still playing the gentleman, Brian stood up and introduced his friends to us. One was John, an Australian, who was a friend of Tara's. Another was Dave, whom I assumed to be Dave Thomson, Brian's Scottish student friend, who looked a nervy and intense type of person. And there were two girls from Swansea called Sally and Mary. Mary was visiting a cousin of hers who had formed a band in Birmingham named the Spencer Davis Group.

I sat down close to Brian; Father and Tara had their tea at the adjacent table.

We were discussing the impending taping when the door opened and Andrew Oldham came in, flustered. Two other men were with him, but they were not the effeminate young men who usually followed in his wake. One looked like a boxer and the other like a sharp, business type.

Brian told me, sulkily, that they were Reg—known as "Reg the Butcher"—who was Andrew's bodyguard, and Philip Wainwright, his publicist.

"Why does he need a publicist and a bodyguard?"

"God knows why he needs a publicist," Brian said. "I know why he wants guarding—Eric Easton's solicitors are trying to serve writs on him. He's suing him for breach of contract. The heavy is there to fend off the bailiffs."

"I thought there'd be some trouble about Eric," I said, recalling Brian's earlier conversations.

"So did I. And it serves that bastard Oldham right. Eric's suing everybody. Nanker Phelge Music, Decca Records, London Records in New York, even Klein. Klein engineered the breach of contracts, he reckons. There's going to be some fun in the courts."

Then we noticed Andrew Loog Oldham hovering over the table. He said to Brian, very coolly, "We're going down to the press reception room now. Are you ready?"

Brian looked at him casually and insolently and said, "No, I'm not going. I'm talking to some friends."

Andrew glared at him, turned and went out, followed dutifully by the Rolling Stones minus one.

Father was beginning to take an interest. "Who's that?" he asked Brian.

"He's the manager of *my* group, the Rolling Stones. Everybody seems to know that except him. He thinks he's God Almighty."

Father smiled at this. Brian was charming even him.

Brian asked Tara Browne about racing cars. The previous November Tara had been offered a twenty-five-dollar-a-week job with the Rootes Group that included a twelve-month dealership course. He had seriously considered the offer and had spoken of selling his $50,000 house in Belgravia and moving to a two-family house near Coventry. In the end he had changed his mind, bringing down the blood pressure of the family elders.

Peter Noone—who was Herman of Herman's Hermits—came in

with Mickie Most, his recording manager. Both were quietly dressed, and when they came to join us, I noticed my father moved over agreeably to make room for them. Apparently he was becoming absorbed. It must have been like another world to him.

Noone and Brian were perfectly friendly—interesting because the press made the two groups out to be archenemies.

"So you've got Allen Klein looking after you now?" Noone said. "You know he's Mickie's manager as well?"

"Klein seems to be into everything," Brian said.

"Well, he's done us proud. Us and the Animals. He's come up with some amazing contracts."

"Good luck to you then," Brian said.

Brian seemed as if he weren't entirely with us; now and then a faraway look came into his eyes. I felt he was building up to a big scene.

"Have you heard that record, 'Hang on Sloopy'?" Peter Noone asked him.

"No, should I have?"

"It's by an American group called the McCoys. It'll make number one over here. I thought you would have heard it. Andrew Oldham's releasing it over here on his own label, Immediate Records."

Brian shrugged. "That's probably why I haven't heard it then. They don't tell me much, that lot."

Peter Noone, mystified, said, "What lot?"

"Oh, a group called the Rolling Stones. And Andrew Oldham. I only seem to be on the fringes. Yes, that's a pretty good record label, Immediate. He only announced he'd formed it two weeks ago. I had to read it in the papers."

I said to Brian, "It sounds as if Andrew's aiming to be like Phil Spector in the States. I was reading about Spector in a mag."

"You don't have to tell me about Spector. I met him over there. Of course Andrew was all over him. Spector goes about surrounded by muscle men, rides in swish limousines with darkened glass in the windows. He taught Oldham all the tricks of the recording game."

Noone said, "Doesn't sound as if he's exactly your 'man of the moment.' What tricks did he learn from Phil Spector?"

"It was Phil who told Andrew that on no account should he use Decca's recording studios but instead hire an independent recording studio and then sell or lease back the tapes to Decca."

Most of us looked blank.

Mickie said, knowingly, "A lot of them do that now. It gives them more control. And they can make a bigger profit out of it."

Soon after this, everybody left the table except Tara, Father and me. Peter Noone wanted Brian to meet some people who had just come in. One of them was apparently a local fan-club leader.

Father was looking through some LP record sleeves of the Stones that Tara had put on the table.

"Why on earth do they make them look so repulsive?" he wanted to know.

Tara grinned. "That's another one of Andrew Oldham's obsessions. He's been reading that book by Anthony Burgess, *A Clockwork Orange*."

"Damned disgusting book," father growled.

"You've read it?" I asked.

"Of course not. I've read the reviews and I wouldn't touch it with a barge pole."

Tara and I exchanged smiles.

Father went on. "But these Rolling Stones don't seem half as bad as they're painted. This chap Brian seems quite civilized."

"Oh, he is," Tara said. "Actually he's become a good friend of mine. But it's Oldham's idea to mix their image in with the *Clockwork Orange* nonsense. I've read the book and think it's nauseating. Brian's really a sensitive sort of chap, and very talented musically. Much more so than the others. He's really getting a raw deal, in my opinion."

"Have you known him long?" Father asked.

"Only about a year. The first time I met him he was in a hell of a state. He was telling me that Andrew and the others were trying to take the group away from him. He said that they were more interested in being rock stars than being musicians who played the blues. He said they'd even moved his microphone over on stage so that people couldn't hear him so well. He was very upset, even burst into tears while he was talking to me."

"Good Lord," Father said. "He must have been badly brought up."

"No, I don't think so. He's just a very emotional person. Ironically it was just one month after the Stones had released 'It's All Over Now'."

Father grunted, which was indication enough that he had other ideas.

Philip Jones, who was apparently the supervisor of light entertainment and a member of the "Thank Your Lucky Stars" team, came in and hustled Brian out. Brian called over his shoulder to us, "See you back here after the show."

To me there was something odd about the expression on his face. It was as if he were reluctant to be leaving us. I noticed Tara give him a wink and a nod as if to encourage him.

Almost immediately, there was a crackle from the speaker system and a voice told us all to take our places for the taping. I asked my father if he wanted to come into the studio. He said he would rather be shot from a cannon, and I left him with a pile of Sunday papers that he'd found on the canteen windowsill.

The studio resembled an old theatre, but in March 1965 the show's format had changed so that a hand-picked audience was now able to sit all around the walls and in front of the backdrops, while the cameras operated from the center of the room. The balcony, however, was still used, and it was up there that the wilder fans lucky enough to obtain tickets were confined.

I found myself in the center among the technicians, cameramen and executive staff. In conversation with Tony Borer, the set designer, and Keith Beckett, the director, I learned that work on the program had begun on the preceding Saturday. Artists appearing were always booked at least three weeks before the taping. Each was given a time of arrival and the number of his dressing room. Discipline, it appeared, was strict, in spite of the anarchic image projected by the finished product. It was now nearly six in the evening but rehearsals had been going on since early in the morning.

Our conversation was violently terminated by the admission of the studio audience. About fifteen hundred fans, mostly shrieking girls, soon filled the gallery, while the less hysterical two hundred or so filed into the seats downstairs around the walls. These latter were people who were known to producers, stars or other members of the production team and could be relied upon not to do anything too irresponsible on camera. The crowd upstairs were those who had written in for tickets and were usually invited in strict rotation.

Herman's Hermits opened and closed the first part of the half-hour show. They were lip-synching to their records, "I'm Henry the Eighth, I Am" and "Just a Little Bit Better." "Henry the Eighth" had just knocked "Satisfaction" off the U.S. number one spot; at this stage Herman's Hermits were far more popular than the Stones in America. Mick and Andrew were hoping to remedy that on the forthcoming tour.

I was standing with Tara when Herman's Hermits went into their lip sync of "Just a Little Bit Better." Someone tapped me on the shoulder; it was Mick Jagger.

With mock cockiness, he said, "'Ello, fruity."

Before I could reply, Mick went into a series of gyrations designed to distract the performers on camera, Herman and the Hermits. Mick pranced and posed and contorted his face while looking at Herman; it was evident that he was trying to create a grotesque caricature of the man. Was his aim to distract or to insult Herman? Surely Peter Noone wouldn't be able to see Mick beyond the glare of the stagelights. Mick and Noone had a mutual dislike for each other, but Mick's behavior now was childish. Tara watched him with disdain.

Peter must have seen him because his face suddenly flushed with anger. Mick kept up his absurd prancing and face-making for perhaps thirty seconds after that and then he disappeared from view.

At the start of the second half of the show, Mick and Peter Noone had to come on together to receive awards from the American magazine *Cashbox*. The golden trophies were awarded to any non-American artist who hit number one in the *Cashbox* Top Hundred in the USA.

Peter looked triumphant as he received three trophies. Mick looked put out at having achieved only one—for "Satisfaction." He managed a little smile, accepting the award, then mumbled something about, "We try hard," and went off camera.

After the taping, Brian and Andrew Oldham were glaring at each other furiously. Brian's face was white; Andrew's red and angry. The intensity of their emotion frightened me. It was as if there were murder in the air.

Brian was snarling and saying through his teeth, "So you bloody well think you can do without me in L.A. Okay, you can do without me in Ireland as well. And in Germany and Austria. In fact you can do without Brian bloody Jones from now on. This is my last date with this bloody outfit, okay? I'm quitting. So you've got what you've been scheming at all along. You've got me out. But by God it's going to cost you, Oldham. You've wrecked something that I built up and it's going to cost you."

"Don't threaten me, you little shit," Andrew snarled back. "Just go, just bloody take off. You've been nothing but a pain in the ass to me the whole time. It's always you that has to cook things up, stir up trouble. You can bloody quit right now. You might be God's gift to musicianship. You might think you're the answer to every virgin's prayer. But to me you're nothing but a shit. If it hadn't been for Mick I'd have got rid of you a year ago."

"Yeah, well Jagger and you are damn lucky I did this show. I'm not bluffing. I was going to quit right before we went on tonight, just leave you right in the shit. Tara talked me out of it. I shouldn't have listened to him." Brian leaned forward and stuck his face close to Andrew's. "I'll tell you something, Oldham, you'll have to come crawling back to me, because without me the Stones are finished. Just take my word for it. And when you come crawling, I'll kick you in the teeth."

I was startled by a cry behind my back. I hadn't noticed the elevator doors open. I turned and saw Mick Jagger standing inside. His face was a picture of anguish and apprehension, like the face of a child about to be deprived of a favorite toy.

"Andrew," he said, "has he started again? He has, hasn't he?" All that cockney whine was missing now. He was speaking in clear southern English. "He's threatening to quit, isn't he?"

Brian turned on him. "Yes, too bloody right I am. I'm the trouble-maker, I'm the pain in the ass. I'm the one whose songs are not good enough to play. And you're the sodding great genius by the look of it. Okay, just get on with it. But count me out."

And then, to my astonished perplexity, Mick Jagger burst into a flood of tears and went flouncing over to the other two, wailing, "Andrew, he can't. He can't quit. We need him. I need him. Do something, you can't let him go." Then, to Brian: "Oh, hell, Brian, what's wrong? Why can't things be like they were between you and me at Edith Grove?"

Brian slowly and deliberately turned to Andrew Oldham and looked directly into his eyes. He said, "Two's company, three's a crowd." Then to Mick: "And we know threesomes don't work—don't we Mick?"

Brian stormed out, slamming the door behind him.

Mick looked accusingly at Andrew, who appeared very uncomfortable for a moment and then went after Brian.

Mick turned around with his shoulders slumped, pulling a handkerchief from his sleeve. Evidently, he was startled to see me standing there.

"Oh," he said, dabbing at the tears on his cheeks. "Sorry about all that. Sorry you had to see all that drama." Still the voice was quiet, the tone well modulated, the accent standard southern.

I was bemused that this reputed lout with the nasal whine, this emblem of anarchy and revolution had suddenly changed as if by magic into a pleasant, sincere, respectable and vulnerable young man.

Mick Jagger sniffed, blew his nose, put away his handkerchief and leaned against the wall as he spoke. Instinctively I moved slightly away, though he probably didn't notice. "You know, Nicholas is a nice name. If I have a son I shall probably call him Nicholas. Did you know Keith used to have a mouse called Mr. Nicholas? He used to bring it to school in his pocket. Reckoned he had saved his life or something."

He and Keith Richard had been to school together in Dartford. Both had been born in 1943, Mick in July, Keith in December.

They had both gone to Wentworth County Primary School. However, I hadn't heard about the mouse, and wasn't all that keen on sharing a name with it.

I said, "You're expecting a son?" I was thinking of his "open secret" romance with twenty-year-old Chrissie Shrimpton, the sister of Britain's top model, Jean Shrimpton.

"Oh no," Mick said. "No, what I meant was I'd like to have a son one day. If I do I'll call him Nicholas." There was something patronizing in the smile of those big fat lips.

Then he added suddenly, "Do you like girls?"

"Of course."

"You like the Shrimpton girls?"

"They're very beautiful."

"Yeah, you know David Bailey, the photographer? He was going out with Jean at one time. But now he's gone and married Catherine Deneuve. Mind you, she's gorgeous, too. I was David's best man. Did you know that?"

"I read it in the paper." I said this as coolly as I could, sensing he was name-dropping and being patronizing again. David Bailey was the most fashionable photographer of the time. In retaliation, I said, "You must find that life's pretty dizzy for you now, after those early days in Edith Grove."

He looked at me for a moment, then quietly said, "You're so right." He stared, as if reflecting on the old days.

I studied his face. He looked as if tears were about to brim over. He seemed to have genuine feelings after all. Yet Brian had told me that his ambition was insatiable. He wanted to be *the* Rolling Stone. Brian had said he was ruthless and unscrupulous and wouldn't let anyone stand in his way; that he would get rid of anyone who tried to—as he had done with Eric Easton; that he needed to dominate not only the other Stones but the entire international rock scene.

Yet he didn't look like that to me—not now. He seemed sad and lonely, in the way that Brian did sometimes. And if he was so anxious to dominate the Stones surely he would not have been pleading with Andrew—as he was a few minutes ago—to stop Brian from quitting the group. It was obvious to me that as long as

Brian remained, there would always be at least two points of focus in the front line of the Rolling Stones. And there would always be, in Brian, a challenge for the ascendancy.

As I continued to study that interestingly ugly face of Mick's, and as he continued to gaze blankly at the milling crowd beyond the hallway inside the canteen, I tried to make sense out of what Brian had said about "three's a crowd" and "threesomes don't work." I was feeling, right now, a sexual attraction to Mick. Standing face-to-face with him, I found it impossible to ignore or deny. Still, I tried to drive any awareness of it from my mind. I said, "Do you think Brian is really going to quit, Mick?"

With a sad, dreamy air, Mick Jagger smiled seductively at me and said, "I really don't know." He was now acting as if he were too cool to have lost control only minutes before.

Andrew Oldham barged through the canteen doors and strode over to the elevator, pressing the button.

"That bastard's going to get what's coming to him one of these days," he growled as he stepped in. The doors closed behind him and he was gone.

Mick looked to be on the point of tears again. I made some excuse and went in the canteen to look for Brian. He might be needing a friend around. The canteen was full and noisy. Brian was at a table with John, Tara and the two girls from Swansea. They looked subdued and thoughtful; there was an air of crisis around Brian.

Father went off with Tony Borer, who said he was going to show him around the studios.

In total silence, Brian sat staring, unblinking, down at the table-top. He glanced up as I sat down, his face pale, his jaws moving as if he were grinding his teeth. I looked around the table and realized everyone was tense and waiting for someone to break the silence.

Tara, probably the most socially adept of any of us, tried by asking, "Shall I arrange for some tea or something, Brian?"

Brian snapped, "Bugger the tea."

Tara raised his eyebrows, shrugged and got up, saying to me, "I think I'll try and catch up with your father and Tony. Have a nose around."

The two girls, Sally and Mary, taking advantage of the moment, escaped by saying they had to get back to Sutton Coldfield and there were no late buses on Sundays. Brian barely managed to acknowledge the departures. John, who seemed the most embarrassed, also got up and went after Tara. Now it was just Brian and myself.

"Where's Dave?" I asked, realizing I hadn't seen him since the taping.

Brian sneered and said, "He doesn't like arguments. Said he was going back to London. Don't bloody blame him. If I had my own car here I'd have buggered off before the show."

That triggered a lot of jealous questions in my mind about *Dave.* Tara and John were still here and surely they must have all come up together. So how had Dave managed to go back? If he was really a student he could hardly afford to run a car of his own.

Instead of asking about this, I stupidly—though no doubt out of subliminal curiosity—said, "What's Dave's surname?" I wanted to make sure it really was Dave Thomson, I suppose.

"What d'you bloody well think it is?" Brian growled. "Don't ask damned stupid questions. I'm not in the mood."

For a moment my instinct was to get up and leave him. After all, I owed him nothing. I was my own man with my own income, and he had done nothing for me but provide entry into the rock elite, which I could have bought anyway and which had turned out to be disillusioning at best. I stayed with Brian out of loyalty. Everyone else was turning their back on him. But now there was something else. I was falling in love.

A young man suddenly appeared at our table. "Brian," he said, "can you come downstairs? There's one hell of a row going on. Mick, Andrew and Keith are going at each other like wildcats. Charlie and Bill won't get involved. They look scared out of their wits."

Brian looked up slowly. "So?" He spoke softly but there was so much menace in that one word that the guy's confidence drained away.

"Well," he stammered, "er, you know, can you come down and try to sort it out. Sort of mediate?"

"Sort of mediate, eh?" Brian said, still softly. But then his voice gradually increased in volume until at the end it drowned out all other sounds in the canteen. "Sort of fucking mediate, eh? The only way I'd mediate would be to give them knives and let them cut each other's bloody throats. So just fuck off back and tell them that, okay?"

"Who was that guy, Brian?"

"Norman Taylor," he said. "Peter Noone's road manager."

It suddenly struck me: What was Brian going to do if he left the Stones? This was 1965 and there were very few solo rock stars. True, he could sing. He had a pleasant, folk-type voice but it wasn't nearly as powerful as Mick's, and in any case he didn't *like* to sing.

"I can't see the Stones going much further without you, Brian," I said.

"Thank you very much. But I can't stand it any longer. All the songs are Keith's and Mick's. Mine aren't the kind they want."

"But it's you and Mick the fans want, isn't it? It wouldn't be the same without you two vying with each other for the screams of the kids."

He put his head to one side and said mildly, "Is that how it looks to you?"

"Oh yes, I don't think the others—even Keith—get a look in. You and Mick seem to be flirting with the kids and—" I broke off. I felt I was just one step off a minefield.

"Yes, go on. Don't be embarrassed. I think I know what you're going to say."

"Well, you seem to be flirting with *each other*." I added hastily, "Of course I know it's only a gimmick—"

Brian laughed. "I wouldn't be too sure of that as far as *he's* concerned." More seriously, he said, "Mick and I have had a good relationship. Like Mick said, 'Why can't it be like the days in Edith Grove?' But that was before Andrew moved in. Later, Keith, Mick and Andrew went to live in an apartment in Kilburn, Mapesbury Road. That broke it up."

A threesome *again*, I thought.

Brian was quietly chuckling to himself. "That was funny. Andrew's girlfriend, Sheila Klein—no relation to Allen Klein, by the way—asked Chrissie Shrimpton if Mick Jagger and Andrew Oldham slept in the same bed. Chrissie's a bit innocent. She looked surprised and said, 'Not when I'm there, they don't.'"

"You think Andrew and Mick's relationship busted up the good feeling between you and Mick?"

"Yes, I suppose that's the way it happened. Andrew used to behave like a bitchy old queen whenever Mick and I were hitting it off well. But that's only part of the story. On top of that, Mick seems determined that he is going to be *the* guy that everybody thinks of whenever the Stones are mentioned. He wants to dictate policy. People are beginning to accept that Mick Jagger is the Rolling Stones."

Brian relapsed into total depression. At last, I felt I had some insight into Brian's problem. He had built up a great company, the Rolling Stones, and now they were trying to kick the chairman of the board upstairs. A new kid was taking over. My business analogy would only work so far. These rock stars were all in their twenties. There were no old farts ready for retirement. Why couldn't Mick, who looked like an intelligent, sensitive man, see that Brian needed part of the limelight? But Mick, I could see at close range, was an indecisive man.

When I got to know Mick Jagger better, I was to discover that he had great agility in sidestepping personal problems. He would procrastinate by pretending to believe that a problem shelved would gradually disappear. The way he put it was that he "abstracted" himself from emotional situations.

Yet now, in 1965, I sensed that there was still an underlying and deep personal bond between Mick and Brian—an old affection intensified by escalating careers. Or could it be that Andrew Oldham—in his own interest—was trying to break up their friendship?

It seemed that Brian had been dwelling on the relationship as well, because he now looked up and said, "Anyway, I did do something recently that pleased Mick. Of course, he wouldn't be pleased

if he knew the truth about it." He gave me his mischievous smile.
"You know that soppy little song by Mick and Keith, 'Play with
Fire'?"

"Soppy? I thought it was great. The music anyway."

"Yes. Well, that's the way it turned out after I had kind of doctored it. The critics are calling it a minor pop classic. What they
don't know is that there were two versions of it. The one Mick liked
was a kind of heavy rock version. So did Keith. That was called
'Mess with Fire.' I didn't like it. And it vanished."

"Vanished?" I said.

"Yes, vanished." The smile broadened. "It was too late to re-
record it, because it had to be the B side of 'The Last Time' so they
had to use the other version. It was, as they say, well-received.
Mick complimented me on the way I had played."

"It was marvelous." I said. "What happened to the other version?"

"Well, it wasn't really Chrissie's fault."

"Chrissie Shrimpton?"

"Yes. She works for Andrew as some kind of secretary. She'd
been told to send the master tape of 'Mess with Fire' to the studios.
She didn't know which one it was, so as I happened to be in the
office at the time I sort of helped her. I gave her 'Play with Fire'
instead."

"So the studio got the version you preferred?"

"Yes." Brian looked very pleased with himself. "It was very unfortunate, don't you think?"

"Not really. But what happened to the other tape?"

"It got mislaid. Mick and Andrew thought Chrissie had made a
mistake and gave her a bollocking. After that nobody could find the
other tape."

"So you are a bit of a troublemaker at times," I said.

To my surprise, Brian continued to smile smugly. The song "Play
with Fire" had made a deep impression on me and many other
people, and it was at least as good as "The Last Time." Of course
the lyrics were quite childish (it was meant to be a boy from a slum
background telling an upper-class girl not to play games with him),

but musically it was a sensitive and intricate construction, with Brian's Mellotron weaving delicate patterns over the basic notes.

"You know what that song was all about, Nicholas?" Brian said. "It was a message from Mick to Marianne Faithfull. He first met her last year. Paul McCartney threw a Good Friday party at his apartment in Paddington. Mick took Chrissie. All night, Marianne treated Mick like dirt. Someone said she described him afterward as a dreadful, spotty, uncouth, London-speaking slob." Brian evidently drew some bitchy satisfaction from this and I smiled with him. Then I saw his expression change as he spotted someone approaching.

"Oh," he said, "here comes another messenger. They've sent Bob Bonis."

"Who?"

"Bob Bonis. He's the guy they replaced Mike Dorsey with as road manager."

The man—a short, brown-haired, chubby type—came up to the table and told Brian that Mick Jagger wanted a word with him downstairs.

Brian scowled and said, "If he wants to talk to me, tell him to come here and talk, not send bloody commands by messenger."

"No, it's not like that, Brian," said Bob. "He wants to talk somewhere quiet, not in front of a crowd."

"Right. Well, tell him to come and ask me himself."

Bob continued to persuade and cajole Brian. By now, the pressure of all the arguments and tensions of the evening were beginning to tell on me. On top of that, I needed to go to the john, and I had a headache. I thought, *Just as I've managed to calm Brian down this secondary messenger is about to work him up into a lather again.*

I left them and went toward the door. As I neared it, I thought I saw a face on the other side of the glass suddenly disappear to one side, but the light outside was dimmer than in the canteen, so it could have been an optical illusion. But then, when I pushed open the left-hand door, it collided with someone outside. That someone, to my amazement, was Mick Jagger, who, it seemed, was lurking out there and peering in at Brian.

I apologized to Mick, saying, "I didn't see you hiding behind there."

"I'm not hiding," he said haughtily. "I was looking for something in my pocket." He suddenly plunged a hand into his trouser pocket and pretended to fumble in there.

How very childish this superstar was. How disenchanting. I found myself talking nonstop, speaking on Brian's behalf.

"What's going on?" There was something so irascible, so callow in Mick's young voice. "Is Brian going to leave?"

"I don't know," I said to Mick. "Why don't *you* ask him? I'm sure Brian won't bite. But I'll tell you one thing. If Brian does leave, it's going to be mainly your fault. Why do you let Andrew rule you? Haven't you got a mind of your own? If you really care about Brian, you'd better do something to help him before it's too late."

Bob Bonis came storming out of the canteen. I stalked off, enormously elated.

I wandered back towards the canteen. I was hoping Mick Jagger would be gone. But he wasn't. He stood talking animatedly with Bob Bonis. I tried to ignore them, but Mick said, quietly and in that cultured accent he often used offstage, "Oh, Nicholas, please see what you can do to get Brian to change his mind. You seem to be able to communicate with him better than I can."

I stopped and looked at him. He seemed to be pleading. Bob Bonis was eyeing me up and down, with suspicion as well as a gleam of hope. I wondered if Mick's concern was really for Brian or for the future of "his" band, which Brian's defection would put in jeopardy.

As I hesitated, Mick went on, "By the way, my invitation still stands for you to come to the 'RSG' studios on Thursday. That's if I—" he pulled himself up sharply—"that's if we still have a band on Thursday."

His gaffe angered me.

"I'll have to see what Brian says."

As I pushed through the swing doors, I heard Mick say to Bonis, "That bastard's on Brian's side all the way."

Yes, all the way, I thought. If there had to be sides to be on, I was on Brian's. But why did it have to be like that among lovers? It didn't make sense.

Tara, John and Father were sitting with Brian, who now appeared to be on his best behavior.

Tara, looking at my father's disgruntled face, laughed and said, "Cheer up, it won't be long now. The police have just got Herman's Hermits out. They'll be getting the Stones out soon, and after they've gone all the kids will go home and we can get out."

"I just hope they haven't damaged my car," Father said.

Charlie Watts walked in and ambled over to us. He looked, for him, rather apprehensive, as if worried that Brian's rebellion might turn on him.

"We're ready for the off now, Brian," he said. "The police are all set."

"Okay." Brian got up cheerfully and started saying polite good-byes to everyone. His constant changes of mood never ceased to astonish me.

When it was my turn, I half wanted to tell him about the conversation with Mick and about the invitation, but there were too many people around. I said I would telephone him tomorrow.

It was decided that we should all go down to the cars and see the operation—almost a military operation—necessary to move rock stars safely through their fans.

We all trooped down the stairs and into the long, narrow loading bay at one side of the building. Two cars had been backed in and were waiting behind the closed roll-up shutter gate. The one in front was a silver Rolls-Bentley and the one behind an Austin Princess.

The screaming and chanting of the fans outside came to us muffled by the door. The atmosphere inside was electric. A policeman and a captain stood on each side of the first car.

It appeared that Andrew, Mick and Keith must have already been in the Bentley, which had tinted glass all around. Brian was ushered into the Princess with Charlie and Bill and two other people whom I couldn't see clearly. As Brian got in, he said to me, "Don't forget to ring." I nodded. The car door slammed.

The policeman's voice sounded hollow as he shouted, "All set? We go after three."

The captain prepared to operate the rolling shutter.

"One, two, three. Now."

The engines purred. The shutter gate clattered up, and as it did so, the clamor of the fans—mainly girls—outside entered and came like a great overwhelming wave of sound into the garage. A sea of faces, a surge of youthful humanity, with here and there a struggling, sweating policeman floating in it, faced the first car as it crawled into the crowd, with the second car almost glued to its tail. Somehow the cars groped their way through the seething mob and turned left down the narrow side street and away from the main road, pursued by determined fans. Some of the girls threw handbags and shoes after the cars as they quickly gained speed. I followed out into the street, which contained mostly old, run-down terraced cottages, and saw the older people standing outside their front doors witnessing this almost weekly spectacle. It must have brightened up their humdrum lives whenever some well-known pop group visited the studios, I thought. Or did they resent the wealth of these jumped-up kids, while they lived in squalor?

As I rode home in Father's car, I wondered if tonight I had witnessed the beginning of the end of Brian Jones' Rolling Stones. Or would something happen to change Brian's mind about leaving? There was no telling with that amazing, irritating, delightful and unpredictable man. But I cared very much. I knew Tara did too. He was following Brian down to London. I hoped he would look after him till I saw him again.

WHEN I SPOKE TO BRIAN on the phone the following Tuesday, he sounded like a man who had won a million dollars. He was going to buy George Harrison's Rolls-Royce Silver Shadow. The thrill of that seemed to absorb him totally.

"What about the trouble?" I asked.

"Trouble? What trouble?"

"About you leaving the band."

"Oh, that's all right. Allen Klein's sorting everything out. Things are really happening. Allen fixed for me to be able to buy the Rolls. I've always wanted a Rolls-Royce. He's also promised we'll record some of my songs on the next LP. Listen, on Friday we're off to Dublin, Saturday Belfast and then direct from Belfast we're going to Los Angeles for recording sessions. That's great. I love L.A., but we're only there for two days and one night, then directly back to the Isle of Man for a dance hall gig. That's living isn't it?"

"So there's no fear of your leaving now, then?"

"Not now. Klein said without me the Stones would collapse. I said, 'I know.' He said the Stones are now at a critical stage in their development. I didn't say 'I know' to that because I didn't know what the hell he was talking about. Anyway, he arranged for a fair bit of cash for me, which I can use at this moment. I expect it was a kind of sweetener to stop me from leaving. But it wasn't that that stopped me."

"I know you well enough to realize that, Brian," I said.

"Yes. I think you do. Anyway, at last they're going to admit I can write songs, too."

"I hope you make a number one with one of your compositions. That'll teach them. If you do, perhaps you can teach me how to write songs, too."

He laughed. "Yeah, maybe we'll collaborate. Listen, we're at the 'RSG' studios again this Thursday. Can you come?"

I must have hesitated longer than I thought. Mick had already invited me, but I couldn't tell Brian and bring him down.

"Nicholas?" he said. "Can't you come?"

"Yes, of course. I'll see you at the studios, okay?" I was about to say goodbye, but he now launched into a kind of monologue about songwriting.

"It's not easy, you know, writing songs. Mick and Keith didn't find it easy at first. One useful thing about Andrew, he told them if Lennon and McCartney could do it, so could they. When they all lived in the apartment at Kilburn, Andrew locked them in the kitchen and said he wouldn't let them out until they'd at least tried. Funny thing, neither Keith nor Mick, in the early days, thought for an instant that they could write songs. They seemed to think that was a songwriter's job. Theirs was to play and sing the songs."

"What about you?" I said. "Have you always written songs?"

"Always tried. I've written quite a few, but mostly in blues style. I tried to get Mick and Keith interested when we were living in Edith Grove, but Mick thought you had to be black to write blues songs. Shows how much of a musician he was back then. Anyway, Andrew finally got fed up searching for numbers in Chappell's R & B catalogue and got Mick and Keith writing at last."

"But not you?"

"Not me, no." Brian's mood was getting lower. "Not me, not Bill. He writes songs and music, you know. And he's good. Of course, it may be because we weren't living with them. The three of them cozy in one nest seemed to be working it all out between themselves. Well, it may happen yet. Maybe one day there'll be Jones and Wyman on the sleeves, instead of Jagger and Richard."

It was a surprise to me that Bill Wyman, impassive, calm, unassuming, a part of the furniture of the Rolling Stones, was also a frustrated composer. Many years later, he was to come into his own.

"You've never had a credit for any of the music, have you?" I said, knowing the answer. "But who wrote the B side of 'Little Red Rooster'? The one called 'Off the Hook'? It's credited to Nanker Phelge."

"That was Bill and me. So was 'Play with Fire,' credited to Nanker Phelge. That's the name they used when it was supposed to be a collective effort. The proceeds go to the five of us plus Andrew."

"But how did you pick a name like that?" I was thinking of the guy who said he was a freelance journalist.

Brian said, "'Nanker' is my name for pulling a grotesque ugly face, pushing up your nose and pulling down the skin under your eyes. That's a nanker. And Phelge is this weird guy who used to use the Edith Grove flat sometimes. Jimmy Phelge. You know, we had to find some collective name for our first publishing company, so we just came up with that. The other two numbers ["Empty Heart" and "2120 South Michigan Avenue"] on *12 × 5* came out under Nanker Phelge as well. I figure they did that just to stop Bill and me getting our names on the sleeves. Bastards."

"By the way," I said, "what's the significance of '2120 South Michigan Avenue'?"

"The address? Oh, it's where the legendary Chess Studios are in Chicago. We were there last June. That's the only significance. The track is a sort of tongue-in-cheek thing we did in a hurry because Muddy Waters stopped by that day and we wanted to dedicate a tune to him. I'm a great fan. We called it '2120 South Michigan Avenue, Muddy Waters Was There,' but the last bit was dropped by the recording company."

"Sounds like an exciting visit. Anybody else there?"

"Oh yes, Chuck Berry, Buddy Guy and Willie Dixon all stopped by. He's great, Willie."

"You must have had fun," I said, aiming to hang up soon, before my father complained about the telephone bill.

"Fun, but damned hard work. It was our first American session.

We started in the afternoon and went through the night. Thirteen tunes we did, all mixed, completed and ready to be mastered. That was some hard day's night."

"Yes," I said, "I read about it somewhere, I think. Didn't you record 'It's All Over Now' there?"

"That's right."

"Brian, I'll have to go now. My father will be complaining about the phone bill. You don't mind, do you?"

"Please yourself." He was huffy again. I should have known.

"See you on Thursday at 'RSG' then."

He put down his receiver without another word.

Thursday, September 2, 1965 was a red-letter day in the life of Rediffusion TV's "Ready, Steady, Go" at Wembley Park. The whole show was to be devoted to the Rolling Stones, an accolade never before bestowed on any other group—even the Beatles.

One of the reasons for this honor was that there was an easy and growing rapport between the Stones and their team, and the production team at "RSG." Another was that the show's director, Michael Lindsay-Hogg, was absolutely carried away by the group's music.

Even Andrew Oldham, who was notoriously difficult to get along with, seemed to mellow when working with the "RSG" team.

When I arrived at the studio, rehearsals had already begun. Looking around the noisy, crowded room for Mick or Brian, I suddenly caught sight of a TV monitor and became riveted to the spot. What I saw was Andrew Oldham, wearing a bobcat vest and a long black wig, lip-synching to Cher's voice singing, "I don't care if your hair's too long," while Mick in reply mimed to Sonny's line, "With you I can't go wrong." And Andrew was lovingly stroking Mick's hair. Surely it wouldn't go out in the broadcast, or if it did, they'd have a woman—maybe Cathy—doing the girl's part. My adolescent mind was really shocked at the way those two were camping it up on the monitor.

It was only recently that I had realized just how camp Mick was getting. I had seen a photograph of him, taken in a BBC make-up department, sitting in front of a hairdryer smoking a cigarette, with his hair in a net like some middle-aged housewife.

Just as the Sonny and Cher mime ended, Brian tapped me on the shoulder. It was his usual way of greeting me, coming up behind me and tapping lightly with two fingers on my right shoulder.

"They're not going to do that on the show, are they?"

"Yep. They said we could do more or less what we wanted. You wouldn't believe it, but they're letting Mick produce the show even. Lindsay-Hogg's still the director, of course. And we've been allowed to choose all the artists. We all chose one each."

"I bet you chose Manfred Mann," I said.

"You're getting to know me."

"Who else is on?"

"Mick chose Chris Farlowe, Charlie chose Cilla Black, Keith chose Goldie and the Gingerbreads, Bill chose the Preachers and Andrew the Small Faces."

I noticed Brian was wearing a light-colored sweater with a strange motif on the front. On top was a kind of inverted crotchet and the logo "88.3" on top, and then a larger crotchet beneath with "Radio Syd" written on its base. I asked about it, and Brian said it was the sign of a Swedish radio station.

Mick was talking to Cathy McGowan close by and they were horsing around. It was pretty obvious that Cathy was very attracted to him.

"Yeah," he was saying, and his voice and accent were of the kind he used onstage—utterly different from when he spoke to me in Birmingham. "Yeah, I fink we'll have a new presenter, seein' as I'm producing. Yeah, we'll replace you, love, and all the rubbish we got workin' 'ere. You can all clear off."

Cathy was laughing. "Okay, producer, I'll clear off."

"Yeah?" he said, and took her hand, pulled her toward him and put his arm round her waist. Her eyes shone with sex and pleasure.

My mind went back to something Brian had told me about Cathy in the early days of the show. She had received hundreds of letters—some very abusive—asking how she could stand being close to those filthy louts, the Rolling Stones, and especially the ugliest one, Mick Jagger. Now, it was said, she got abusive letters from jealous girls every time she stood too close to either Mick or Brian.

There was lots of activity going on in the huge studios. The various groups were setting up their instruments, lights were being adjusted, cameras were moving about like strange-looking vehicles and there were echoing, shouted instructions going on.

Brian introduced me to Vicki Wickham, the assistant producer. We were talking when Mick Jagger looked over at us and came to us with that almost mincing walk he sometimes affected. When he reached us he stared blankly at me as if he didn't know who I was. Then, but very slowly, recognition dawned on him.

"Oh, 'ello," he said. "You made it then?" And before I could make any comment he turned to Vicki and asked, "Where's Michael?"

She said, "I don't know. He was with Cilla a few minutes ago."

I looked at Mick's eyes and saw that they were oddly glassy and the pupils were dilated. He was vague. In fact it was being borne in upon me that all these pop people were vague about most things. It was surprising they ever turned up for their various gigs or remembered the words to their songs. The reason for this—though up until that evening my innocence about such things was still intact—was that most of the people I was meeting were "stoned," but not on booze. I knew all about booze. They were stoned on drugs.

Mick didn't move away but stood with us, looking around, and then Brian came back with Keith Richard in tow. Today there seemed no bad feeling between the three of them; at least not yet. Brian introduced me to Keith as "Nicholas, a friend of mine." Keith was very easygoing and relaxed, quite different from when I had met him briefly in the Hilton. They all three were relaxed and affable—and slightly glazed in the eyes. It surprised me the way they all seemed to keep changing in relationship with one another, in the way they spoke and even in their personalities.

The first thing Keith said didn't endear him to me. "I used to have a mouse called Mr. Nicholas." *Damn that bloody mouse,* I thought.

"Oh, really," I said in a deliberately bored tone. "I think somebody told me about that before."

"He was a good little chap," he said, smiling. "I've seen you before somewhere, haven't I?"

"I've been to the studios before. And in the canteens and various places with Brian."

"No," he said. "No, it wasn't connected with the Stones or with music. Somewhere else."

I shook my head; didn't want to bring up the meeting at the Hilton. But it was odd he should have recalled that, however vaguely.

Changing the subject, I asked Brian if he'd had his Rolls-Royce delivered yet.

It was an ingenuous question; and yet it was received by all as if I had made a serious accusation.

Keith's face turned as black as thunder. "What bloody Rolls?" he growled.

Mick's eyes bulged and those fat lips formed into an ugly sneer. "You buying a Rolls? What with?"

I glanced at Brian, thinking he'd be angry with me for putting my foot in it again.

But Brian regarded them with a hostile cockiness and said, "Would you believe money?" He tossed a coin in the air and caught it in the same hand. "Yes, I've decided to take the lead again."

With a greater confidence than I had seen in him before he outstared both Mick and Keith and added, "The leader shall have a Rolls-Royce. I'm having George Harrison's."

He certainly looked the best of them. He was the most arrogant, the sharpest dresser, the hippest hipster and the best-looking. Only the previous week the readers of *Record Mirror* had voted him Most Handsome Pop Star. They had put Paul McCartney in second place.

Brian was the Rolling Stone who originated things. He was the most daring and most innovative. He was the Stone who wore his hair the longest and the first to smoke dope—the quintessential anarchist Stone. All the same, now that fame had really caught up with them, Brian would find that Keith and Mick could be powerful opponents. From my observation of the Stones at work and play, it

appeared that all of them, as well as Andrew, were a little frightened of Brian's moods and tempers. And as time progressed I was to
find that these three often found themselves, in various permutations, in situations of two against one. One week Mick and Keith
would be in alliance against Brian; another week Keith and Brian
against Mick; and so on. But as a threesome they never got along
well for any length of time. Someone was always out in the cold,
and in the final stages before Brian's death it was usually him.

The taping was about to begin. Brian touched my arm and said,
"See you later," and I went to look for a good vantage to watch the
show.

It proved to be quite eventful. The first act, introduced by Keith
Richard, was Goldie and the Gingerbreads. They were an all-girl
group that had toured the U.K. in March that year as a supporting
act with the Stones.

After he'd introduced them, Keith came and sat next to me. They
sang a song I didn't recognize but assumed to be their latest record.

We listened for a while and then Keith turned to me and said,
"What do you think?"

"Very good. Better than a lot of the male groups in this country
at the moment. Their organist is marvelous. It was a bit of luck the
Animals discovered them, wasn't it?"

Keith raised his voice and said irritably, "The Animals didn't
discover them, I bloody did."

I had seen Chas Chandler and Dave Rowberry—two of the
Animals—sitting somewhere nearby earlier, and I looked around to
make sure they weren't in earshot. They weren't.

"Oh," I said, "I'm sorry. I read somewhere the Animals had discovered them."

"Yeah, well, you can't believe all you read. I found them in New
York. They were playing at a party given in our honor by Jerry
Schatzberg. It was in June last year at the start of our first North
American tour, and that was way before the Animals heard them. It
was when I got back and mentioned them to Alan Price that they
came to know them. Right?"

"Okay," I said. *Anything for a quiet life,* I thought.

Later, during one of the lulls between numbers caused by technical requirements, Keith said, "Talking of what you read in the papers, that's Keith Altham over there from the *NME*. And that's his ever-faithful dog Napier."

I looked to where he was indicating and saw two men chatting to Cathy McGowan, but there was no dog. Later I was told that the second guy was Altham's photographer and that this was one of Keith Richard's odd jokes. The photographer was Napier Russell, so maybe the reference was to a Russell terrier.

The subject of reporters made me wonder aloud whether that strange guy Phelge was around.

Keith gave me a quizzical look and said, "Jimmy Phelge? I'd hardly think so. God, I don't think so. I don't think I've seen that cat since we left Edith Grove." He smiled then, as if reminiscing.

"D'you know, Dave," he said (why he called me Dave I couldn't think), "that guy would nail up the john while a visitor was in it and lower a tape recorder in through the window to capture the moment when his victim couldn't get the door open. He ended up with a reel of tape, which he doctored so that everytime the flush operated there'd be a round of applause. It was a great tape. Pity nobody kept it."

I smiled and recalled Phelge telling me something about nailing up doors. "He must have been a bit of a menace to live with, though" I said. "Was it him who drove you out?"

"Ironically, no. He might have been the catalyst that worked on the rest of us, but I guess I was the one who really brought things to a climax. I got back one night rather the worse for wear with drink and found I was locked out. So I smashed a window to get in. That woke Phelge, Mick and Brian and also let in a cloud of London smog. The window never got mended and the London weather continued to seep in the rest of the time we were there. I was also responsible for breaking the only piece of functional apparatus in the place—Brian's trusty old record player."

Keith's way of speaking, quite formal and almost pompous, struck me as odd—as if he were trying to give the lie to the Stones' reputation for illiteracy.

"How did you do that?" I asked.

"One night I plugged the leads into the mains through a damp socket and the whole contraption exploded in my face."

"Oh, God," I said, though I couldn't help laughing. "What did Brian say?"

"I didn't dare to tell him. I just said it had packed up like everything else in the damned hovel. And don't you dare tell him the truth. Even if he has now attained the Rolls-Royce status."

Just after that Keith excused himself and went over to talk to Keith Altham.

Bill Wyman was now getting ready with his choice of guests, the Preachers, about whom I knew nothing. People still continued to mill about all around the studio, which resembled Grand Central Station with all the comings and goings.

Brian came and flopped into the chair that Keith had vacated. "How's it so far?"

"All right," I said.

"I saw you having a heart-to-heart with our Keith. What did he have to say?" Brian spoke lightly, though I could tell there was at least a hint of distrust behind the question.

"Oh, we were discussing Edith Grove. He was saying what a dump it was."

"Dump is right. I tell you, in that bedroom there was a species of fungus that Alexander Fleming would have given his right arm for. Where's Keith now?"

I pointed him out.

"Oh, I'm glad he's talking to Keith Altham. He's been good to us. He must have been the first reporter to interview us. Hey," Brian added, as the Preachers were introduced, "listen to this. Get the drummer."

The Preachers performed their "Hole in My Soul," which Bill Wyman had produced.

When it finished Brian said, "Now, you're the expert. The drummer is Tony Chapman. Who did he used to play for?"

"Don't know," I said.

"So you don't know everything." Brian was euphoric now, quite high. "He used to play for something called the Rolling Stones."

That surprised me, because I'd never heard of Tony Chapman.

"December 1962," Brian went on, "when I was still forming the Stones, my bass guitarist, Dick Taylor, quit, so I put an ad in *Melody Maker* for 'an enthusiastic bass guitarist to play in an established R & B group.' Tony Chapman saw it. He and his mate, Bill Perks—an ex-RAF serviceman—both played in a band called the Cliftons, but they weren't doing very well. They were just playing youth clubs, doing three or four gigs a week for peanuts. Later, Bill Perks changed his name to Bill Wyman. Bill Wyman sounds better than Bill Perks, doesn't it? Tony suggested Bill apply and he did. In fact he was the only suitable one to apply. On the phone, I told him we were also without a regular drummer. He mentioned Tony and I told the two of them to come down and audition."

Brian grinned. "Bill must have thought we were a well-off group as we could afford to advertise and because the audition was in the awfully fashionable King's Road, Chelsea, in the Weatherby Arms. Actually, we were skint.

"Bill turned up at the pub looking like a seasoned old professional compared with the rest of us. Remember he was seven years older than Mick and Keith. He came in lugging his guitar, a huge 60-watt amplifier and a Vox 850 amplifier (which he said was his 'spare')— all the right equipment that some of us had hardly seen before. Behind him came Tony juggling with his drum kit. There were only Mick and I in the room and they obviously weren't very impressed by us. We were our usual scruffy selves, but they'd apparently taken the trouble to dress up a bit for the audition.

"Then Stew came in and started playing a few notes on the piano, and it was only then that Bill and Tony realized they were there to audition for *us*. They seemed amazed, especially as we were soon scrounging drinks and fags from them."

Brian was called before the cameras to be interviewed by Cathy McGowan.

In the spotlight his mood changed, and he was the handsome, confident, charming and slightly raffish character his fans loved.

Cathy asked him how he felt about being voted the Most Handsome Pop Star by the readers of *Record Mirror*.

He said, "It's terribly embarrassing."

Mick Jagger plunked himself in the seat next to me, grunted and sneered, "I suppose we'll never hear the bloody end of that now."

Cathy went on. "You've had a great deal of bad publicity lately. A considerable number of people have accused you of going after bad publicity."

"Well, no, that's ridiculous. We obviously wouldn't seek bad publicity just to create a name for ourselves, because we all have friends, parents and relations, so it's very embarrassing for people we know well."

As the interview ended a record of "Hang on Sloopy," which had been playing in the background, increased in volume. Brian stepped into a crowd of reporters and cameramen.

The record by the McCoys had crashed into both the British and U.S. Top 30's the previous week.

I made some remark about it to Mick.

"It was a bit of luck for Andrew, this one," he said. "Andrew was in Bert Berns' house one day in the States. Bert Berns is an American record producer. Produced hits by Ben E. King, the Drifters, Solomon Burke and Them. He also wrote 'Twist and Shout.' He had a new record label called Bang and he was playing a few new releases for Andrew. Andrew heard this one and he wanted it right away, first hearing. He's like that, Andrew. He released it under his own label, Immediate, and now he's purring all the way to the bank."

Manfred Mann—Brian's choice—was the next act. Their singer was Paul Jones, who had changed his name from Paul Pond for the peculiar reason that he thought being called Jones might bring him some of the success that Brian Jones was achieving. Paul, of course, was the singer Brian had originally wanted instead of Mick Jagger. Paul had turned down the opportunity.

Brian introduced them, and after a guitar opening the Manfreds exploded into their record of "If You Gotta Go, Go Now (or Else You'll Have to Stay All Night)," which had a fast and tricky beat emphasized by the skillful use of the tambourine. Manfred on the organ gave extra power and gusto to the rhythm, so that the whole building seemed to be rocking with it.

Paul Jones now seemed to have many of the mannerisms of Mick Jagger, and perhaps it was unfortunate that he hadn't stuck to his own individuality. He even followed Mick's style in doing a harmonica solo midway through the number, which was a Bob Dylan composition. Although it had some of the plaintive style of Dylan it had been arranged and speeded up into something more in Brian's R & B concept—which is probably why he asked them to perform it.

The Stones closed the show with a frenzied version of "(I Can't Get No) Satisfaction."

While this was being performed, Michael Lindsay-Hogg floated among cameras and engineer, arranging fantastic new camera effects. He looked as if he'd be more at home in a bank or a city office. He had quite short hair, a very young-looking, pinkish face, and he wore a sober suit and tie—hardly anyone's idea of a TV director—and yet director he was, and a brilliant one. This was to be proved over and over during the next three years, during which he was closely associated with both the Stones and the Beatles.

I watched Michael devise tricks as he directed the Stones today. He was adopting the technique used for soccer games—stopping or slowing down the visuals while the Stones continued to play, which undoubtedly increased the excitement for those watching at home.

It was obvious from the amount of work, the amount of activity and the contortions which the technical people were subjecting themselves to, that this method of presentation was far from easy, but it was extremely effective—and everyone of the Stones was always pleased and enthusiastic about any kind of innovation on-screen.

In the "RSG" club afterward I sat with Cathy McGowan, Chas Chandler and Dave Rowberry. Brian joined us long enough to say that tonight's "RSG" was the best show ever. He went off to the viewing room.

Chandler said, "'RSG' is easily the best thing on the air. There's nothing to compare with it in America."

The Rolling Stones in 1963, when Brian Jones, center, was still considered the group's leader. Surrounding Brian clockwise are Bill Wyman, Mick Jagger, Charlie Watts and Keith Richard.

▼

Brian reading the New Musical Express, 1964.

Signing autographs in Regent's Park, 1964.

◀

Rehearsing for the television show "Ready, Steady, Go," 1965.

▶

The actual "Ready, Steady, Go" performance.

A break during the taping of "Ready, Steady, Go," 1965.

U.K. singer Anita Harris hands the Rolling Stones an award aboard a Thames steamer, 1965.

At the Glad Rag Ball, Wembley, 1964.

Brian—a happy, candid moment, 1965.

Bill Wyman and Brian, 1965.

The Rolling Stones outside their London office, 1965.

Brian on drums(!), 1965.

Brian in Regent's Park, 1966.

The whole band at
Green Park, 1966.

The Rolling Stones
with manager Andrew Loog
Oldham and Ian Stewart.

Dave, another member of the Animals, agreed. "I only hope they'll come up with something half as good. But tonight's 'RSG' has got to have been the best ever."

Cathy beamed with pleasure, but in a moment Brian was back. Cathy's smile disappeared as Brian told her Cliff Richard was on "Top of the Pops" that moment with a haircut so short it made him look like the guitarist Jet Harris. Cathy said she didn't believe it and went off to check for herself. It was well known that Cliff was her favorite male singer.

Chris Farlowe and Keith Altham came by and said they were going to look for Eric Burdon in a Wardour Street pub. Chas and Dave said they'd go along for a drink.

Brian and I were alone at the table with half the British rock 'n'roll world swarming around us. Last Thursday, Brian and the Stones had appeared on BBC-TV's "Top of the Pops," which I had caught at home in Edgbaston.

What had intrigued me, I told Brian, was the fact that he and Mick had worn almost identical clothes—light and dark striped sweatshirts and light colored slacks. I asked who was trying to upstage whom.

"Oh, I was the one who changed at the last minute," he said, with an air of mock innocence.

"It must have upset Mick."

"Too bloody true it did. I thought it might make him a bit less anxious about his dressing up. He spends so much time nowadays agonizing about the particular image he wants to convey on the various shows that I thought I'd take the piss a bit. I waited till it was too late for him to change, and have his precious hairdo and makeup altered, and then I slipped into something as near as I could get to his outfit. He just had to grin and bear it—in front of the cameras, at least."

"And away from the cameras?"

"He sulked, of course."

"Didn't burst into floods of tears?"

Brian's face clouded over with suspicion. "Why would he do that?"

I hadn't told Brian about my encounter with Mick outside the elevator at "Thank Your Lucky Stars" in Birmingham.

To avert another lapse into moodiness, I said, "Oh, I just heard he was prone to tears when upset."

"Yeah, I suppose he is sometimes. Anyway, he had something more to be tearful and to sulk about on the Wednesday. The *NME* chart was released, and his great pet, 'Satisfaction,' only entered at number three. Everyone assumed 'Satisfaction' would knock the Beatles off the top spot. Nobody guessed it would be Sonny and Cher. Nobody except me."

"And you didn't confide in Mick?"

"Nope. Nobody asked my esteemed opinion. But I did say to Mick when the chart came out Wednesday that it proved the Stones were taking the wrong direction."

"You mean getting too far off the R & B stuff?"

"That's exactly it. We're off the right path. We need to get back to the real stuff, like 'Little Red Rooster.' I told him that."

"What did Mick have to say?"

Brian shrugged moodily, "Nothing, as usual. Just grunted and walked away. Seems that I spend a lot of my time these days watching peoples' backs as they walk away."

Brian and I fell into a discussion of the TV show "Top of the Pops," which Brian didn't like because it always meant dragging up to Manchester and, even more odious, it required lip-synching, which he hated.

All the same, I thought, "Top of the Pops" had done the Stones a lot of good. They had appeared on the very first production of this new BBC show back on January 1, 1964, when they performed their second single release, "I Wanna Be Your Man," written for them by Lennon and McCartney. It was then in the *NME* Top Twenty at number twelve. Also on that show were the Dave Clark Five, at number two with "Glad All Over," and the Beatles themselves at number one and number three with, respectively, "I Want to Hold Your Hand" and "She Loves You." What a terrific debut for a show.

Brian looked up as somebody hovered beside him, looking diffident and nervous. He was a lad about my own age and was quite strikingly pretty for a boy. He said, "Excuse me for interrupting you, Brian."

Brian was bowled over by the boy's good looks. He stood up, put a hand on his shoulder and helped him into the chair next to his own. "Nice to see you. I can't quite remember your name, but we met somewhere, I believe."

"Well, not actually met," the boy said, modestly, and he gave me a friendly not. "My name's Marc Bolan."

Brian gave me a knowing kind of smile, as if teasing me a little and at the same time asking me to agree about the boy's alluring good looks. The name Marc Bolan meant nothing to me, and I didn't think it did to Brian until he said:

"Marc Bolan, yeah. Got you. You signed a recording contract with Decca. It was about the end of July this year and it was the same day we renewed our contract with them. Right?"

Marc beamed proudly and said, "That's right. Fancy you remembering that."

"Oh, I don't miss much." Brian subjected him to a long deep gaze, which I thought ought to embarrass the boy, but he just gazed back with patent admiration, a case of idol worship. For a moment it made me feel I was playing fifth wheel and ought to leave.

Brian's manner changed. He glanced at me, then asked Marc, "Well, is there anything I can do to help? I haven't actually seen you perform yet."

"Really, I just wanted to ask your advice about the way music is going generally. Everyone knows you're the man who really knows about music. I play finger-style guitar and sing my own songs. I've just done a gig at the Pontiac Club in Putney. It isn't all that well known. It's in Zeeta House, near the railway station. I met Donovan there in June, and Joan Baez. I've heard you're a great friend and fan of Bob Dylan; is that true?"

I went off to get more drinks as Brian went into a eulogy about his guru, Dylan.

At the bar I came across Vicki Wickham and Cathy McGowan

having a joke together. Cathy said to me, "I see you've been having a little talk with Brian. What sort of a mood is he in tonight?"

"Quite good," I said.

Vicki said, "Who's that he's talking to? Is it that singer, Marc Bolan?"

"Yes."

"Good Lord," Cathy said. "He's changed his image. He used to be a model of a mod when he was younger. I believe they even used him in *Town* magazine as an example of the breed."

Vicki said, "Well, he's an example of the folk-singer breed now—scruffy."

When I went back I saw it was true. Marc was wearing a floppy red sweater with a shirt that was untidy and open at the neck, ill-fitting cord trousers and a duffle coat.

He and Brian appeared so intimate in conversation that I hesitated before joining them. Brian was leaning toward him, saying something about fantasies.

Then Brian noticed me, pulled back and smiled. "Ah, come on, Nicholas. More booze."

As I sat down, he went on with a hint of mischief in his eyes, "Marc was telling me he writes songs about his fantasies. I bet if you or I did that, they'd be banned."

"Speak for yourself," I said, smiling but feeling awkward.

Marc said, "Perhaps I don't use all my fantasies. Anyway, what future d'you think there is for my kind of music? Folk music."

1965 had been the year of folk—Dylan, the Byrds, Sonny and Cher, Peter, Paul and Mary, and Donovan, as well as the lesser-known Dana Gillespie, who had been secretary to Joan Baez until Donovan brought out her talents.

"Oh yes," Brian said, confidently. "Even the Marquee Club is having a folk night now. Every Wednesday. As for the blues side of folk, there's a guy Bob Dylan introduced me to in Greenwich Village, John Hammond, who's handling that like an angel."

Marc was silent for a while. His expression was doubtful, pessimistic. Then he said, "Some are making it great. But the other kind of sounds look like they're taking over. Look at the Walker Brothers."

The Walker Brothers were three good-looking, shaggy-haired Americans who had been touring British ballrooms to the delight of local kids for about six months without much publicity, but just now they had romped to number four with "Make It Easy on Yourself" in only three weeks.

Brian grinned to himself. "Yeah, that's bugged Mick. He seems as jealous as hell of them. Yes, but just because they've got in and we got in, it doesn't mean that folk is out. To me it looks as if there's room for everyone. All you've got to do is be good at what you do."

"D'you like their latest record?" I asked him.

"No, I don't," Brian said. "Mind, I am not saying that because I'm jealous of them, like Mick. They're nice guys and I think the lead singer is vocally good but they ought to produce better material; they sound too similar to the Righteous Brothers. I prefer them, anyway, Marc—don't let it worry you." He put his arm around Marc. "There's plenty of room for folk for a—"

Brian broke off and looked toward the bar, and his eyes narrowed. I turned and saw Mick Jagger just detaching himself from a crowd there and beginning to come in our direction, holding hands with Chrissie Shrimpton, his current girlfriend, whose face had so often appeared in the popular press since her relationship with him had begun. Following Mick came Keith Richard, who also had his girlfriend, Linda Keith, in tow.

Then Mick saw Brian, with his arm around this handsome young man, and me sitting opposite him, and he stopped dead in his tracks. His face turned pale, his overstuffed lips parted and anger and jealousy were written all over him. What the hell sort of a guy was he? Here he was with an attractive, long-haired girl with a peach of a figure—and he was jealous of Brian sitting with two young men. It seemed to me that he was so indecisive he couldn't even decide whether his proclivity was for girls or boys. Even if it was for both—as in Brian's case as well as my own—then surely he could stick to one at a time.

Keith, who was relaxed and smiling, eased around the stricken Mick and sat at an adjacent table, winked at Brian, nodded at me and then turned his attention to Linda. Mick sat down opposite Chrissie. He was sullen and kept looking over at Brian. Brian pretended to ignore him, but did withdraw his arm from Marc's shoulders. Brian flashed Chrissie a bright smile.

In return for this, perhaps, Mick turned his eyes on Marc Bolan and kept them there for so long that the boy, flushed and confused, eventually fled into the crowd. Mick watched him till he was out of sight.

Brian and I exchanged a few words, but now I noticed that his glance kept straying to Linda Keith, and when, some ten minutes later Keith went off somewhere, he leaned over and said, "Where's Ratbag?"

Mick, overhearing, gave him a sour look. I wondered who Brian was insulting now.

But Linda said, "Oh, he's in Keith's car."

Brian gave her a wink and a lustful leer, and she smiled before turning away. She was another long-haired girl, quite similar in looks to Mick's girl Chrissie, though with darker hair. Also Chrissie had greenish blue eyes, while Linda's were hazel. Both were chic as hell and about nineteen.

"Who's Ratbag?" I asked Brain quietly.

"Keith's dog. She looks after it for him most of the time. Damned flea-bitten mongrel, but he seems to like it. Pity it can't drive. Keith still hasn't passed his test."

Brian said later, after Keith had come back, "You ever seen a photo of Linda Lawrence? My ex-girlfriend."

"I don't think so. Why?"

"Oddly enough she's like those two, Linda Keith and Chrissie Shrimpton. Same sort of hairdo. About the same height, same sort of figure. Maybe we three have the same tastes. In women anyway." Those bedroom eyes again—and more of Brian's cocky homosexual innuendos? How was I supposed to follow these up, I wondered. Fall in his arms? What did Brian want of me?

The Stones' women. What was the essential they all—from Chrissie Shrimpton to Linda Lawrence—had in common? While the girls were all probably pretty and attractive, they were not really stunning; not the kind of glamorous, sparkling girls one would associate with high-flying pop stars like the wild and raucous Rolling Stones.

"They're none of them in the same sort of league with Marianne Faithfull, are they?" I said quietly, but apparently not quietly enough, because Mick turned and looked at me the instant I uttered Marianne's name.

Shortly afterward, Brian was called away to the telephone and I was left to study the others. Keith was leaning back in his chair, carefree and easy, glancing about the room idly and occasionally acknowledging people. His girl, Linda, was engrossed in a letter of some kind, while Chrissie was sulking. Mick was avidly scanning the faces in the room; young Marc Bolan was probably out there somewhere in the crowd. Suddenly, both Brian Jones and Mick Jagger seemed crazy to me. Their whole world was absurd—a bad joke.

Brian, lately, had been dating a succession of beautiful girls and perhaps was looking out for one to adorn his new Rolls-Royce, yet at the same time he liked to taunt not only Mick but Andrew Oldham by flirting, or pretending to flirt, with young, pretty boys. Mick, on the other hand, made a point of often being seen out with Chrissie Shrimpton, with whom he had now been going steady for about two and a half years.

Brian came back and said to me, "Come on, let's go, Nicholas."

"Where to?"

"The Scotch, I thought."

"Not the Scotch of St. James?" I said, excited. I had heard so much about the place but never yet set foot inside.

As we got up and said goodbye, Mick said, "See you," to me. It was only the second time he'd spoken to me all night, in spite of the fact that I was supposed to be his guest.

I was Brian's guest at the Scotch. If it hadn't been for him, I would have stood more of a chance of getting into Buckingham Palace than into that most fashionable and expensive nightclub. It was in the very heart of the West End of London in Masons Yard off Duke Street and close to Piccadilly Circus. A good half of the membership was connected in some way or other with the music industry. It was the kind of place where young dukes rubbed shoulders with pop idols and where the scions of tycoons danced with rock drummers and guitarists who had just climbed out of the slums.

It was eleven when we arrived, early by the standards of the Scotch. Brian knocked on the formidable wooden door and a 1920's speakeasy-type routine ensued. A panel slid open, someone looked out, saw who Brian was and let us in. Nervously I worried lest the fifty dollars in my pocket was not going to be enough even to gain entry. But I needn't have worried, because Brian signed me in as his guest. I learned afterward that there was a long waiting list for membership, and no amount of money could have gotten an uninvited outsider past the door.

The action at the Scotch took place at the bottom of a flight of stairs. It was not a large place. The dance floor, as well as the stage, was tiny. Tables surrounded the floor and there was a raised area that ran around three of the walls. On one side there was a bar the entire length of the room. There were framed areas of tartan cloth covering the walls.

The club was packed—the rock star's entrance absolutely smashing, Brian aglow, the trendiest person alive, a kind of pop deity who had created fashions, blurred genders, helped launch the drug and sex revolutions, changed rock, altered morals. The energy waves he generated as we made our way through an adoring crowd left me dazzled with Brian's public flair. Brian ordered two double Bacardis with Coke, although I was already quite drunk. Brian seemed to be hitting the bottle to a greater extent every time I met him.

The first person who came to speak to Brian was Allan Clarke, lead singer with the popular British group the Hollies, who, like Herman's Hermits, had originated in Manchester. Brian congratulated him on the success of their latest record, "Look Through Any Window," which had come in at number sixteen in the British charts yesterday.

Allan said that he'd just been a panelist on BBC 1's TV show "Juke Box Jury." This was a panel game program in which four personalities from the entertainment world were invited to listen to newly released records and vote them either a "hit" or a "miss."

Allan laughed. "We voted the entire bloody lot a miss," he said. "Apparently that's never happened before."

Brian laughed too, and Allan said, "I thought that would amuse you."

But I wondered whether Brian might have been laughing at something else.

On Saturday, June 27, 1964, I had watched on my TV set at home that disastrous edition of "Juke Box Jury" on which the Stones appeared as the panelists. It was the only time ever that the studio had been enlarged to house five and not four. The program went on at five-fifteen and was quite a favorite with both young and older viewers.

It was introduced by the very suave and sophisticated David Jacobs, whose neat appearance, dark good looks and easy smile made him a perfect TV commentator. On this occasion, though, the show turned out to be a complete shambles. The five Stones grunted in their worst accents, lolled about in their seats and over their desks and generally acted like the ignorant louts they were reputed, at the time, to be. I read the next day that hundreds of telephone calls had come in to the BBC protesting their insolence. To be honest, I hadn't been at all enamoured of it myself. Many years later David Jacobs was to say in a broadcast, "They conducted themselves as ignorant, moronic imbeciles."

Now I said to Brian, "Remember that time you were on it? You and the other Stones?"

The smile immediately left his face and I knew then that it wasn't the memory of that broadcast that had been amusing him. "Yes," he said, very seriously. "That was bloody Andrew's idea. Told us to act like rebels. Louts more like it. I felt quite sorry for David Jacobs, who's a hell of a nice guy. I half decided not to go along with the antics. And as David came on before the show started I stood up and shook hands with him and said, 'Good afternoon, sir.' He was quite astonished. No, I don't think that show did our image any good at all, but it did get publicity, which was all Andrew was out for. We were even asked about it six months afterwards in Australia. But it's not something I'm proud of at all."

Later Brian introduced me to Allan, and I asked him about the records that had been put on in the show this time.

"It was an atrocious selection of records," he said. "And they got a truthful response. Pity I wasn't on the week before, because they had disks by us and the Stones." He laughed again, but Brian was morose, and like a drunken man, wanted to persist with the one subject.

"In many ways," he was droning, "I regret that show more than anything I've ever done. That bloody Andrew has pulled stunt after stunt to make us look like scum, but that was the worst and I'll never forgive him for that. I'll never go along with that again—anything like that. He can get stuffed."

Allan could see Brian was getting maudlin and with some lame excuse he moved away.

Just as I was going to suggest something to eat or some coffee to sober us up, Brian started introducing me to someone else. He was a wiry character with a thin, intense face and untidy, curly hair. His name was Michael Cooper and he was a photographer for *Vogue* magazine. In the course of a conversation that lasted for some-time—throughout which Brian popped off at intervals to greet people, sign autographs and buy yet more Bacardi—I found out that Michael was also a friend of my cousin Tara's. I asked Michael how long he had known the Stones.

"Oh, since way back," he said. "Let's see, I started working for *Vogue* in 1962, and it was a Thursday in that July that I went along to the Marquee Club—Alexis Korner's group Blues Incorporated was playing. However, they weren't appearing that week, because they were making a live appearance on BBC Radio's Jazz Club. Instead Long John Baldry was appearing. Plus the Rollin' Stones, as they were known then. The Stones had been booked to support Baldry. That was when I first met Brian and the others. Of course Bill and Charlie hadn't yet joined them."

"When did you next see them?"

"At the *Vogue* offices last year. They'd come to have their photograph taken."

"By you?"

"Oh no. By David Bailey." Michael smiled. "Only the best for the boys by then."

Brian had been circulating, floating on oceans of good will, the trust of every glamorous table. Periodically he would return to us, his guests and home base. On one such occasion, Michael Cooper opened a large flat envelope he'd been holding. "I've got the sleeve of the new LP here, Brian, and some shots for the British tour."

While Brian studied the LP sleeve, Michael handed me the promotional photographs. I was quite intrigued that they showed Brian standing alone on the left of the shot with the four others standing in a group and looking away from him, leaving him isolated. In fact, he was the one looking into the camera, appearing rather insecure, while the others seemed to be talking among themselves.

I then asked to see the sleeve while Brian examined the photographs. The LP, due to be released in Britain next week and in the States next month, was titled *December's Children (and Everybody's)*, and had a picture on the front of the four other Stones standing in what looked like the entrance to an alley, while Brian crouched in front of them so that his head was at their waist level. On this, too, he appeared detached, the odd man out, the enemy almost.

Brian, sounding puzzled, said, "Well, these are all the same shot. Where are the others?"

Michael said, "Oh, I didn't bring them now it's been decided."

"What's been decided?" Brian was getting angry.

"Well, that that's the best one to use. Mick asked me to bring a few over here. Is he here, by the way?"

I recognized the signs that Brian was seething again, as he had been that time in the Hilton foyer. His fists were clenched and his face was deathly white. And suddenly he was completely sober. "Mick told you to bring the pictures over here?" Brian asked.

"Yes." Michael looked nervously from me to Brian and back again.

"You have decided, haven't you? It is the right one because it's got the green line on the bottom. We always use the green line when the right shot's been agreed."

"It's been agreed, has it?" Brian said through clenched teeth.

"Yes, it's gone to the printers. I'm positive it's the one Mick—" Michael looked down and then continued, "the one you all wanted to use."

We were so near another crisis that I felt both supportive and apprehensive for Brian. At last, Brian exploded. "It's the first time I've seen the fucking thing!"

Michael started hastily putting the photos and the sleeve back in the envelope as people all around us turned to see what the ruckus in Brian Jones' group was about. "Well, I'm sorry. Brian, I hope you don't think it's my fault." Michael had put the envelope under his arm. "The posters are being printed up now and it's too late to do anything about it."

"Too late," Brian growled. "It's always too bloody late when I'm told anything these days." He stormed over to the bar again.

Michael Cooper seemed genuinely upset. He struck me as a sincere and modest sort of man, sensitive and obviously talented. He looked at me, crestfallen.

I shrugged and said, "Don't take it too hard, Michael. He's up and down like a yo-yo these days."

He sighed. "Yes, you're right. He always has been moody, ever since the early days, but he's getting worse. But then, maybe he's got good reason to be. I don't think it's all paranoia with him. I've watched Brian build up that band with so much patience and hard work. It's as if you've watched a man build a house with his own bare hands, only to have someone else claim the credit."

In a moment he spotted a redheaded woman and said, "Excuse me, won't you, there's my wife."

I stood alone for a moment near the rail that separated this area from the floor below. I watched the band playing, the people dancing. Dusty Springfield was there and I noticed Vicki Wickham dancing with someone. There was a well-known member of Parliament sitting with a party of pretty girls at one table. I wondered in my naive way if they were all his daughters.

A little later I found Brian at my side again. He was subdued now. Yet another two Bacardis were in his hands and one of them was for me.

Although I was pretty stoned myself by now, I studied him for a while as he looked down over the scene to try to guage the state he was in. Oddly, he did not appear on the surface to be very drunk at all, but when I looked at his eyes I saw his pupils were hugely dilated.

"What's the matter with your eyes?" I said.

He turned to me. "What? Eyes? Oh, I just took a couple of Duraphits. They calm me down."

"A couple of what?"

"These." He took some black pills out of a pocket and held them in his hand to show me. "You want to try one?"

"What do they do to you?"

"Make you 'hang loose,' as the Yanks say. You'd better just have one, as you're not used to them; otherwise you'll hang so loose you'll lose your strings."

I took one and swallowed it with a gulp of Bacardi.

"Look at this lot," Brian said suddenly, waving his hand to indicate all the people—the rich and the elegant—who were his fellow club members. "A few years ago they wouldn't have given people like John Lennon, Paul McCartney, Eric Burdon, Mick or me the contents of their trash bins. Now we're all part of a kind of aristocracy of pop and everyone wants to know us. You've got top models, fairy hairdressers, debs, Hooray Henries, rich men's kids . . . And the scene shifts from here to the King's Road, where a lot of them live, to the Chelsea Antique Market, where everyone goes for breakfast, to the Baghdad House in Fulham Road—near my place—where everyone goes to dinner. And if you want an 'in' place for coffee it has to be the Kenco Coffee Bar, near Chelsea Barracks. We're all part of a little elite, I suppose—at least the young ones."

"D'you think they're all anti-Establishment, like the Stones are assumed to be?"

"Well, let's say they think they are. It won't make any difference if they are. There'll always be an Establishment. But this Sixties scene is changing things a little bit maybe. The class thing—at least with the young—seems to be dying out. And I don't think the young are ever going to be put down again the way they were. Seems that with the young the classes are getting something from each other and are going to make bloody sure they don't get stuck in different slots."

It was prophetic and beautiful. This euphoria of mine might have had something to do with the little black pill. My mind was perfectly clear, so clear that at last I recalled the magazine cutting I had been carrying around to show Brian. I hoped I still had it. I groped in my pockets and there it was among my twenty-pound notes, which all so far remained unspent.

Steering Brian to a table, I opened out the article and showed it to him. It was by a top British journalist, June Southworth, and it had appeared in *Fabulous* in March 1965. The article described Brian's growing popularity and even listed some of his quirkier antics, such as having imaginary conversations with Mozart and playing requiem masses on the harmonica.

Brian smiled as he read it. "Yeah, somebody showed me that before," he said. "She's good fun, June. It was shown to Mick too, and he wasn't well-pleased." Brian chuckled. He seemed in a great and friendly frame of mind. He was at peace with the world. So was I. He leaned closer to me across the table and said, "Hey, have I ever told you about Tangier?"

I shook my head, thinking how striking he looked with his long fluffy hair.

"I'll really have to take you there sometime. The colors you wouldn't believe. I love the colors there under the sea. You can't describe it, you have to see it. When I look into it I hear music in my head. Did you know Tchaikovsky complained to his nanny about that? When he was a child he complained to his nanny about the music. She said she couldn't hear any music, and he said no, it was coming from inside his head."

I laughed.

He disapproved. "No, it's true, I hear it. Not other people's music. I hear my own out there. New songs, new melodies." His face saddened. "Then there was poor old Beethoven. He ended up stone-deaf. They say his last words were, 'I shall hear music in heaven.' Don't you think that's sad?"

I nodded, trying to look sad; actually I wanted to laugh.

He gazed into space for a while. Then he said, "Last time I was in Tangier I was with Robert Fraser. I don't think you know him. He owns an art gallery in Duke Street. Old Etonian and all that. I think Robert understood about the color—"

"How come you were hobnobbing with old Etonian art dealers?" I said. The idea, for some reason, seemed ludicrous.

Brian raised his eyebrows, slightly indignant in a drowsy way. "I know all sorts of people." Then he sniggered. "Now that I'm famous I do. Teddy, the deejay from the Ad-Lib Club, brought Robert Fraser over to Paris to see us play at L'Olympia. When was that? April this year. Teddy brought Robert backstage afterward and introduced us. We hit it off quite well."

"What sort of art is Robert Fraser into?"

"Pop stuff. Modern. Andy Warhol, Jim Dine, that sort of thing. That's why he appreciated the colors at Tangier."

I was getting sick of Tangier. "What about Paris?" I said. "How did you go down with the audience there?"

"It was more like a riot than a concert. The only difference there is the boys screamed and the girls cried. It was crazy. Two and a half thousand of them. Anyway, where was I? Yeah, after I had met Robert and Teddy after the show we all went on to a party at Donald Cammell's studio apartment in Paris. I told you about Donald and his girl Deborah Dixon?" Brian's eyes were getting more glassy by the minute, and seemed to be focused on something behind me.

"I don't think so," I said.

"Well, Donald's a great painter. Deborah's a beautiful girl. They all joined Linda and me in Tangier. Hey, d'you fancy a bit of tail?"

"What?"

"There's a girl over there I know, and she's sending out signals. She's got a friend. Come on."

I remember standing up. After that I have a series of memories interspersed with whirling gray pools of unreality. The memories come now as fleeting vignettes. The face of a blue-eyed, blond young girl . . . submissive and flattered . . . the more challenging face of a brown-eyed, suntanned brunette . . . a short altercation with staff in the foyer of the Kensington Palace Hotel . . . Brian naked . . . the two girls wearing only their pants . . . more black pills . . . more Bacardi and Coke . . . writhing bodies . . . a consummation . . . the joyous sound of an orgasm—and in the morning, still sleepily stoned, I found myself naked between two sleeping, naked girls. And Brian gone.

In the bathroom, written in lipstick on the mirror, was the message: FLOWN TO DUBLIN'S FAIR CITY.

CHAPTER
9

*D*URING THE NEXT THREE MONTHS the Stones toured Great Britain, Canada and the USA, as well as Ireland, Germany, and Austria. The number of concerts during that short period was staggering. It made me wonder if they could keep it up without at least one of them cracking up. In North America alone they made something like fifty appearances.

Understandably my visits and telephone conversations with Brian became infrequent and brief, but Brian thoughtfully and regularly kept me up to date with what was happening and on occasions ranted about the latest slight or insult—real or imagined—to which he had been subjected by the others.

"Get Off of My Cloud" by Jagger and Richard was released on October 22, and by November 2 was a number-one hit in both Britain and the USA.

Just before Christmas, Brian started a hot new romance with a twenty-three-year-old German model named Anita Pallenberg. The press reported their every move. I saw pictures of them together at London Airport. She looked quite attractive, with blond hair, a pretty face and a slim figure, but I had learned by now that people can't be judged on pictures in the paper. I was intrigued and was hoping to meet her soon. Brian, directly after the U.S. tour, whisked Anita off for a vacation in the Virgin Islands.

To celebrate my eighteenth birthday, Brian took me to a riotous New Year's party. The occasion was one of the rock events of the year, the New Year's Eve edition of "Ready, Steady, Go." It was the best birthday celebration of my life. As it turned out, there was no time for talking with Brian. He was off-color with some tropical bug he'd picked up, and things were so hectic I never did get to meet Anita Pallenberg.

What a party—the Stones performed with a fantastic supporting cast, including Tom Jones, Dave Clark, Dusty Springfield, and Eric Burdon. There was booze by the bucketful, and long after the live TV show ended, the party roared on and rolling, reeling people collided and kissed and danced till daylight. Somewhere, sometime, I crashed out alone in the house of a male acquaintance with whom I had staggered up the street, singing lustily.

The only real disappointment was not having met Anita and not having had the company of Brian.

It was nearly three months before I heard from Brian again. On a Sunday, March 20, Brian telephoned me. I knew he had arrived back in the U.K. on the previous Thursday and I had been living in hope since then. He sounded enthusiastic and happy, so I was careful not to ask if any of his songs had been recorded. I'd read in the music press that the Stones had recorded twenty-one Jagger-Richard songs in Hollywood—and not a one by Brian Jones.

"Hey, listen," he said, "can you make it to Paris on Tuesday week? That's the twenty-ninth. We're playing L'Olympia. You just gotta be there. I'll arrange for you to get in and all that."

At that time I had been to Paris only once in my life; in fact, I'd never been anywhere else in Europe. But Brian made it all sound so enticing I instantly agreed to go.

"That's fixed then. I'll make the arrangements for you. We're actually leaving for Amsterdam on Saturday. It's the start of a European tour—five countries. But Paris is going to be the one you'll like. Don't forget, the twenty-ninth. I'll try to call you before that, but if not just go backstage at L'Olympia and I'll have fixed for the staff to let you in."

"Great," I said, almost breathless.

"Hey, d'you know what I've bought?"

"Not another Rolls? Or a Cadillac?"

"No, a sitar. D'you know what a sitar is?"

"Not exactly, but I heard George Harrison play it on a disk."

"Yeah, he played it on the 'Norwegian Wood' track. Well, now I've got one, a beauty. I'll show it to you."

I congratulated him on winning the Carl Allen award—Most Outstanding Group of 1965—and asked him if he was going to the TV presentation.

"Dunno yet," he said, "We're on a schedule as tight as a duck's ass. Must go now. See you in Paris."

Damn, I thought, *he didn't give me the chance to ask about the great romance.* The press was plugging the story for all it was worth. It was rumored that a wedding was imminent and that Brian had asked Bob Dylan, with whom he had spent a good deal of time in the States during the last six months, to be his best man.

I would soon see for myself what it was all about.

As the cab approached the George V Hotel, where I was staying as Brian Jones' guest in Paris, I was amazed to find it beseiged by young fans all demanding to see the Rolling Stones. Apparently, the Stones were already inside.

It took me a good half hour to heave my way through the seething mass of humanity, convince gendarmes that I had a reservation, and reach the welcome peace of my room. Faintly, I could hear the chanting of *"Vive les Stones"* from outside.

After a shower and a change of clothes, I tried to call Brian's suite. I was asked to give my name, and the receptionist said she'd call back if Brian would agree to speak to me.

After a while the phone rang and it was Brian. "Well done," he said. "You made it. Listen, I'm like a bloody prisoner up here. They're sending a security guy down to fetch you up. You'll have to show him your passport. There's also a gendarme outside my door. You'll have to show it to him, too. I don't know whether I feel like a king or a convict."

When at last I was let into the suite, I expected to find Anita with him in his princely living room, but he was alone.

"Hi," he said, handing me a Bacardi and Coke he'd already mixed. "We flew in a day early. Jumped straight on the plane after the Brussels gig because Mick thinks Brussels is a drag. Well, compared to Paris, it is. None of us has been to bed all night, except Charlie. All the rest of us went out on the town—Mick, Keith, Bill, Stew, and Mike Gruber. We ended up in a place called La Castelle. It's Paris' equivalent to the Scotch of St. James. They didn't turn us out till gone five."

I had not heard of Mike Gruber before and asked Brian to explain.

"Oh, I suppose you could say he's another road manager. We seem to have three now. Nobody consults me. He seems a decent chap, though, in his early twenties. He likes a good time and maybe Andrew likes him. We picked him up when we were on the last North American tour. He was working with one of the bands who were supporting us. But he says he only did that to get to know us. Flattering, isn't it?"

I looked around the room, taking in the luxury of the furniture, which managed to look comfortable and at the same time antique, the elaborate cornices and the cut-glass chandelier, the ornate architraves on all the doors, the velvet curtains and flock wallpaper.

"You seem to do yourself proud on tour," I said.

"Probably the best hotel in Paris."

"Yes, I was told that by my parents. That's why I came."

"It's certainly the most famous. But we have to stay at the best places. We keep odd hours so we have to have twenty-four hour service for food and things. They can also lay on proper security. After all, the Royal Family and the U.S. presidents stay here."

Brian rang down for some "goodies," as he put it, for lunch, and we settled down for a chat in two of the lovely chairs.

Tactfully I asked how much truth there was in the extensive press coverage of him and Anita Pallenberg.

He shrugged. "How much truth is there usually in that sort of talk?" he said.

"But what's she like?"

"She's very sweet."

Obviously he didn't want to talk about it, and the last thing I wanted was to nudge him out of his present equanimity, so I asked him how the various tours had gone over the previous six months since we'd last had a chance to chat.

"Well, there were riots everywhere we played, but we got used to that. I think Ireland was probably the worst for that, but there was a lot of it everywhere. Even in Brisbane there were five thousand fans waiting for us at the airport. In Sydney it hadn't rained for nine months until the day we got there. Then it persisted down for five days. In Germany, on our last tour there, we nearly started World War III. The fans got so worked up they pulled a railroad train to pieces. A mob. Unfortunately, although it happened in the West, it was an East German train. The Reds started demanding compensation from the West." Brian chuckled. "Oh, so much has happened. Half the time it's a job to remember what country you're in when you wake up in the morning." He poured another drink. I refused any more.

Soon afterward, there was a tap at the door and a waiter was allowed in with a load of cold food on a tray. I helped myself to the meat, prawns and French pickles. Brian said he wasn't hungry yet and sipped at his drink as he talked.

"Andrew and Klein reckon we could stay at the top now for at least another three years and that by then Charlie, Bill and I will all be dollar millionaires. But Mick and Keith, of course, will be sterling millionaires before that 'cause it's only their bloody songs that get recorded now." He sounded as if he was down in the dumps again. "Do you know Bill and I spend endless hours helping Keith transform one of his riffs into a basic song? But when either of us has an inspiration for a song, then we're bloody lucky if Keith spends, say, twenty minutes before getting bored and saying it won't bloody work."

"Steady up," I said lightly.

"What?" He looked puzzled.

"I don't want you getting depressed again."

"Oh, I don't do that too often now, Nicholas. I have ways of making me happy. That's one thing about being in the money. It makes it easy to get a spot of grass, or whatever turns you on."

Quickly, I took a look into his eyes, recalling our orgy at the "Kenny Pal" (Kensington Palace Hotel). We started to talk about that night and, strangely for me, I didn't feel embarrassed at the memory of the two of us naked together.

"You were a bastard, creeping off like that," I said.

He shrugged and held out his arms, continental style, "So? You're complaining? Waking up between two chicks like that? A lot of guys would give their right arms for that."

Yes, I thought. And yet my first reaction had been to wonder where he had gone.

We talked on then about records, especially "19th Nervous Breakdown," released in the U.K. on February 4, which again, like "Get Off of My Cloud" reached number one in Britain in two weeks. But in the USA it was now still only at number two in the *Billboard* Top 100.

To anyone but Brian this might have been splendid, but it was not good enough for him.

"It should have crashed straight in at number one in the U.K. and should be number one by now in the States," he said. "Mick and Keith blame that bloody 'Green Berets' record ["The Ballad of the Green Berets" by Staff Sergeant Barry Sadler], but I don't know. To me its failure in the States shows we're not taking the right path."

"Aren't you contradicting yourself a bit?" I was taking a chance on his temper. "Sometimes you say you'd rather play your kind of music even if it isn't commercial enough."

He leaned forward earnestly but without anger. "No, I'm not saying that. What I'm saying is that if we're going all out for commercialism let's do it right. We've got all the best gear in the business, we've got the musicians and we're used to each other—we know how to blend with one another. And yet when we put out a real humdinger bestseller it takes weeks for it to climb feebly up to number two in the States, and now it will probably drop down again like a dying spider."

"All right, I see that point, but you must admit—"

The telephone interrupted me. Brian picked up the receiver irritably. After listening for a few seconds, he said, "Right, I'll be down shortly." He banged the receiver down and leaned back in his seat. He was silent, as if thinking or planning something. Then he turned his attention back to me with a small smile.

I said, "What was 'Breakdown' about anyway?"

"They're not Bob Dylan, are they? It's not supposed to mean anything. It's just about a neurotic bird, that's all."

Brian obviously didn't intend to go anywhere, so we carried on talking. I mentioned Marianne Faithfull now being on Klein's books with Andrew handling her management again. I told him I had seen her on "Juke Box Jury" a few weeks back, in February. He showed little interest in her now. Once his eyes had shone like moonstones at the mention of her name. Maybe he was serious about this new girl, Anita Pallenberg.

He was leaning back, stretching himself luxuriously while telling me of the wild and sometimes frightening escapes they had had from concert halls around the world when the telephone rang again. He cursed and answered it. He snapped, "No, I'm not talking to anybody. I'm busy." He put the phone down and said, with a smile, "I'm busy relaxing with a guy who wants nothing from me."

I leaned back, too, feeling at ease with him. It struck me then that he had changed in some way over those past six months. He was probably just as mercurial in his moods, just as much of a pain in the backside to his fellow Stones, but in some indefinable way he was a different Brian Jones from the one I first met at Leamington Spa.

And then I thought I realized what it was. He no longer gave the impression of flirting with me. Yes, no more looks that said, "Let's get it on, baby."

"No," he said suddenly, "Ireland wasn't the worst. The place that was the worst was the place everyone might imagine to be the quietest and the gentlest of all the places we've been. It was Wellington, New Zealand. They frightened the bloody life out of me there. The cops absolutely lost control of the situation. We did two shows the same night, but had to abandon the second when the fans got onto the stage. The only way out was down a staircase at the side of the stage. Charlie and I nearly didn't make it. As we reached the stairs the fans swooped on us. All we could do was throw the instruments to one side and push microphones over behind us as we ran down. Yeah, that was the worst."

I remember Brian and I talked about the Spencer Davis Group, who had supported the Stones at their Birmingham gig on October 14, 1965. Their latest record, "Somebody Help Me," was at that time number fifteen in the British Top Thirty. While the Stones were away touring, the Spencer Davis Group had been number one in Britain with "Keep On Running" on January 12 after only six weeks. I suggested their tour with the Stones must have boosted their subsequent progress.

Brian just shrugged. He was never the kind of person who would accept flattery or claim credit for assisting other groups.

"Actually," he said, "and not wishing to be pedantic, 'Keep On Running' hit number one two days before we flew to New York for the 'Ed Sullivan Show.'"

"I'd love to have seen that show," I said, imagining what an effect Brian would have had on American teenagers. "Tom Jones was on, too, wasn't he? The same night."

"Yeah, He's great, Tom. He's a straight Ernie. You can have a chat with him over a pint as if he was just an ordinary sort of guy you meet in a pub. Completely opposite to P. J. Proby. I met him in Mr. Smith's Club—in Manchester. I just couldn't get onto his wavelength. He ignored me—well, all of us. Weird guy."

"Good performer, though," I said. "Apart from when he splits his trousers."

"Well, it's a gimmick. Bloody odd one, but it gets him in the papers. Anyway, we were talking about the Spencer Davis Group. The morning I got back from New York Spence turned up at the mews with Stevie Winwood—Stevie plays guitar and does vocals and a load of other things in Spence's group—and they were waiting there for me to let them in. I couldn't find my key. I hadn't slept for about fifty hours and there was this welcome home committee and I couldn't bloody well get in. Must have lost the key somewhere between Sydney and New York. What a bloody day that was. A week last Thursday."

Brian fished in his pocket and brought out a pair of rose-tinted glasses. He put them on. "You like?" he said.

They looked comical to me. I said, "What are they for?"

He shrugged. "Well, it's another paradox, I guess. At first I thought they'd be a help in disguising me. But now I'm getting to be a bit of a Narcissus about them. Never mind."

"So how did you get in that day?"

"I was so uptight that day, I climbed up a drainpipe and put my fist through a window in the first floor. Then we all got pissed. And still no sleep."

"Well, why? What the hell had kept you up all that time? Fifty hours, did you say?"

"Yeah. Well there was this guy called Hari." Brian spelled the name out. "I met him in a club in New York before we went to L.A. They stay open twenty-four hours a day there. Well, this Hari was a fascinating character, half-Welsh and half-Indian, he reckons, and absolutely bananas, but he plays the harp like an angel. Anyway, I stopped off in New York and spent a few days with him. The other Stones cleared off four days before me, and I just hung about in the clubs with Hari. It was him who introduced me to the sitar and taught me how to play it. I told you about it, didn't I?"

He got up and went into another room. He came back carrying a strange-looking instrument that looked to my unprofessional eye like an elongated mandolin with a lot of knobs up its stem. It was made of red mahogany.

Brian settled himself on the floor cross-legged and held the thing up between his legs. I began to wonder if Hari's state of being bananas had been contagious. He began plucking at it with his fingers, producing very odd and eerie sounds.

"It's a bit wearing on the fingers," he said. "I've cut most of the ends off mine. I reckon if I carry on playing my fingers will get rather short." He got up and handed the instrument to me, warning me to be careful how I handled it. He set off toward the other room again.

Over his shoulders, he said, "I used that on one of the recordings we did over in L.A. It's called 'Paint It Black.' I used a dulcimer on another track." He came back with another instrument, which looked like a piece of wood with banjo strings on it—something like a zither.

"If you think it's odd sitting cross-legged to play the sitar, this is one better. You have to lie flat on your belly to play this—according to Hari, anyhow. I used this on a track called 'Lady Jane.'"

It kept coming into my consciousness how different Brian was in his demeanor since the last time we had been alone together.

Somehow he seemed to have come to terms with himself—or perhaps with the others. We had been here talking for an hour, and he hadn't made one sour remark about Andrew Oldham or Mick Jagger. There had been no more talk of his leaving the band either. He seemed even enthusiastic about their recent recording sessions in L.A. Brian always insisted that anyone who has traveled says "L.A." and not "Los Angeles."

He told me he thought they were the best recordings the group had ever done, coupled with the previous one.

"We've really got a different sound now," he said, as he sat fingering the dulcimer. "It's almost—not quite—coming round to the kind of sound I want. But it's bloody hard work, Nicholas. I remember my dad used to nag me and say nobody ever got anywhere except by hard work. I thought it was a load of bullshit, but it seems to be true. We did four sessions lasting from about five in the evening till five in the morning. Nobody else was there except Andrew, Dave Hassinger and Jack Nitzsche, who played piano on some of the tracks. Oh, and Hari, who had come along for the ride."

"You sound as if you've found a new guru in Hari," I said, thinking of Dylan.

For the first time that day there was a scowl on his face. "What?" he said.

Hastily I tried to extricate myself from whatever mess I'd now put my foot into. "I was only referring to Dylan. You seem to like this Hari almost as much as you like Dylan."

His face cleared. "Oh, I see. Well, it's not really in the same way. I admire Hari as a musician. Dylan I admire as a poet, and almost as a philosopher. But I do owe a lot to Hari. He's very knowledgeable about music and he's very talented. He told me that in the north of India they play instruments called vinas, whereas in the south it's the sitar. I bet you didn't know that."

Truth was, I didn't much want to know, either. "What else did you do in L.A.?"

"Bought loads of things. Clothes, records. I had to buy an extra trunk to bring it all back. And pay excess baggage, of course."

"Did you go to any shows?"

"Yes, I went to see Martha and the Vandellas. And the Lovin' Spoonful. I hear cousin Tara is booking them for his twenty-first birthday party."

"Yes, he did mention it."

Brian gave me a very odd look through his kinky glasses. "And now you're wondering why the hell Brian Jones isn't behaving like Brian Jones?"

He continued to stare at me, almost challengingly, but I spurned the challenge and said nothing.

"You know everything we recorded there was by the two ge- niuses, Jagger and Richard?"

I nodded.

"And you know something else? I don't sodding care. I've built a new image. 'Hey, you, get off of my cloud.' You ever notice how he looks at me when he's singing that? Pointing the finger at me as if it's a gun? It used to bug me, like the other one—'I've told you once and I've told you twice.' Now I don't let them bug me. I smile. I act as golden boy among the yobbos. And now it's them that get bugged, because it's me upstaging them instead of the other way. And I flirt with the audience, and to them, now, I'm the cool one. There's Keith ducking and diving with his guitar as if he's trying to spear a shark, there's Mick strutting and posing like a bloody great poof—and then there's me, the golden boy and the boy with the talent, the boy who now and then looks up like a cherub and gets the girls crossing their legs to stop themselves peeing. I've worked at it, Nicholas, and it's getting noticed."

"I'm glad about that," I said. "I was afraid you were getting neu- rotic about Mick. But everyone in the business knows that it's your contribution that makes the Stones' music unique."

He took off his glasses and leaned forward eagerly. "You're damned right. And that's not blowing my own trumpet. I've resigned myself to their not using my songs, but I have the power now to alter their stuff so much that I'm gradually bringing the music back to the style I've always wanted." He sat back and looked composed and full of confidence. Then, for the third time, the telephone rang.

He picked it up and looked as if his newfound composure was about to depart, but then his face and his eyes softened. Whoever was on the other end evidently had the power to melt him. It must be the latest love of his life, Anita, I rightly assumed as the conversation transpired.

After saying "Yes, dear" and "No, dear" a few times, he hung up and said, "Excuse me a moment, Nicholas. I have to go and see someone."

He went out. I relaxed, glad of the interlude because my stomach had begun to rumble. But Brian didn't return for a surprisingly long time. It was over an hour before the phone rang; Brian said "everyone" was going shopping. Did I want to go?

Feeling particularly groggy by now, I declined the invitation. Then, putting down the receiver with the intention of going back to my own room, I decided to go down to the foyer just to meet the fascinating Anita Pallenberg I'd heard so much about.

When I reached the lobby, none of them were to be seen, but then as I went to the entrance I saw Bill Wyman ducking and diving through a crowd of fans, photographers and gendarmes. He rushed out into the road and, obviously forgetting that the traffic flow was opposite to that in Britain, looked the wrong way. He narrowly missed being hit by a car. As the car driver cursed at him, he vaulted over its hood and ran off, presumably to one of the cars hired for the Stones.

Suddenly I was ill, doubled over with stomach pains. I went to my room, vomited and fell asleep. Waking at ten-thirty at night, feeling better, I ran down to find out where the Stones were, and was told they had been back but had now gone out again. Then I recalled Brian saying he was going to see Marianne Faithfull that night at L'Olympia. Well, it was too late to join him now. I went back to sleep.

In the morning the house doctor diagnosed mild food poisoning and advised me to rest. After he had gone, Brian breezed in, grinning broadly and trying to talk to me in French, which I told him was a waste of time because I couldn't understand even good French.

"Hey, you sick?" he said.

"Just a bit of food poisoning. Something I ate on the plane, I expect." Sitting up, I stared at him. He had on those tinted glasses again, and now he was wearing red corduroy hipster trousers, a white sweatshirt with some motif in French printed on it and a full-length coat, which I later discovered to be made out of kangaroo skin.

"Well, you better get ready to get better," he said. "You're coming to the concert tonight. I've got you two tickets and a chick. They'll be in my room from two o'clock. You missed Marianne last night. I tried to get you on the phone but there was no answer. She was sensational."

Before I could ask whether the chick or the tickets or both would be in his room, he marched out. Then he stuck his head around the door again and said, "Hey, after the show tonight there's going to be a great party here. You're invited. So get yourself together. Okay? Ciao."

It was two forty-five by the time I was showered and feeling fit enough to move about. I headed for Brian's room to collect the tickets—and maybe the chick.

The gendarme on the door was the same one I had seen the previous day and remembered me. He allowed me to knock on the door. For a long time there was no reply, but I thought if Brian were out, the gendarme would have had the sense to tell me. I knocked again, feeling a little foolish, with the gendarme standing, uninterested, with his back to me.

Then, faintly, a female voice said, "Come in."

I opened the door and went into the beautiful room that Brian and I had spent so much time in yesterday. And standing by a small table carved out of oak was the most stunning girl I had ever seen in my life. The photographs of Anita Pallenberg had led me to the conclusion that she was a conventionally attractive female, but nothing had prepared me for what she was really like close up, in the same room. Something warm and exciting seemed to emanate from her.

Her eyes were a very strange color. The dominant color was amber, yet there was a tint of green in them, too, that flashed when the light caught them. The bone structure of her face was magnificent. Her hair was blond and shoulder-length, and she had a lean and tempting body, slim and tanned legs. She wore a blouse that looked to be of silk combined with lace, and it was a gold-brown-russet color, redolent of an autumnal scene. Her short skirt was the color of amber that dominated her eyes.

I suppose I was gaping at her. At last, she said, "Can I help you?" Her voice was low in tone, and there was an elegant trace of a European accent.

"I've come to collect some tickets. Two tickets. Brian—Mr. Jones said I was to collect them here."

"Your name?" She sounded like an imperious duchess.

"Nicholas."

"Nicholas what?" Again it was a command.

"Fitzgerald. Sorry."

She picked up a small pile of envelopes and riffled through them.

Although she had an almost Teutonic formality of manner, there was also about her face an impression that she was concealing an impish sense of humor. Not that she was wasting it on me. She probably assumed I was just another of Brian's fans who had somehow inveigled his way into the presence of the hero.

She held out the envelope and I crossed the room to take it from her. I still couldn't take my eyes away from her and stood there rudely staring and taking in the delicate perfume she was wearing.

"Is there anything else?" she demanded.

"No," I said. "Thank you."

"I hope you will have a good time," she said.

Outside the door, I looked up at the gendarme as he looked down at me, and he smiled.

"*Toujours perdrix,*" he said.

I didn't know what the words meant, but the motion of his hands made it clear he was referring to Anita. I grinned back at him and went away. Later I found out what he'd said meant, "Too much of a good thing," literally, "Partridge every day."

Alone in my room at seven, I was putting the finishing touches to my grooming when there was a timid tapping on the door. Opening it, I found Brian's little present standing on the threshold. She was about sixteen, with shy, big, sultry brown eyes, very long brown hair and a delicate but well-structured face. She was slim and shapely.

"I am Mireille," she said. "Brian has asked me to accompany you to the concert." She spoke English well but very precisely.

I gave her a sherry and asked her how she had met Brian. Somehow I hoped he hadn't just called an agency, or a brothel, and booked her.

"Brian spoke to me in the store where I work. That was yesterday. He asked me if I would like to go to the concert. Of course, I said yes. He asked me to take you because you are not familiar with Paris. Of course, I said yes. He told me you were a gentleman, so I would not have to be afraid of you."

"And are you afraid of me?" I wasn't sure whether to be flattered or insulted by Brian's description. Either way, it didn't look as if I was going to get far with her after the show. But I was wrong.

Suddenly she moved closer to me and put a small hand on my chest. "Oh no," she said. I felt her firm little breasts against my arm. Then she reached up and kissed me full on the lips. "Brian said we would be friends."

She was certainly no longer shy. She took command from then on. In the taxi she pointed out the various places of interest. She told me she worked in a record shop and was a member of the French Rolling Stones Fan Club.

At L'Olympia, the Stones crashed into their first number and the pandemonium gradually increased in volume until a full-scale riot was underway.

The boys gave possibly their best performance yet, and established themselves as at least the equals of the Beatles. In fact, to me the Stones' stage manipulation as well as their blatant love affair with the audience now outdid the Beatles' act. The outrageous gyrations of Mick Jagger were undoubtedly the trigger that sent the kids mad. He was now the star. But Keith and Brian, with his new, cherubic image, provided something more than accompaniment; they each represented a focus for the fantasies of those in the audience who found Mick to be rather strong meat for their taste.

The Stones played fourteen numbers in all and reduced my escort to tears and howls and screams along with most of the other girls.

Through the number "Time Is on My Side" everybody swayed from side to side, and through "She Said Yeah" they chanted like a soccer mob. It seemed to me like mass hysteria; and when someone threw a smoke bomb onstage, I looked nervously toward the exit door. But Bill Wyman, calm and cool as ever, managed to stamp it out before much smoke escaped among the band.

As the last song ended, I grabbed Mireille's hand and headed for the emergency exit, well aware that the mob was fighting the bouncers to get onto the stage. Chairs were being torn up for use as weapons. I saw Mick Jagger throw a tambourine into the crowd before he escaped backstage. Once outside, we found ourselves on the fringes of another battle, this time between gendarmes and frustrated fans, but managed to escape and run up the road, where we persuaded a taxi driver to take us to the hotel. He mumbled something in French, and Mireille giggled.

"He said it's the Jacquerie," she told me.

"What's that?"

"Oh, the revolt of the peasants."

She cuddled up close to me and I put my arm around her. She was wearing a white fur coat that made her soft and warm like a small cuddly bear.

By the time I had played with my cuddly toy in my bedroom it was eleven-thirty and well past the time for the party, which I'd found out was in one of the five suites on the third floor that had been rented for the Stones and their entourage.

It was a party given by the Stones in order that the rich and famous of Paris could have an opportunity to meet the group.

The irony of the situation struck me as Mireille and I entered the grandly paneled room full of elegant men and women. Only three years ago, Brian, Mick and Keith had been living in abject poverty in an Edith Grove slum, where the only people who wanted to meet them had been the bill collectors. Now here they were, the toast of Paris, fawned upon by some of the most lovely of Europe's women; and at worst patronized and at best admired by some of the richest men on the continent.

Mick, Bill and Keith were there in a group containing Marianne Faithfull and another raving beauty, Françoise Hardy, the French singer and socialite. Charlie was in a corner chewing at some of the snacks from one of the well-laden tables and looking a bit off-color. There was no sign of Brian and Anita.

After a while, Mick saw me and came loping over, his hair, his silly makeup and his clothes all immaculate. I couldn't help wondering whom he was out to impress tonight.

He shook me by the hand and said, "It's Nicholas, isn't it? You see, I remembered this time. And who is this little beauty?" He took Mireille's chin in his hand and held up her face. I introduced her. She seemed on the point of fainting—meeting the great man himself.

"And where is friend Brian, I wonder?" Mick went on. "Playing with Anita, I suppose. Or maybe the journey back upset him. Do you know they brought us back in a riot wagon? The bold gendarmerie bundled us in the back and we came screaming along the Champs Élysées, sirens blaring like we were firemen late for the holocaust."

"What's the matter with Charlie?" I said, and we all looked over at him. He really did look sick and it seemed he was finding it hard to stick the party out.

"Oh, poor lad, he's suffering from a bit of blood poisoning. Nearly had to cry off the concert. But he's waiting to get a look at the lovely Brigitte Bardot. She specially asked to be invited. She'll be here soon. At midnight."

I looked over at Chrissie Shrimpton, Mick's girlfriend, wondering how she was feeling about Mick's evident excitement over the imminent arrival of the great sex symbol of the age. I had a feeling then—a premonition—that as a Stones girlfriend Chrissie was nearing the end of her run.

Mick spotted somebody else not far off, excused himself and said, "See you at Tara's party—but probably before."

At twelve o'clock, just as the huge, antique grandfather clock struck the hour, the doors opened and in she swept—Bardot, the original sex kitten. Everyone was struck by Bardot's childlike beauty that night. She wore a flame-colored dress and held up her chin with that inquiring innocence that somehow always, to me, seemed to override whatever other expression was on her face.

Then another beautiful woman joined her. It was Anita Pallenberg. Behind Bardot and Pallenberg, to Mick's obvious fury, came Brian, smiling brightly.

The atmosphere between Brian and Mick was charged with menace now, but I'm not sure whether anyone else noticed it. The only thing that tore my gaze from Brigitte Bardot was the glimpse of Brian's mischievous smile at Mick. I had already seen Brian upstage Mick a few times on the stage tonight; now he was upstaging him at the much-vaunted social gathering.

Mireille and I mingled for a while, but it was more fun just hanging out with Mireille. I was finding she was great fun to be with on her own. She noticed the most interesting things, especially about women. She informed me that Brian and Anita were hopelessly in love, and as I looked at them—totally engrossed with one another—at last I acknowledged it myself. Brian had never looked this happy—or this devoted to anyone.

I pointed out to her the various characters associated with the Stones. I noticed that Chrissie Shrimpton was steered away by Mick every time she got anywhere near Brian or Anita.

We stood by as the introductions were made to Brigitte Bardot. Both of us noticed that Mick was excelling himself as a poser, retaining some of his raffish, hell-raising, Rolling Stone image, but blending it a little to fit in with the exalted company he now kept.

As Mick joked and posed with Brigitte, Mireille said, "You call them—people like him—social climbers in Britain?"

"I suppose so," I said.

"But surely he is as high as you can get in the world of entertainment. People should be socially climbing to him."

I smiled. "It doesn't seem to work that way with the British."

It was her turn to shrug. The inscrutable British.

Keith was being introduced now. He appeared to be totally overcome, as if he were being introduced to the Queen. Brigitte said something to him and he muttered something in return, backed away and melted into the throng.

"He is a shy one, that," Mireille whispered to me. "And I think he is attracted to Anita, too."

Now that she mentioned it, I had noticed Keith eye Anita in a shy, furtive way. Could this kid be right? If so, it could lead to one hell of a bust up.

Charlie was the next to be presented, and he was even more embarrassed than Keith had been. He muttered and disappeared, blushing.

Bill, the quiet and retiring Rolling Stone, was positively suave when he met Brigitte. They were quite close to the same age—Brigitte was thirty-one, though she could easily have passed for twenty, and she had more in common with Bill, who was twenty-nine. Maybe she saw the other Stones as crude, callow parvenus.

Mick never moved far from Bardot's side, though he usually had Chrissie in tow as well. Brian would chip into their conversations regularly—deliberately to annoy Mick. Whenever Brian moved away, Mick's eyes would trace Anita's figure from head to toe. Was Mick after her as well? Or just jealous again? Maybe he thought that because Brian had a new, classy, glamorous girl, it was time he had one, too. Perhaps he'd even make a play for Bardot herself. He was certainly working at impressing her.

I was standing close enough to hear Mick say to Brigitte that he had an apartment in Montague Square, a brand new Aston Martin on order and a dog called Dora. He did not neglect to reveal that he'd paid £5,000 for the Aston Martin, worth about $15,000.

It was unlikely she'd be impressed by any of that bullshit, I thought. She'd more likely think him the French equivalent of a flashy bastard.

Just as I was thinking that, the familiar tapping on the shoulder came, and Brian was standing behind me with Anita.

"It's a deformed Yorkshire terrier," he said in my ear. "Much too big, not the right color and it's front legs are bent."

"The dog?" I said.

"Dora. She's a bit of all right, isn't she?"

"Who, Dora?"

"My present." Then he took Mireille's hand and said, "I hope you're enjoying yourself."

"Oh, I'm having a wonderful time. Thank you."

He introduced us both to Anita, who still sounded a bit formal, but was very friendly. "She's a bit of all right too, don't you reckon?" he said, and we all laughed because of what seemed like his cheekiness in talking about her like that. Brian then took us away to a window, where we overlooked the million twinkling lights of Paris.

"So he's getting an Aston Martin," Brian said. "You see how they all copy me?"

"You haven't got an Aston?" I said.

"No, I mean because I get a flash car, they've all got to have flash cars. Keith bought himself a Bentley Continental in January. And Andrew's got himself a bloody great Phantom V Rolls. $35,000 worth. He bought it at the garage Brian Epstein uses. Nothing but the best, eh?"

I nodded. I'd never been much impressed by people flaunting wealth.

"But I'll tell you something, Nicholas. There's none of them got a chick like Anita to ride alongside him."

So the Stones actually *did* compete to see who could get the best-looking girls. That still seemed crazy and pointless to me; and unfair to the women. I looked at Chrissie Shrimpton. Mick was still talking a lot to Brigitte. Chrissie looked happy enough, perhaps because it was obvious to all that Brigitte was more interested in Bill

Wyman, standing there with confidence and style, pleased, as any straight man would be, to have snared Bardot's undivided attention.

We were joined at the window by Françoise Hardy, the sultry French singer, who knew Mireille. She also resembled her rather closely; they had the same long brown hair. But she was quite a bit taller and had a pretty, snubbed nose. Her eyes were very brooding as she looked out over the shimmering Paris night.

Brian, Anita and she had met earlier. "It's a beautiful city," Brian said. "So full of life."

"London, too, is so much alive," Françoise said. "To me it is a second home. Here I live near the Élysée Palace. In London I like to be near to Buckingham Palace, and so I stay, when I can, at the Hilton."

Brian said, "But the architecture here is so exquisite, all over. In London we have grand buildings, but they're mostly confined to the center, where the tourists go. All the rest of it is dull and slummy. Here, everywhere you go is fascinating. And the atmosphere is so exotic. I'd love to have an apartment in Paris."

Bardot and Mick and the others were moving closer to us to take in the view from the window.

Françoise was saying that she liked to spend a lot of her time in St. Tropez. "You can dance through the night in clubs there, and in the day the weather is so much nicer. In the daytime you sleep all day on the beaches outside the town. In the town you have to pay a lot to use the beaches. Outside they're free."

Behind me I heard Mick, still trying to impress Bardot. The London School of Economics was part of London University and he had been a student there, Mick explained. Having had enough, Brigitte edged away from Mick and moved closer to the window, between Bill Wyman and Françoise Hardy. The two women knew each other; Françoise said, "We were talking about St. Tropez, Brigitte. Do you still love it there as much as you did?"

"Oh, yes. But you must come down and stay again soon."

Mick said bitchily to Chrissie, "Then she won't have to pay to go on the beach, poor girl."

Everyone except Chrissie ignored him, but she hissed, "Oh, be quiet."

Brian said, "I suppose all the 'in' crowd still hang out there? Alain Delon and his crowd?"

Brigitte nodded.

Mireille said, "He's great. So handsome and husky." Then she tightened her grip on my arm as if to reassure me.

Brian went on, "Roman Polanski, Sharon Tate, Catherine Deneuve. They were all there when I went last."

Brigitte said, "Don't be too shy to mention Roger Vadim. We are still good friends." Brigitte was divorced from Vadim.

Mick was boasting again. "I was best man," he said, "when Catherine married David Bailey." Mick added, "Bailey [the name by which he was affectionately known to his friends] is one of my closest friends."

"Mick hasn't got many," Brian said in an audible aside to Anita. A malicious smile came over Anita's face.

Brigitte turned to Mick and regarded him coolly. "I heard. Catherine happens to be one of *my* best friends."

"One of mine is Sharon Tate," Brian piped. Brigitte turned and smiled at Brian. He was high and he beamed his satisfaction over upstaging Jagger.

"Sharon Tate and I were going together last year," Brian said, oblivious to the green highlights that were flashing jealousy out of Anita Pallenberg's amber eyes. I held my breath as Brian went on. "Sharon was in London last year making that film *The Eye of the Devil.*"

I couldn't take my eyes off Anita. God help any woman who touched what was hers. The veneer of gentility was extremely thin. Underneath was a tigress. She could be wicked. That was part of her animal magnetism. It was so obvious why she was attractive to men even in the midst of this feast of feminine charm.

Under Anita's fierce gaze Brian was rambling on about Sharon Tate, running out of steam. "I didn't think a lot of her producer friend, Marty Ransohoff, or whatever he was called."

Mick saw his chance and stepped in. "I suppose you all know how Bailey and Catherine Deneuve came together?"

Nobody answered until Brian said, "I bet you're going to tell us." It was like a sparring match between them.

Ignoring him, Mick said, "Catherine was doing a photographic session for an American magazine, and Bailey was doing the photographs. Trouble was, the magazine people wanted her to strip off nude." He paused for effect.

Brigitte put on a seductive look. "And she did?" Brigitte asked. Bardot of course knew very well what the answer was.

Mick was in his element. He had the floor. "Well, yes, she did. But only because Roman Polanski was there and he persuaded her. Anyway, Bailey could see she was a bit upset and uneasy about it, so he took her out to lunch. Then they fell for each other, and that was that."

A quiet, cultured voice was heard to say, "Nobody would ever persuade me to pose nude."

Everyone turned. It was Marianne Faithfull. It had been eight months since I'd seen Marianne. She had prematurely given birth last November to a son, christened Nicholas. Her husband, John Dunbar, was not present. He was an academic, not a socialite. "Perhaps he's looking after the child somewhere," Brian whispered to me.

The party drifted on and, as usual for me, began to seem like a merry-go-round, a carousel spinning amid bright colors and beautiful faces. Parties had that enchanting effect on me. Periodically the carousel would halt and there would be a kind of slow-motion picture before me that would etch itself into my memory.

One of these was of Bill Wyman slowly leaving the room as if he didn't want the bother of saying goodbye to everybody. He had spent a long time in deep conversation with the great Bardot, and now, clearly, Bill was tired. Marianne and Anita both deliberately avoided talking to Bill. As he slipped away tonight, it was clear to me for the first time that Bill Wyman was an outsider in the band and had been all along.

"He's written several good songs," Brian said, "but Mick, Keith and Andrew ignored them. Several unknown groups were only too keen to record Bill's compositions. He's also comanager of a group called the End. He does a lot of reading and lives up to his reputation as the Rolling Stones' steady type. Bill spends a lot of time collecting press cuttings on the various tours."

As Brian and I talked, I noticed Mireille dancing with a dark, swarthy man. She winked at me.

Later Brian and Anita settled onto a chintz sofa. They were smiling and talking intimately. He brushed his fingers over Anita's cheek. I regarded the scene with mixed emotions. Above all, what kind of influence would Anita exert on Brian? To me, they looked in love to the point of lovesickness. She could become the great woman behind a great man—could conjure great music out of Brian. The only odd note was that two such obviously lovesick creatures hadn't already flown the party to the sanctity of their love nest. But then I saw that Brigitte was still present, and at parties such as this you do not leave before the great one. It would have been alien to Brian's basic good breeding, but Mick Jagger seemed to have disappeared, at least for the moment. Charlie Watts had left long ago.

Mireille joined me. The guests had become aware of Bardot's impending departure. Everyone was standing near the doors, which were open.

Keith was there and so were Mick and Chrissie. Anita and Brian stood at the door like the true host and hostess.

Brigitte said to Keith Richard, who was now feeling bold, "Well, you'll have to see if you can do the music for my next film. It's a spy thriller."

Mick jumped in immediately. Before Keith had a chance to respond to Brigitte's invitation, which could have been personal and exclusive, Mick Jagger said, "Yeah, that's great. We'll have a bash at it, won't we, Keith?" Mick put his hand on Keith's shoulder. Brian gave an ironic smile.

"If they do it," I said to Mireille, "it will be Brian's music that fetches it alive. With his new confidence, he might be thinking the same thing."

When Brigitte left, everyone else started saying goodbyes and making arrangements. The Stones were due to fly to Marseilles in the morning. Brian said, "Nicholas, why don't you stay in Paris until Friday? 'Ready, Steady, Go' is being televised live from La Locomotive Club. I'm coming back especially for it."

I thought of home and studies. Mireille said, "Oh, yes. Please stay, Nicholas, and let's go to bed soon." That did it. We'd stay.

There was a strange, questioning look from Anita Pallenberg when we said good night. Brian's eyes shot us a randy invitation. But in bed I soon forgot about them.

On Friday, April 1, Brian Jones returned to Paris for the "Ready, Steady, Go" TV show. Brian arrived at 5 A.M. on a sleeper from Lyons, where the Stones had performed in concert, stirring up a riot. At 2:30 P.M. Brian called the George V. I had been lying in a state of drowsy euphoria, my arms around the firm, naked body of Mireille. At first she wouldn't let me go and we continued to hang onto each other, hoping whoever was calling would eventually give up and go away. Finally and reluctantly I detached myself.

"Hi," Brian said. "What are you doing?"

"What d'you think I'm doing?"

"Well, that depends. If you've still got that little present I sent you, you're either screwing her or passing your rough, workingman's hands over her smooth, virgin body."

"I've still got your present," I said, smiling as I looked down at the girl's small, upturned breasts. "Where are you?"

"Back here in my suite. I'd have to be. There's a telephone strike outside. A national telephone strike. I tried to ring you from the station. Have you seen any papers?"

"Haven't seen a paper since I got here. Why? What's happened?"

"Mick's got hurt. Hit by a flying chair when the riot started in Marseilles. They rioted in Lyons too, but not as bad. In Marseilles it was the fans against the gendarmes. This is getting to be a habit. Mick had to go to the hospital. Eight stitches under his right eye. He's not a pretty sight, but then he never was, was he? Also, the Labour Party won the election, back home. In the English papers the two stories take up about the same amount of space."

Brian was at his most tranquil. He now accepted he was an

instrumentalist and he wasn't any longer interested in the songs; he could take almost any song, he said, and "pretty it up."

"You know these beauticians," he said. "They reckon they can pick up any old dog off the streets and turn her out after a couple of hours looking like a Cinderella on her way to the ball. Well, at the moment that's what I'm doing to their songs. And if you can do that you're doing something more than writing a boring old song. I don't even know the words to most of the songs Mick sings. I'm an instrumentalist, a beautician. Mind, it would take a bloody good beautician to do anything for Mick."

"So what's on the agenda for tonight?" I said, hoping to end the conversation and cuddle up to Mireille again. "Where shall we meet? The La Loco?"

"Yes. You know where it is?"

"No, but Mireille will—"

"It's in the famous Moulin Rouge building. Toulouse-Lautrec and all that. Come early. This is going to be wild—we're going on the show. They want Bill to dress up as a barman, me as a priest and Mick as a gendarme."

"What did Bill think of that?"

"He said he'd rather be a gendarme. I'm going to crash out for a while now. See you later."

It was absolute chaos at "Ready, Steady, Go." Besides the Stones, there were to be star turns by the Who and the Yardbirds. Bands were rehearsing and noisy technicians were running sound and lighting tests in a blitz of shouted French.

Jimmy Phelge accosted me at the bar. Batting his eyes, he said, "Monsieur Fitzgerald, fancy meeting you here."

Resignedly, I introduced Mireille and he acknowledged her perfunctorily, like a woman dismissing a rival. He introduced us to Paul "Sam" Samwell-Smith, the bass guitarist with the Yardbirds, the group who'd had the great hit, "For Your Love."

Sam looked glum. "The way things are going, the other boys are not going to be here for tonight. The Yardbirds have gotten themselves stranded in Amsterdam."

"I bet Giorgio's having a whale of a time," Phelge said, referring to Giorgio Gomelsky, manager of the Yardbirds and founder of the Crawdaddy Club, where he'd given the Stones their start.

"The last thing I heard, he was going to charter a plane," Paul Samwell-Smith said.

A few minutes later he was called away by an announcement on the intercom. "That'll be a cable," he said, hurrying off.

When he returned, Paul told us Giorgio had managed to charter a plane for $7,500.

Cathy McGowan of the "Ready, Steady, Go" staff said, "That's one problem almost solved. So far it's been one disaster after another all day. Now someone tells me Mick Jagger isn't coming. Have you seen him?"

"The last I heard, he was trying to get to London."

"He's got a bad memory, but surely he can't forget us, the 'RSG' team. God, I've got a feeling this show is going to collapse around my ears tonight."

"I think you can count on Bill and Brian," I said.

"Another problem—I can hardly speak a word of French. They *promised* me a personal interpreter—"

"Perhaps Mireille can help," I suggested, and introduced them.

They started chatting like old friends. Cathy wanted some help with the French male dancers. Phelge said, "O là là! Can I come?" He went mincing off after them, leaving Paul Samwell-Smith and me alone at the bar. I congratulated him on the Yardbirds' latest single, "Shapes of Things," currently number five on the charts. Paul had been with the Yardbirds when they'd cut one of the classics of the 1960's—"For Your Love." The greatest guitarist in rock, Eric Clapton, had also been with the Yardbirds then as their lead guitarist.

Paul Samwell-Smith looked more relaxed now, and we fell into conversation about how the Yardbirds had continued success in the charts even after Eric's departure. I took a deep breath and said to Paul, "I have always wanted to know why Eric Clapton left the Yardbirds only two weeks after your first major hit. 'For Your Love' was on its way to number one in the British charts."

Eric Clapton, who had celebrated his twenty-first birthday only two days ago, had recently been voted—by other leading artists—

Britain's number one guitarist. It was a popular verdict, and I knew no one who was quarreling with it. The fact that he had only taken up the guitar four years ago, after having fallen in love with rhythm 'n' blues music, made it all the more remarkable.

Eric Clapton joined the Yardbirds in 1963. They played regularly at the Crawdaddy Club and later toured the Continent with the American blues singer Sonny Boy Williamson.

"Eric Clapton hated 'For Your Love,'" Paul said. "In fact, he despised the whole 'business competition,' as he called it, that had crept into the music profession. When the talk of finance companies, promotions, began, Eric said, 'We're being turned into machines, money-making *machines*. I'm pulling out.' And he did. I admired his guts. Most of us think like that now and then, but it takes incredible moral courage to pull out, especially when the money is just starting to pour in with a solid gold hit."

Eric sounded not unlike Brian, and I said to Paul, "I suppose you know Brian Jones asked Eric if maybe they could get something together. That was a couple of years ago."

"No, I didn't." He thought for a while, then said, "Hey, what a combo that would have been."

"They would probably have ended up fighting the whole time. Brian's a difficult guy to get along with. What d'you think of Pete Townshend as a guitarist?"

"Oh, he's good. But I resent the myth that's grown up that he invented the 'feedback' technique. Even the *Observer's* color supplement fell for that, Sunday before last. You'd think a paper like that would get it right. The Yardbirds had been using feedback on our disks well before the Who started it. Our guitarist Jeff Beck was using feedback in the days when we played at Richmond Athletic Ground. Pete Townshend and the rest of the Who used to come along and watch. I'm not knocking the Who, but let's give credit where credit's due."

"D'you think Eric is happy now, then?"

"He's with John Mayall's Bluesbreakers and they play his kind of music. But happy? Somehow I don't think so. But I'm sure he'll find his niche."

I wondered if Brian Jones would ever find *his* niche. After the nightmare in Birmingham, Brian seemed about ready to "step off the bus." But he seemed a different Brian now. There had been no more of that wild talk since he met Anita.

Cathy and Mireille returned, and it was obvious 'RSG' was still very much in crisis. "I wish the Stones were here instead of the Who," Cathy said. "The Who are all right when they decide to cooperate, but at the moment I'm not sure they're going to tonight. It just isn't my day."

"Well," said Paul Samwell-Smith, "at least the Who are here."

"Yes," said Cathy. "That's something."

"And," said Paul, a bit huffily, "it looks like it's only us and the Who pulling new stuff out of the bag at the moment. And if the Who are any good it's got a lot to do with them watching us and learning from us."

Paul got up and walked off.

"Oh, my God," Cathy McGowan said, hardly knowing whether to laugh or cry. "Now I've gone and upset Paul Samwell-Smith."

Phelge sauntered up and said in his lilting, lisping voice, "Very sensitive, those intellectuals. He reads those kinds of books, so deep you can drown in them. Wouldn't like to sleep with him; he might try to psychoanalyze me in my sleep. Gawd!"

Everyone regarded Phelge as a pest, but we were glad enough to have him now, to give Cathy a good laugh and relieve her tension.

The Who lined up to rehearse a song. Their latest record, "Substitute," stood at number twelve in the British Top Thirty.

The Who had abandoned their Carnaby Street gear for ordinary slacks and T-shirts. Keith Moon, probably the smallest of the group, was at his drums; he had the reputation of looking like Hitler without the moustache (he would die of taking fifty shots of vodka).

Michael Lindsay-Hogg was fighting with his French codirector. While Michael was issuing instructions in English, the Frenchman was countermanding his directions in French.

Mireille and I agreed that the show was going to be a disaster.

Phelge had been abandoned by everyone else. Now he approached me and said in a knowing, leering manner, "And what of the sweet Anita?"

"She's very attractive," I said.

"If you care for that sort of thing," he said.

Not really wanting Phelge's company but interested to hear what he knew of the girl who, at least for the moment, was having such a pacifying effect on Brian, I said, "I suppose you know all about her?"

"An arty type from way back. Father and grandfather were painters and she was brought up among all the arty types throughout Europe. She speaks four or five languages, my dear! Would you believe it? And all I can speak is Chelsea camp. Well, she studied all the art subjects in Rome, then went off to New York with some photographer boyfriend. And there, through meeting various artists and photographers, she began to emerge as a model. So let that be a lesson to you, Nicholas. Never mess about with artists and photographers."

I was getting impatient. "How did she meet Brian?"

Phelge ignored me. "Gradually she became much sought after all over Europe as a model. She even made a couple of films, those boring continental-style things where the camera hovers on someone's hand for half an hour and nobody smiles or says much. Anita liked the Stones' music. She first went to see them at L'Olympia, Good Friday last year. And that's when she announced she was going to *have* Brian. You know what those calculating females are like—or perhaps you don't?"

"How d'you know all this?" I demanded. "How can you possibly have known that? Did she tell you?"

"It so happens that a friend of mine was with Anita that night at L'Olympia—Françoise Hardy."

"I just met her with Brigitte Bardot."

"My, my. We are flying *high* these days."

"She is also a friend of mine," Mireille chipped in from my other side.

"Please, spare me the name-dropping," Phelge said, putting Mireille down in a typically camp manner. "According to Françoise, Anita turned to her during the show and said, in ref our Brian, 'Give me four months and I'll be with that guy.' They couldn't get backstage that night because of the rioting, but she did finally meet him in Munich—"

"No, they met before that," said Mireille confidently.

Phelge was huffy. He raised his yellow eyebrows and said, "Oh? And *where* was that, pray?"

"At a party in the Rue de L'Ambre. At Donald Cammells' apartment. I was there. Brian Jones was with a girl called Zou Zou and he did not take any notice of any other girls that night. But he met Anita there."

"Well," said Phelge, "that was hardly a *meeting*. They really got together in Munich in September last year. Mick had goose-stepped while singing 'Satisfaction' and started a riot. The police used water cannon on the fans. Fifty rows of seats had been torn out of the theater. After the show Anita managed to get someone to smuggle her backstage. Brian was the only one of the Rolling Stones who would talk to her. Brian was having one of his fits. He'd fallen out with everyone else in the band and wanted to cry on someone's shoulder. Anita told somebody I know that they ended up in his bed and he cried all night, poor dear."

"I always was taught that Englishmen do not cry," Mireille said. "That is why they do not make good lovers."

"Then it must be the Welsh in him, love."

"I'm half-Welsh," I said.

"That is why you are a good lover, perhaps?" Although Mireille was only sixteen, she knew exactly how to please a man.

The other four Yardbirds had arrived. They were trailing behind their corpulent manager Giorgio Gomelsky like ducklings behind their mama. Giorgio was the reincarnation of the prewar Hollywood movie tycoon—dark glasses and the unmistakable air of one who hires and fires.

There was still no sign of Brian and Bill, but the show finally got going. The production team had given up all hope an hour ago of getting the Stones on.

The show went out live and the Who gave it a strong opening with their hit, 'My Generation.' When the sound system broke down, Pete Townshend stormed offstage cursing the technicians' incompetence, then came back toward the cameras with a chair over his head. One of the Who diverted him at the last moment. Cathy, sitting in front of the cameras in an attractive Parisian hat, looked on in horror for a moment before regaining her smile and professional composure.

Keith Relf, the sensational vocalist with the Yardbirds, took the stool next to me when Phelge scurried off.

He had a glass of milk in front of him, and I wondered if the barman had made a mistake.

Keith looked at me as I stared at him. He was a Brian type, at least in looks, in the same way as Mike Clarke was. In fact I wasn't sure then that Keith wasn't the best-looking of all. He was about five feet eight inches, blond-haired and blue-eyed, and he had a sparkle about him that gave an impression of vitality and a great love of life. I smiled and asked if he always drank milk. He said he had a bit of stomach trouble and thought it best to keep off the booze.

We both turned as a great whoop went up and half the audience began swarming to the place, just within the doors, where Brian Jones and Bill Wyman, who had just arrived, were standing. Cathy ran over with a mike and did a short interview with Brian and Bill.

The fans were about to crush Brian to death, but some guards rushed in and pulled them off. He and Bill were then taken to some special seats behind the cameras, where the fans were kept at bay by a circle of bouncers. I couldn't even see them from where I was.

Keith said, "Thank God we haven't come to that stage yet where they try to lynch us. But it's getting almost as bad when we turn up somewhere unexpected." He finished his milk and excused himself, saying his father was in the hospital and he was going to call and find out how he was.

The Yardbirds went on and roared through a string of their hits, including "Shapes of Things." Unfortunately the set was totally ruined by the faulty sound system.

After the show, Brian and Bill were pursued through the building and then whisked away in a police car; I didn't see them in the hotel. In any case, it was my last night to enjoy my "present," Mireille, before I flew back to London tomorrow.

She was still naked in my arms when about 12:30 P.M. Brian called to say a protracted goodbye. Mireille was depressed and close to tears at the prospect of the fun, the excitement, the glamour and the sex coming to an end.

"I'm off to Stockholm later today with Bill," Brian said. "We meet up with the other three there. We're playing at somewhere called Tungliga Tennishallen. Now then, try to get your tongue around that at this time of day."

"I'd rather not," I said.

"Coward. Anyway, it seats ten thousand, so it'll probably be another riot. Then we're off to Copenhagen on Tuesday for the last of the five-country tour. That's to give a concert at the K.B. Hallen. Where did you get to last night?"

"Came home here with my present," I said.

"Randy sod. We went up the Eiffel Tower. There's a restaurant there on the first floor. Had a good feed, then ended up at La Castelle again. Sleep seems to have gone out of fashion in Paris. Hey, I forgot to mention. You remember Mike Dorsey? Used to be our road manager? You know he disappeared last August and everyone said he was in the States. Well, I bumped into him the other day. He'd flown in from South Africa of all places. Says he got his own club out there, and a house with a pool, servants and an Alfa Romeo. Can't stop now; I'll ring you in London. Ciao."

Only half the story as usual, I thought. Where had he bumped into Dorsey? Where was Anita? Was she going to Scandinavia? Anyhow, I was pleased that Brian was happy at last and hoped things would go more smoothly for him now that he appeared to have found his mate.

CHAPTER

10

T HE LOVIN' SPOONFUL WERE GOING to play at my cousin Tara Browne's birthday party in Ireland on Saturday, and we were all going. Brian also wanted me to come to the Marquee Club in London on Monday, April 18, where the Lovin' Spoonful were appearing. "They're four crazy boys I first saw in Greenwich Village," Brian told me.

Back in January, Tara had booked them for his party for $2,500, which the family considered outrageous. Actually, Tara had got them cheap. Since January, when they were virtually unknown, the Lovin' Spoonful had rocketed to popularity in Britain; "Daydream" hit number seventeen in the British Top Thirty, and now they were at number two in the States for the second week in a row, chasing the Righteous Brothers with their "You're My Soul and Inspiration."

At the Spoonful's club debut at the Marquee, rock royalty was out in force—Brian, John Lennon, George Harrison, Spencer Davis and Stevie Winwood.

"You have a hit on your hands with *Aftermath*," I said, congratulating Brian on the Stones' new album, which the music press had hailed as "the best value for money of any LP record ever produced;" there were no fewer than fourteen tracks, unusually long for 1966. No wonder Brian had been so excited in Paris about the recording session. His contributions elevated what were adequate songs into wild music. With every instrument Brian played, he snatched up the basic melody, danced around with it, then handed it back, enhanced, while he continued to flirt with it on the outer edges. On "Lady Jane," it was the dulcimer, which he had shown me in Paris. "Lady Jane" had a slow, elegant rhythm and, for a Stones number, was relatively restrained. Jack Nitzsche played the harpsichord on this one. On "Under My Thumb," Brian played the marimba, turning a minor instrument into something major. On "Think," Brian used a fuzzbox for his guitar, which made it sound like anything but a guitar.

Although all the compositions were credited to Jagger and Richard, clearly the star of this marathon record was Brian Jones. His claim to that could rest on one track alone, "Going Home," in which he played the harmonica.

On first playing *Aftermath*, I picked out "Mother's Little Helper" and "Under My Thumb" as possible commercial singles. My personal favorites, keepsakes of Brian's genius, were "Lady Jane" and the riotous "Going Home."

Tara's birthday party was held at Lugalla, near the village of Roundwood, in County Wicklow, outside Dublin. The house was described in a nineteenth-century handbook for Ireland as "one of the sweetest summer villas in Wicklow." It is known as a "lodge," which meant it was once used for shooting, but, as Mick Jagger was to say at the party, "When you come from Dartford, it's more like a palace."

The walls were castellated and on the corners there were curious stumpy towers or turrets. The upper-floor windows were triangular, and from the roof there sprouted, in various places, little pinnacles and huge chimneys. It looked as if the architect had built the ground floor as a Georgian villa and on the way up had gradually grown more fanciful until he had constructed an amalgam of fortress, decorated Gothic cathedral, Spanish villa and Eastern temple. But there was no denying it was impressive, especially on the night of the party, with its white stone walls floodlit, starkly standing out on the empty hillside in the vale of Lough Tay.

The Honourable Tara Browne was the son of Lord Oranmore and Browne and of the former Oonagh Guinness, his second wife. Relationships were rather complicated in that family. Tara's mother, Oonagh, who was the Earl of Iveagh's niece, had married Lord Oranmore in 1936. Their marriage, however, was dissolved in 1950. She was next married to a Cuban dress designer, Miguel Ferreras. But that marriage had also been dissolved in Mexico last year. She then made an extraordinary decision. She dropped the Cuban's surname and reverted to the name of her second husband. So she was now known as Oonagh, Lady Oranmore and Browne. Lord Oranmore and Browne was now married to a former actress, Sally Gray. About a year and a half ago Tara had secretly married a farmer's daughter, Nicky Macsherry. There was a big fuss in the family when this came out, but now Nicky had been accepted.

The inside of Lugalla was as magnificent as its shell led one to expect. There were tapestries and priceless paintings, ancient and modern. There were busts and statues dotted around between columnar pillars that led up to Doric arches. In the music room, a seven-piece orchestra started scraping away at violins and cellos. My God, I thought, what are the Rolling Stones going to make of that? A society orchestra for deb dancing.

Three hundred people had been invited, but there seemed more to me. It is the tradition in Ireland on the big estates, in the rich houses, that employees—gardeners, grooms, stable-boys and cow-hands—are invited to any party held by the family. Since feudal times it has been the custom to treat them as members of the family on these occasions. This evening, all the rough-clad people of the estate mixed freely and without self-consciousness with the aristocracy of Ireland, Great Britain and Europe. And these in their turn mixed with the strangely garbed, long-haired Chelsea-type pals of Tara. The result was an unlikely conglomeration, and it was interesting to study the way the different types regarded one another. The estate-workers and the genuine aristocracy hit it off very well and had a lot in common. But the workers regarded the youngsters with undisguised disapproval and thought them insufficiently respectful to their "betters," while the "betters" themselves appeared either amused or highly curious about the clothes, habits and talents of the new generation.

Among the upper crust were lords and ladies by the score—Aberconway, Astor, Balfour, Beatty, and on through the alphabet. There were Fitzgeralds, FitzRoys, and FitzHerberts. There were countesses and viscounts, barons and baronets, an odd duke and a count, and even two couples of foreign royalty. And there were all the permutations of the divorced Guinnesses and their new wives and husbands.

Among the young and talented were Brian with the magnetic Anita Pallenberg, Mick Jagger, Chrissie Shrimpton, and Victoria and Alice Ormsby-Gore, the daughters of the former British Ambassador to Washington. Tara was with his pretty, petite young wife Nicky, greeting everyone in the hallway. Tara had now grown his hair quite long.

Most of the younger people were gathered in one of the drawing rooms, where drinks were being served. Brian was with Anita and the four members of the Lovin' Spoonful. He called me over to meet them. Anita flashed a smile at me.

John Sebastian wore old-fashioned-looking steel-rimmed glasses and seemed very polite. He was only twenty-one. The others looked younger and more mischievous. Joe Butler was a nice-looking, friendly, boy-next-door type, while Steve Boone and Zal Yanovsky were the kind who clown around a lot.

Later in the evening I heard Zal, the lead guitarist in the group, talking to one of the employees of the estate, called Jonjoe, a little, wise-looking old fellow with sparkling eyes—a leprechaun.

"You mean they make all this dough outa black beer?" Zal said.

"Ah now," said Jonjoe. "I wouldn't say it was just black beer. It would be more like a mixture of cream and the kind of water you'd expect to get in heaven if ever you visited the place."

"Wowee!"

"I beg your pardon, sir?"

"That must be some kinda drink. I'm gonna get me some."

Later the Lovin' Spoonful took the place of the orchestra. Their music was restrained and pleasant to most ears. Even the older members of the family didn't appear to dislike it.

Brian and I managed to have one of our heart-to-hearts in a quiet room while Anita was off being shown around the house by Oonagh, who seemed to have taken quite a liking to her.

"Still going well with you and Anita?" I asked Brian.

"Marvelous. She's the one I've always been waiting for. Don't want anybody else. Not any other woman." The impish smile was meant to reassure me. "She's something else again."

I was going to say I hoped it would last, but realized in time that would be tactless.

"Day after tomorrow I'm taking Anita to Paris for a bit of a holiday," Brian said. "Mick's going, too, with Chrissie, but not with us, thank God. I don't think there's anything really big coming up till May Day."

"Yeah, the *NME* concert," I said, having read about it. I was hoping to be able to go.

"There's us, the Beatles, the Who, the Walker Brothers, Spencer Davis, the Yardbirds, et cetera. That ought to be some show. Then on the tenth of May Bob Dylan's British tour opens in Bristol. I've got to try to get down there and see him."

I sensed now that Brian was so happy with Anita, he had less time for me. It was only natural, I told myself. Before he met her he would have said "We've got to try—" Never mind. It was good to see him so tranquil. When Anita came back, he said, "Ah, here she is," and I drifted away.

In the music room, when I saw Mick Jagger sprawling over one of my relative's antique armchairs with Chrissie perched on the arm, I experienced a momentary sensation of snobbish resentment. The bloody upstart, I thought. But the feeling soon passed and I stood behind him as he chatted to a group of young London people.

"Nearly everyone you meet claims to have an Irish grandmother, d'you know that? Ask anyone and they'll at least have an Irish great-grandmother."

Somebody asked, "How d'you fancy being a film star Mick?" The Stones were due sometime this year to work on the film from David Willis' novel, *Only Lovers Left Alive*.

"Looking forward to it," he said, putting a languid arm around Chrissie.

"What's it about?"

"Well, everybody grown up suddenly commits suicide and only young people are left. Then Britain becomes a fascist dictatorship. Don't you think I'll make a good fascist?" He did the fascist salute with his other arm. Steve Boone, up on the stage, stopped playing the bass for a second or two to return the salute.

An elderly aunt nearby said, "Well!" and swept, duchesslike, from the room.

Chrissie noticed this and removed his arm from her waist. "You fool, why d'you have to do that?" She stood up.

He wagged a finger at her. "Careful, careful. The next one's the twentieth."

She looked down at him, angry and pale. Almost under her breath she said, "You bastard," and she ran off.

Mick stretched himself out, undismayed. "Contrary to popular belief," he said, "my parents were respectably married."

The others giggled. But I wondered how many of them knew what he had meant about the twentieth. Brian had told me that Chrissie always believed that the song "19th Nervous Breakdown" had been written about her. She used to worry about Mick, and when she nagged him, he would accuse her of being paranoid or being near to a nervous breakdown.

The party lasted all night, and the last I saw of Brian he was sitting quite stoned on the floor in the music room demonstrating to Zal Yanovsky how the dulcimer was played.

In Paris, Brian had shown me the Indian sitar, and now, with the Friday, May 13, release of "Paint It Black" b/w "Long, Long While," it was clear that Brian played with far greater effect than George Harrison had achieved in "Norwegian Wood." Brian seemed able to become a part of the instrument itself and conjure from it an exotic, primitive jangle that transformed the song.

On the day before the single was released, the twelfth, Brian, Keith, Bill and Charlie flew to New York (a day early, avoiding the unlucky day) to appear the following Sunday on the "Ed Sullivan

Show." Mick Jagger, who claimed not to be superstitious, flew out on Friday because, he said, his clothes were not ready—and his obsession with clothes was more important than any old superstition. And this from the guy who, when the Stones had started, urged that they should all appear in scruffy jeans and sweaters.

"Paint It Black" was their fastest-selling record to date in the U.S. Brian called me with the good news and invited me to Bob Dylan's Albert Hall concert. We had not made it to the Bristol opening.

On May 26, the day of Dylan's concert, "Paint It Black" moved into number one in the British charts. That night the Stones and their party occupied several boxes. Dylan had been receiving mixed and sometimes poor responses from his fans. His music had changed, the papers claimed, and in Britain the tour had been a flop. People had even been walking out in the middle of his concerts, or shortly after the intermission.

Perhaps that was why Brian and the other Stones and their women had come in a body—to give moral support and encouragement to their guru.

Brian was in one of his fits of despair, a far cry from the sparkling and confident image he had presented in Paris. Was it all going wrong again? Anita was standing close to him at intermission, looking concerned. I hoped she was going to stick by him.

Mick and Chrissie were looking moody, too, obviously discontented with each other's company.

The Royal Albert Hall revealed the reason for the disaffection of purist Dylan fans. He used an electric guitar and a rock backup group. The performance of "Leopard Skin Pill Box Hat" was deafening and completely out of character for this man whose reputation had been that of poet and philosopher. There was a rustle of discontent and only scant applause at the end of it.

He went on to sing new arrangements of his old songs—"I Don't Believe You" and "Baby, Let Me Follow You Down"—which bore only a vague, and perhaps vulgar, relationship to the originals.

"Judas!" someone shouted from the audience, just before the last number.

Dylan hesitated, then stepped up to the microphone. "I don't believe you!" he yelled angrily. "You're a liar." Then he stepped back, looking defiant as he and the band began to beat out the song, "Like a Rolling Stone."

There was booing in some parts of the audience, but Dylan glared at them as if saying he was right and they were wrong.

Backstage, Bob Dylan looked depressed as Brian introduced us. Dylan barely nodded. The atmosphere was strained and unfriendly.

Brian steered me over to a table where drinks were being served, then over to a corner. Anita was not around.

"Sorry about the mood," Brian said. "Maybe it'll pass."

"You haven't fallen out with Anita?"

"No, no. She's just gone to the loo. No, it's the setup that's getting me down. Mick and Keith deciding on the songs, and me— like any old sit-in musician—being told I've got to learn to play them."

"But you were happy enough in Paris," I said. "I thought you'd got yourself together. And I think you were doing the right thing. God, you're well ahead of anybody else as a musician, and the fans know it. And you've got that new image where you shine out as the nice guy, the good-looking one. Why can't you be contented with that?"

"No, I want to do my own thing—write some songs, write some music. I can do it, but they're holding me back. They keep trying to put me down. Mick reckons I'm schizoid. Maybe I am."

"Well," I said, "nobody can deny 'Paint It Black' was your record. You might not have written it but without you and the sitar it wouldn't be number one today."

"Maybe," he said gloomily.

I saw Chrissie go up to the bar, looking upset. Mick came up beside her and they both got drinks. He said something to her and she turned away. Then he saw us and came mincing over.

"Here it comes," Brian said. "God's gift to the music industry. What the hell does he want?"

Mick wasn't his normal, flirting self. He looked almost as un-happy as Brian. He nodded at me and said to Brian, "Do you think Dylan is doing the right thing? I'm not sure."

"Maybe you better go and tell him," Brian said. He was being vicious. "D'you want me to call him over?"

"Oh, don't be stupid. Anyway, you're the one who's supposed to be his friend."

"And you're the one who's supposed to be the expert on commercialism. I thought you'd be all for him dropping his standards to make some money."

"All right, all right." Mick was backing down as Brian grew more angry. "Well, you got your way with 'Paint It Black.'"

"And it's number one."

"Yes, but it took two weeks to get there. It should have gone in straight to the top when it was released."

"Balls."

"I'm not blaming you." Mick looked tearful, like a child trying to make friends with somebody who hates him. "Andrew will have to sort somebody out."

Things might have gotten worse, but we were interrupted by Anita, who asked Brian if he was ready to go. Before he could answer, Marianne Faithfull came up to Mick and asked if he had seen her husband, John Dunbar. I caught the twinkle that came into his eyes as he looked at her and the shy smile Marianne gave. Chrissie's eyes snaked over and back again. She looked as if she didn't much care anymore. Then John came over, and Marianne took his arm, clutching it tightly to her as if to assure herself as well as him that the Mick Jagger scene was not for her.

In June, two weeks before the Stones were to leave on their fifth North American tour, Mick Jagger collapsed and was taken to a clinic where doctors diagnosed nervous exhaustion. During the tour, on July 10, Brian collapsed. Although the press diagnosed "exhaustion," news quickly spread around music circles that drugs were available in all forms, twenty-four hours a day and Brian, with his appetite for anything new, sampled everything he was offered, with the result that he freaked out and was taken to the hospital. When he emerged his depression deepened still further with the news that the Stones had managed to thrill the crowds at two concerts just as well without him.

Brian made it to the big one, the Hollywood Bowl, where a capacity crowd raved to the music and screamed for more.

The tour concluded in Hawaii. And there it appeared the Stones were stuck.

Brian told me what happened, calling me, two days after he'd gotten back, from his Chelsea mews. It was August 16.

"There was some sort of strike involving the main airlines. I don't really know what it was about, but it meant you couldn't get to the States. No jets. Well, we were due at L.A. for a recording session. We were all uptight—especially me. I felt like kicking all the other bastards in the teeth. Anita got it sorted, though, all by herself. She was on the phone for an hour or two. We could get to Honolulu, she said, by steam plane."

"What's a steam plane?"

"Those things with propellers and things. The jets were flying from there but not to the States, only east. Then from Honolulu we could get to Hong Kong and from there to Tokyo . . ."

"Tokyo?" I said. I thought it was one of his weird jokes. For all I know now it might have been.

"Yeah, Tokyo. Then we could fly direct to L.A. from there."

"And you did it?"

"Mick moaned like hell about the money, but none of the guys who are paid to sort these things out came up with any better idea so, yes, we did it. Halfway round the bloody world instead of a thousand miles or so."

"Must have cost a fortune," I said.

"Tax deductible, as the Yanks say. Hey, you should have seen this big guy at Honolulu. He came up behind Mick, towered over him, tapped him on the back and when Mick turned, said, 'Hey, are you Herman of the Hermits?' Mick was nervous and thought he'd better humor the guy. 'Yes,' he said, 'I'm Herman.' Then the guy said he wanted fourteen autographs, so Mick gave them to him, signing Herman's name. Mick didn't think it was funny. Our Mick likes people to know who he is."

Brian spoke at length about Jimi Hendrix, who was unknown at the time. Slumming in New York, Brian had drifted into a dive called the Cafe Wha. "It was in the afternoon, but it was dark down there. And there was this guy on the guitar. The sound hit me straight between the ears because he was playing 'Like a Rolling Stone.' And God, could he play. Robbie Robertson [Bob Dylan's guitarist] is good, but this guy was way above his class. I got talking to him and sort of asked him what's a nice guy like him doing in a dive like that, and he said it was a place where unknown artists could come and audition. He said if the management liked you or the people clapped, you might be asked to play in the evening for money. I thought, my God, what a waste of talent. You ought to call in there. It's on MacDougal Street."

"Yes," I said, "but it's a long way to go."

"Nonsense. Compared with where we've been it's a five minute walk."

Brian said he was going to Tangier with Anita for a rest on Saturday. He would call when he got back. Then he added ominously, "If I bother to come back."

In Tangier, Brian had a "climbing accident," according to the press. But when he called me, Brian explained that he had been wrestling with Anita and his arm had hit a metal bedframe. He broke two tendons in his left hand.

The Stones had met in New York on September 9, after Brian had left Tangier, for another appearance on the "Ed Sullivan Show" on the 11th.

"I had just had my plaster taken off," said Brian, "but my hand was too stiff to play so Mick had to sing to a prerecorded backing. He didn't half look a burk."

Brian had stayed with Jerry Schatzberg, a fashion photographer he'd first met in 1964, when the Stones had been guests of honor at the New York party of the year, the Mods and Rockers Ball. Jerry was the proprietor of the exclusive discotheque Ondine.

"We had to do a photograph for our album cover in New York as well," Brian said. "Jerry did the photos outside his studio on Park Avenue. It was broad daylight, people walking up and down and there we all were, dressed in drag, Bill in a wheelchair and the four of us standing behind him. Bill and I are in uniforms and the rest are supposed to be typical American mothers. We went for a drink afterward in a bar. Charlie couldn't get away with drag for sure. We all got stared at by the barman, and he seemed to fancy me."

"I can imagine," I said.

He laughed. He sounded in quite a high mood again. "Jerry threw a party after the 'Ed Sullivan Show,'" he said. "Allen Klein was talking about the film we're going to make, *Only Lovers Left Alive.* He told some reporter that Charlie and myself were going to be the best actors out of the bunch of us."

"Maybe you'll become a famous film star."

"No," he said, his voice lowering, sounding sad. "I could only play a musician. That's all I am, a musician."

"When d'you start making the film?"

"October the first. He said it'll either be a disaster or a fantastic success that'll do as much for us as *A Hard Day's Night* did for the Beatles." This, of course, was not to be.

1966 was without doubt the peak of that phenomenal decade known as the Swinging Sixties, which, to those of us now in our mid-thirties and early forties, was a landmark in our lives. Just as older people speak of before or after the war, we say before or after the Sixties.

And the high spot of 1966, as far as the British pop music scene was concerned, came with the Rolling Stones' Royal Albert Hall concert on September 23. After Ike and Tina Turner warmed things up with "River Deep–Mountain High," and the Yardbirds completely blew their set—Keith Relf's voice was drowned out by the band—the Stones came on. Fans managed to break through the security guards and climb onto the stage. Keith was pushed to the floor and Mick was almost strangled, while Brian was grabbed around the neck by some well-built girl and received a large, wet kiss.

After an announcement was made that the concert would be abandoned unless order was restored, the fans returned to their seats.

Brian was holding his own now with Mick as the star of the Rolling Stones. Brian was outstanding not only in his performance

190 / BRIAN JONES

but in his extravagant clothing. He wore a purple velvet jacket and a red shirt with a white cravat and gray trousers.

Not to be outdone, Mick had on a black, Chinese-style jacket with sequins, a bright orange shirt and white bell-bottom pants. They consigned the other three to the shadows. Charlie, I noticed, had grown a moustache.

There were two spotlights, the one following Mick as he pranced about with a tambourine, and the other picking out the elegant, golden-haired musician, Brian, as he played the sitar, looking rather Elizabethan, for "Paint It Black." On "Lady Jane," he changed to the dulcimer.

Keith Relf of the Yardbirds told us about appearing in Antonioni's saga of the Sixties, *Blow-Up*. Antonioni had been unable to get the Who. He liked Pete Townshend's guitar-smashing routine so much that he'd required Jeff Beck of the Yardbirds to do it. In one scene Antonioni had the Ricky Tick Club in Windsor reconstructed in the studio at Elstree.

Reporters asked Brian what he thought of the recent demise of "Ready, Steady, Go." "Very sad," said Brian. "It's been part of our lives."

"Thank Your Lucky Stars" had been axed in June.

Anita turned up then. Feeling in the way, I moved off.

Brian took a new apartment on Courtfield Road, South Kensington. "Frightfully posh," he said. "It's on the second story, so the kids won't be able to shove their noses up against the windows the way they do at the mews."

On December 4, 1966, Brian led me into a huge lounge that was dotted about with the most incongruous furnishings. There were lovely antique chairs, and there was a cinema projector and screen. There was an oak-paneled minstrel gallery with a small but elaborate curved staircase leading up to it, and there was a television set. Three Moroccan tapestries were divided by a 7-Up advertisement hung from the gallery rails. Two huge windows, which took up most of one wall, overlooked the Gloucester Road underground station.

"You like?" Brian said.

"It's certainly big," I allowed.

"I've had fifty or more people in here and it still didn't look full."

He led me into the smart, modern kitchen and down through a trap door to a little wine cellar. He showed me around some rooms that were empty and cavernous; then we went back into the lounge.

"Where do you sleep?" I asked him.

"Up here." He went up into the gallery, and concealed by the tapestries at one end was a large double bed.

There was a rope ladder leading up to another trap door in the ceiling at the other end of the gallery. "There's a spare bedroom up there," he said. "You've got to be fit to get up there. Keith sleeps up there sometimes." I had heard that Linda Keith had split up with Keith Richard.

It was a Sunday, about one o'clock, and Brian suggested we go to the local pub and join Anita and Keith. He opened a built-in wardrobe in the gallery. There were masses of clothes hung up and drawers spilling over with bits of silk and satin. He opened one drawer that was full of costume jewelry. He selected a couple of gold bangles and put them on his wrist. On the lapel of his white, elegant jacket he pinned a cameo brooch.

He turned to face me. "There; is that pretty?"

"Yes," I said. He did look beautiful, I couldn't deny it. He wore black cord trousers, and a white, frilly shirt with ruffled cuffs in Elizabethan style. His hair was shiny and fluffy.

"I might look a bit of a poof but the world needs to be brightened up a little, don't you think?"

The local pub was just across the road. We found Keith and Anita at a table in an alcove. There was something in the way they were looking at one another before they saw us that made me uneasy; but Brian seemed unaffected. We took our drinks and joined them.

Anita gave Brian a warm smile. I noticed that in the fairly crowded pub most of the customers kept a close eye on our table.

"Tara's coming this afternoon," Brian said. "He's got a new girlfriend called Suki he wants to show off."

Tara's marriage to Nicky had broken off in September, and he was currently living at the Ritz Hotel in Piccadilly.

Anita said that Brian's pad was now the headquarters of the London "in" crowd. "Since we moved," she told me, "we've had Paul McCartney, George Harrison, Eric Burdon, Peter Noone, and Spencer Davis dropping in at all hours. It's become the Grand Central Station of rock."

I was surprised. This was more than Anita had said to me since we'd met. Her voice was hypertense, as if she were covering up some anxiety by keeping the conversation going.

We all talked about Marianne Faithfull leaving John Dunbar now Marianne and Mick Jagger were seeing each other.

"The whole scene seems to have changed," Anita was saying. "All the old 'in' places are out. Everyone's going to Alvaro's or Oats to eat now, then on to discotheques like Sibylla's and the Bag O'Nails."

Yes, I thought, *you really are jumpy.*

It was closing time, 2 P.M., and Brian was telling me about Bob Dylan's motorbike accident, when suddenly our table was besieged by youngsters thrusting autograph books and scraps of paper at Brian. Soon we scrambled out and ran across the road for the apartment.

Brian went to a cocktail cabinet and poured more drinks. Keith relaxed in a chair, and Anita went to the kitchen to make some lunch.

"Was Dylan badly hurt?" I asked Brian.

"Oh, a couple of fractured ribs. Nothing too bad. He's had to take it easy, though, and he tells me he's writing a book, *Tarantula.* He refused to tell me what it's about."

He brought over a large glass full of Bacardi and Coke and handed it to me. He gave another drink to Keith. Then, to my surprise, he suggested Keith should go and give Anita a hand in the kitchen. It was obvious by now, at least to me, that Keith had a crush on Anita. Was Brian trying to get rid of her? That didn't seem likely, the way he had been gazing at her in the pub. Or was there a part of him that was geared to self-destruction? Why were he and Keith so close?

When Keith had gone, Brian went up to the gallery and came back. "Talking of books," he said, "have you read this one?" He was speaking softly, confidentially, as if he didn't want the others to hear.

He handed me the book. It was an American edition of the novel *George Arbuthnott Jarrett* by the Welsh novelist Bernard Toms, published by Harcourt Brace and World Inc. I opened it up. Inscribed on the flyleaf was the message, "Hey, Brian. This is about you."

I turned to the photograph of the author on the back of the cover.

"D'you know that guy?" Brian said.

The face looked vaguely familiar, a face I had seen around various pubs in Monmouthshire, where I lived.

"I've seen him around," I said. "Why?"

"He comes from around your way. You haven't talked to him about me, have you, Nicholas?" He looked at me searchingly.

"Never spoken to him at all," I said. "Just seen him about in pubs."

Brian sat down near me. "Well," he said, "you'd better read it. It's about a schizophrenic character—and he could be me. A guy with two totally opposed personalities inside him. The frightening thing is that although he's like me and hates violence he ends up by knocking a woman about with a poker. Christ, could that happen to me?"

"Doesn't sound very likely," I said. "Who wrote this on the flyleaf?"

"That's just it. It came by post from the States. Obviously it's someone who knows me pretty well. I wondered if it was Mick."

Soon afterward, Tara arrived with his girlfriend, Suki Potier. Suki bore an uncanny resemblance to Anita. Everyone around the Stones was beginning to have the same look—the Brian Jones-Marianne Faithfull look. It was incestuous. As soon as Brian set eyes on Suki, I could tell he was spellbound. Later, as we sat down to a light lunch, I could see his eyes moving from Suki to Anita as if he could hardly believe what he was seeing.

Brian spoke of Jimi Hendrix. "He made it," Brian said. "It's not always true that talent will get you fame. But it worked with him."

Tara said, "I hear he's being managed by that chap who used to be with the Animals, Chas Chandler."

"Yes. Him and Mike Jeffrey, that's right, and his first disk is out in a couple of weeks. It's called 'Hey Joe' and it's coupled with 'Stone Free.' The guy certainly deserves a break."

Tara said, "Wasn't Mick approached to sponsor him, or be co-manager or something?"

Brian grinned. "Yeah, Chas did approach him, but Jimi made a pass at Marianne, which buggered everything up. Very possessive, our Mick."

Tara smiled. "I thought it must have been something like that. I met him—Jimmy, or J-I-M-I, as they're calling him now—at the Bag O'Nails the other night. Eric Clapton was there, too. He seems quite enthusiastic about his partnership with Jack Bruce and Ginger Baker."

Tara was talking about the new group, Cream. I had seen them on television last month performing their number "Wrapping Paper."

Anita and Suki seemed to hit it off well together. While they were out washing the dishes, Brian said, "They could be sisters, those two."

"I suppose they are a little alike, in looks anyway," Tara said coolly.

I knew that Tara didn't much care for Anita because of her apparently imperious manner, which made him imagine she was a snob. Tara, in spite of his enormous wealth and his intimacy with some of the world's noblest heads, detested snobbery.

"Yes, I meant in looks," Brian said.

Keith said he was going to help the girls with the dishes, and at last I plucked up the courage to ask Brian about the rumors that he was going to get married to Anita. There had been a report in the *Daily Mirror* the previous day that Anita had quit a Munich film set on Friday to fly back to Brian in London. Brian was quoted as saying, "You can be sure we are not going to marry in the next forty-eight hours."

I said, "I hope I'm going to get an invitation to the wedding."

Brian smiled. "Nobody's invited me yet."

Tara said, "Everyone in London is saying the reason you're going to L.A. on Wednesday is so that Dylan can be best man."

"Yes, I know what everyone's saying."

It was obvious we weren't going to get anything out of him, but he was a relaxed and very contented man, as if everything was at last going right for him. He was full of enthusiasm for the trip to L.A. and the vacation there with Anita and Keith. Why Keith? I wondered. Maybe he was going to be the best man, or since he and Brian now seemed to be great friends, he was to be one of the few guests at a secret wedding. I just didn't know, but as I left that evening it was with a comfortable feeling that my friend was coming into the happiest period of his life.

In the early hours of December 18, 1966, Tara Browne died. His fiberglass sports car—a blue Lotus Elan—collided with a stationary van in Redcliffe Gardens, Kensington. Suki Potier, described in the papers as a photographic model, was with him, but she survived with only minor injuries. Tara's death proved an even bigger blow to Brian than to me, Tara's cousin. Brian flew to Ireland for the funeral, while I decided to attend the memorial service that the family was arranging at St. Paul's Church in Knightsbridge.

Brian then went to spend Christmas, still with Anita and Keith, at the George V Hotel in Paris.

On January 13, 1967, the Stones released their double-A sided single, "Let's Spend the Night Together"/"Ruby Tuesday." Brian toned down the basically clamorous construction of the music by playing cello and recorder.

On the fifteenth, on the "Ed Sullivan Show," the numbers were broadcast, having been taped the previous day. Brian telephoned later in the week, horselaughing, to tell me the directors of the show insisted that the words of the first track should be altered to "Let's spend some time together."

The single reached number two in the U.K. and at that time stood at number three in the U.S.

On January 20, the LP *Between the Buttons* was released. Once again all the tracks were of Jagger-Richard composition and once again it was Brian's musicianship that saved them from mediocrity. On the opening track, "Yesterday's Papers," he was on marimbas and harpsichord; on "Cool, Calm & Collected" he played banjo and kazoo; on "Something Happened to Me Yesterday" it was his crazy performance on trombone that enlivened the performance. Brian had developed by now a style all his own on harmonica, but he aped Bob Dylan's style for "Who's Been Sleeping Here?"

But when I bought my copy I was shocked by the sleeve photograph of Brian. He was a nervous wreck, shattered and haggard.

To promote the record, the Stones appeared on the "Palladium Show," where it was an established tradition that as a finale the whole cast was assembled and took a bow on a rotating stage. I was watching the show at home and was astonished to see that the Stones were not on the stage as it revolved.

However, I was pleased to note, during the Stones' performance, that Brian was again looking happy, and his music was excellent. He was dressed in a white, broad-brimmed hat, an elaborate cravat held together with a large jeweled brooch, and a jacket with velvet collar dotted with badges, brooches, and buttons. Keith and Mick each wore a kind of jacket-*cum*-shirt made of a shiny, sleek-looking material.

The Monday papers were full of condemnatory reports of the Stones' refusal to take part in the show's finale. What they were saying, between the lines and even quite openly, was that these five ignorant louts were getting far too big for their boots.

On Sunday, February 12, the police raided Keith's country home, Redlands, taking some uppers away for analysis. The account by *News of the World* made it clear that one of their reporters had been present at the raid. The paper had been running an exposé of the connection between drugs and pop stars for two or three weeks, and the raid fitted neatly into place.

After the *News of the World* story appeared, Brian, Anita, Mick, Keith and some friends set off, in two different parties, for Morocco. Keith, Brian and Anita went in Keith's Bentley Continental—which he had christened the Blue Lena, after a Lena Horne record. Tom Keylock, then Keith's chauffeur, drove them. At the Minzah Hotel in Morocco they met up with Mick and Marianne and other people.

There are various versions about the events in the hotel, but what really alarmed me was that Keith cleared out with Anita Pallenberg, and everyone left Brian alone in Morocco. Somehow, in shock, he found his way as far as Barcelona, where he collapsed. Then he was in a hospital in the south of France—and now he was in a West London hospital for what was described as postpneumonia checkup. It all sounded ghastly; I knew that losing Anita was going to have a hell of an effect on Brian. On the ninth I went to see him at the hospital.

The day's papers were full of Brian's great success in having composed the music for the German film *Mord und Totschlag—A Degree of Murder*—which was to be entered for the Cannes Film Festival, and in which Anita was the star.

I found him in a private room in the clinic. He was out of bed and wearing a golden-colored dressing gown. Newspapers and magazines were scattered over the bed. He was pale and washed-out, and there were dark circles around his eyes. He smiled as I entered, but it was forced. I had not seen him in three months.

After handing over the unoriginal gift of grapes, I said, "Congratulations. You've really proved you're a composer this time."

The half-hearted smile returned. "It's great news," he said, almost as if we were talking about someone else's achievement.

"But it's tremendous," I said. "It's something you always wanted to do."

"Yeah, I know, Nicholas. But I'm really down at the moment. They're giving me drugs here that they'd bust me for outside, and I'm still down. Please don't talk to me about what's happened." His voice was very flat.

"Except to say," Brian went on grimly, though still with no tone to his voice, "except to say 'if they think I'm going on the European tour in a fortnight's time with that bastard still in the group they must be crazy."

"What about your wearing a Nazi uniform for one of your photos? Whose idea was that?"

Brian had recently posed for photographs standing bolt upright in an old German uniform, with his long blond hair hanging down below the cap.

"That was her idea. It was meant as a send-up." By her, I assumed he meant Anita.

"Wearing that uniform with the kind of hair I've got was meant to take the piss out of fascism, not to acclaim it. But the bloody stupid press, of course, deliberately turned it around the other way. D'you know, I even heard talk in the States that the CIA were keeping an eye on us because they thought we were becoming a dangerous political influence?"

"What happened at Redlands?" I asked him later. I had been told he wasn't there.

"Don't think anything much will come of it," he said. "I blame the bloody rags more than the cops. You know it was all set up by the newspaper people?"

"It looked that way."

"Damn right."

There was a nervous tap at the door. Brian said, "Come in." A small, slim, pleasant-faced woman with a mop of curly blond hair came in holding the hand of a small boy about five years old. The woman looked about twenty-three.

She was holding a box of chocolates and she gave Brian a friendly and sympathetic smile. He smiled rather sadly, I thought.

He introduced us. She was Pat Andrews, and the boy was her son by Brian—Julian.

I knew that Brian had been sued by Pat. But they looked friendly enough now. I left to get out of the way.

T EN DAYS LATER the Stones hit the front page of the *Daily Mirror*:

JAGGER IS ACCUSED OVER DRUGS

Two of the Rolling Stones pop group—Mick Jagger and Keith Richard—have been accused of offences against the drug laws.

Summonses against the two men—both aged 22—were issued after a police raid on Richard's £20,000 farmhouse home at West Wittering, Sussex.

The summonses, due to be dealt with at Chichester Magistrates' Court on May 10, are expected to be served early next week. Two other men, not named so far, are also to be summoned.

The *News of the World,* whose investigation into football corruption had led to the imprisonment of seventeen people, alleged that Mick had been seen by an investigator taking about six Benzedrine tablets at the nightclub Blases, where he also showed a companion and two girls a small piece of hash and invited them to smoke some at his apartment.

Mick said he would issue a writ against the *News of the World* for libel; on the following Tuesday he did so.

In a telephone call to me from his apartment Brian said, "Serves the buggers right. At least they can't blame me for this lot. I was nowhere near the place. Anyway, they can afford the bloody fine. They're getting the lion's share of the loot. Sod 'em." He sounded slow-witted and dopey, and it was plain he was heavily sedated.

"So you're still not going on the tour?" I said. The European tour was due to begin next Saturday, March 25.

"No. Oldham's been around trying to talk me into it. I told him to get stuffed. I'll never play with that lot again till Keith Richard is out of it. Supposed to be such a mate all of a sudden and all the time he was—" His voice trailed off.

"Listen," he said, suddenly urgent, "Allen Klein's flying over from New York to see me today about going on this concert tour. I need some sleep before he gets here. I'll give you a ring later."

Allen Klein managed to do what Oldham had been unable to achieve. Brian went on the tour, which began in a storm of publicity over the Redlands drug raid. The Stones now epitomized the struggle between the young and the old, and the daggers were drawn. There were riots in Sweden, Warsaw and Zurich—police nightsticks, attack dogs, and kids hurling smoke bombs.

As soon as the tour was over, Brian went to the Cannes Film Festival for the premiere of *A Degree of Murder*. Anita went too, accompanied by Keith Richard. The newspapers carried a photograph of Anita, wearing a striped dress with a split skirt and showing a lot of thigh, above a headline: ACTRESS ANITA, 22, SWAPS STONES. Keith said, "Brian's romance with Anita was all over when I started dating her. In a way it's a sort of triangle, but there is no rift between Brian and me."

Anita said, "Keith has been a very good friend to me—but on the other hand so has Brian."

At 4 P.M., May 10, 1967, the Scotland Yard Drug Squad raided Brian's apartment on Courtfield Road and took away "certain substances." Brian and another man were taken to the Chelsea police station.

Later, standing in the doorway of Marlborough Street Magistrates' Court, Brian was a remorseful figure. He wore a well-tailored suit with bell-bottom trousers and a polka-dot tie. He had on dark glasses, and his hair, in relation to the quiet clothing, appeared excessively long. He wore Cuban-heeled shoes. As he was driven away in his Rolls-Royce, cameramen were almost fighting each other for shots.

The court had taken only three minutes to go through the formalities of adjourning the case until June 2, and setting bail at $750 each. This seemed a moderate sum, and I hoped it reflected the relative triviality of the matter.

The first thing Brian did after the court appearance was to send a telegram to his parents at their Cheltenham home.

It read: "Please don't worry. Don't jump to hasty conclusions and please don't judge me too harshly."

Brian called. He sounded sedated, as he had the last time; he also sounded utterly defeated. *He's gone over the top,* I thought. *He's flipped his lid.*

"You heard about the bust, I expect?"

"Yes. How the hell could you let it happen? Especially after Keith and Mick got done. You must have known the Establishment are determined to book someone at the height of pop fame and make an example of him."

"Yeah. Well, I had to have a party. I had a gang around and we took some stuff. I needed it." He gave a weak little laugh.

"You're not still taking drugs are you?"

"Yes. It's all right if the doctor gives you them. Bloody funny old world, don't you think?"

"I know how you must be feeling, but you'll have to snap out of it, Brian. Get on with some work. Write some more music like you did for the film. That got a hell of a good write-up, even in the posh papers."

"Yeah," he said flatly. "So did the other business."

"What d'you mean, the bust?"

"No; I mean the bust up. Anita and me."

"You want to talk about it?"

"Yeah, can you come around?"

"I'm in Abergavenny."

"Oh yeah."

"We can talk on the phone. What happened? How did Allen Klein get you to go on tour?"

"It wasn't him. It was her, the false bitch. She said I'd have to go with them. She rang and said she regretted leaving me. She said that after the tour we'd get together again. I was up in the air about it and I was so pleased I almost got matey with Keith. Then we met up again at Cannes and he was with her. I knew then there was no chance. The way she was looking at him. Later I got her alone and we talked about it. I asked her who had put her up to telling me that cock-and-bull story just to get me on the tour. I was going to bloody hit her but—" I heard a few muffled sobs. "I still love that bloody woman."

"In the long run you'll be better off without her. Any woman who could do a thing like that—"

"She didn't admit to it," he cut in defensively. "No, she said she meant it at the time. She thought she loved me more than Keith— then. But later she changed her mind."

It sounded unlikely to me but I let it pass.

"Mind you," he said, "if it was a put-up job it must have been one of *those* bastards who put her up to it. Oldham or Mick—even Keith."

"Allen Klein?" I put in.

"No. He's been great to me, especially since the bust. It's odd I should have been busted the same day Keith and Mick were in Chichester Court. Allen came straight up from there to see me and bail me out."

At Mick and Keith's brief appearance at Chichester Magistrates' Court, they elected trial by jury and were bailed out.

"They were ringing me when the party was on. Well somebody was. They were telling me I was going to be raided, but I thought someone was putting me on."

"What are you charged with?" I asked. The papers had mentioned every drug you could think of in a speculative way.

"They got me for everything. What the others had brought as well as what I had for myself, which was only Methedrine and cannabis. They found cocaine, but God knows where that came from. Anyway Klein got me out, as I said. He wouldn't let me go home. He brought me here."

"Where?" I said, a bit irritated by his vagueness.

"Oh, the Hilton." There was a small laugh. "They told him here they were fully booked up. You should have heard Allen giving them stick. They got the manager—or someone pretty high up—and when he told them how much he'd spent at the hotel in the past, of course, they quickly found a room. Can't imagine Andrew getting the same respect, can you? I think that's why Allen is taking more of a hand personally. Come to protect his investment, maybe. Seems three of us at least are going to be made criminals. Maybe he thinks we need a Dutch uncle."

When he came back to Anita again, he began to sob. Then the line went dead.

I called the Hilton but was told Mr. Jones had left instructions he was not to be disturbed.

On Friday, June 2, Brian appeared at West London Magistrates' Court and elected to go for trial before a jury at the Inner London Sessions. Bail was renewed and Brian was granted permission to go to the U.S. for the Monterey Pop Festival before the trial date was fixed.

1967 was the summer of love, and the place to be was the Monterey Pop Festival. Monterey was the idea of Alan Pariser, a man of means and a maker of scenes. His dream was a nonprofit festival where ideas could be exchanged and new, unappreciated artists could be heard as well as the famous. New and old styles—in fact all styles—of popular music could be played; and all in the gentle atmosphere of Flower Power, which had now taken over the cities of the California coastline.

Pariser met with John and Michelle Phillips of the Mamas and the Papas, and Paul Simon, who agreed that it was going to be a free concert of love.

A board of governors was appointed, and it included some formidable names: Paul McCartney, Jim McGuinn, Smokey Robinson, Brian Wilson, Donovan and Paul Simon.

The response from every major artist in the pop world was amazing. I knew Brian was going because in the course of a conversation one day he told me Andrew Oldham had asked him.

"I teased him for a bit," Brian said, "I knew he had been asking all the others. Bill and Charlie are married and both busy moving into new houses. Anyway, Flower Power's hardly their scene. Keith's going to Rome with—her."

Anita was making the film *Barbarella* in Rome.

"Mick's too mean to do anything for nothing, and anyway he says he's got this case hanging over him. Well, so have I. But give me L.A. and maybe I'll get out of the dumps there. You staying at my place over there?"

"Thanks, Brian, but I've arranged to stay with a cousin in L.A."

"Male or female?" he asked, and there was a provocativeness in him that had been missing a long time. I hoped he was going to have an uplift for a change.

"Female, as it happens, but it's nothing like that."

"Just good friends?"

"Just good cousins."

We were strolling around Chelsea, where I had recently settled in Cheyne Court, overlooking the Thames. Mick Jagger, the only Stone who didn't want to move away from London, lived nearby, having recently bought a Queen Anne–style house for $100,000. Other neighbors were Paul Getty II and his wife, Talitha.

Brian was the obvious choice to represent the Rolling Stones at Monterey. He loved the U.S., and the kids of the U.S. loved him. He was especially fond of L.A. and he had a house there now. He was also enamored of San Francisco's embarcadero, the Golden Gate Bridge, and the Flower Power generation which had begun there.

The site for the three-day festival, which was to include five concerts, was about one hundred and fifty miles south of San Francisco, about as significant a distance as fifteen miles in England. Monterey, on the peninsula of California, is a resort area whose vast arena had for ten years been the venue for the Monterey Jazz Festival.

Two days before Brian was due to fly out, he was full of bounce and enthusiasm again. "Hey," he said, "what d'you think I'm going to do at the Festival?"

"You're going to cheer up and enjoy yourself. You're going to pick up ideas for a new direction."

"Yeah, yeah. All that, but listen. John Phillips said he'd pay air fares and hotel expenses for the Jimi Hendrix Experience to go to the Festival. And Paul McCartney has asked me to introduce Jimi."

"That'll really put Jimi at the top of the tree."

"I won't be staying at my place in L.A. Too far to travel every day. I'm going to stay near Monterey with Sheila—you know, Andrew Oldham's wife—and Nico."

Nico was a German ex-model who had taken up a singing career in 1965. I had seen her perform her first hit on "RSG," "I'm Not Saying," which was produced by Oldham. She migrated to the U.S. and ended up in Andy Warhol's Factory in New York. Nico was yet another one who had the Anita/Brian look, complete with long blond hair. Was this the start of yet another affair?

"Jimi will be staying with Peter Tork. He's the guitarist with the Monkees."

Brian called me shortly after I'd arrived at my cousin's house in Laurel Canyon in the Hollywood Hills on Monday, June 12, 1967.

"Monterey's crawling with thousands of hippies," he said. "Far more than they were expecting. I've got to be surrounded by heavies the whole time. Meet me in San Francisco Saturday."

I found Brian standing in the middle of a large entourage in the Hilton lobby dressed like a medieval prince. From his shoulders to his knees hung magnificent silk robes, cuffed and collared in white fur.

He was thoroughly stoned. We tried to talk, but people kept crowding us; after a while he excused himself and said he was going to change. He asked me to go with him. Two brawny men in plain suits followed us to the elevator and to the door of his room.

Once inside he crashed on the large double bed and said, "Jeez, what a bloody crowd everywhere." He lay there, looking up at the ceiling.

"Did you go to Monterey?" he asked.

"Yes," I said.

"You like? What about all those bloody flowers, man, coming out of the sky?"

"Yeah. You can trust the Americans to put on a show like that."

"A hundred thousand orchids, they said, flown in from Hawaii. And God knows how many garlands they hung around me."

"Someone even hung one on me," I said, laughing. "Are you staying the night here?"

He sat up. "Oh no, just booked a room for the day—or maybe the night as well." His meaning was unmistakable—let's spend the night together.

I tried to shrug it off. "Can't we go out and see the sights?"

He smiled. "I suppose we could, but we'll get followed everywhere."

"We will with you dressed like that."

Still smiling he got up and went to a drawer in an open trunk. He took out an elaborate gold necklace and draped it around his neck. "Would I look less noticeable if I put on some jewelry? This is from Fifth Avenue in New York, from Saks. There's some more here. Come and see."

I stood beside him looking in the drawer. He was already wearing rings and bangles and brooches, but there was a whole treasure trove of the stuff in there.

"Got to keep up my image, you see. They're all dressing wildly gay now, especially here in San Francisco. Come on, let's go out and I'll show you."

Surrounded by bodyguards, we roamed streets where slums were being transformed by bearded hippies with paint brushes. Bare, ugly walls were sprouting psychedelic patterns. Brian pointed to a girl on all fours, fascinated by the sparkling minerals in the concrete pavement. "They're quite openly tripping on LSD in the streets," Brian said.

Brian talked about the groups that were performing at Monterey.

There were twenty-seven—including Eric Burdon and the "New" Animals, the Paul Butterfield Blues Band, Otis Redding, the Byrds, Canned Heat, Aretha Franklin, the Mamas and the Papas, the Steve Miller Band, Simon and Garfunkel, the Who, the Jimi Hendrix Experience, Ravi Shankar and Janis Joplin.

Brian was happy to a degree that meant he was on something, drugs or booze or both. Back in his room at the Hilton we settled in some chairs side by side. He put something on a sugar cube and chewed on it. Seeing me watching him curiously, he asked if I wanted some.

"Jimi and I've been experimenting with it," he explained. "It's called STP. On second thought, it might be too strong for you. You can have some LSD if you like."

"Not dangerous, is it?"

"No. It just loosens you up."

Feeling careless, I agreed to try it, and he gave me some on sugar. I tasted nothing but the sugar.

He talked enthusiastically about Jefferson Airplane, who were performing at the Festival. I told him I liked the voice of Grace Slick.

"Yeah," he said. "Something sexually exciting about it." He winked. I turned my head away.

We had some Bacardi and Coke. I noticed without alarm that night was falling outside and lights were twinkling around the city. Brian went on about rock bands—Quicksilver Messenger Service, Country Joe and the Fish, the Grateful Dead. "The Dead are a cult here," he said.

Brian helped me into bed. I lay in bed for hours with his arm over me. I guess the LSD had kicked in.

It was broad daylight. I was vaguely aware of an urgent ringing of the doorbell. Brian was gone and a limo had been sent to take me to the final day of the Monterey festival.

The backstage enclosure at Monterey was almost like an arena itself. A vast area had been fenced and securely sealed off for the artists' trailers.

The driver Brian had sent for me flashed a pass for admission and we were waved through. In minutes Brian and I were sitting near the stage on a bench, having a surprisingly private conversation, considering the number of people moving about.

He wasn't very chirpy this morning. I was still torpid from the effects of last night's booze and LSD. Some mention of Anita came up and this led us onto the subject of love.

At one stage he said, "I like women—I think I loved her—but I hate commitments. You know, the kind of commitments that can tie you down to a little house hung about with babies' diapers. God, that would kill me, kill my soul, anyway—if I've got one. No, I don't think I could ever get married. Seems to me I like the sex but not the responsibility. You know I've had three, don't you?"

"Three what?" I said dopily.

"Kids."

"Oh, yes. The first one when you were at school."

"Yes, that one hardly counts. We were both kids. It could have happened to anyone. Then there was Pat Andrews. I liked her. Sometimes I thought I loved her. I was only nineteen. She was seventeen. I was going through a rough patch with my efforts to break into the music business. I think making love to her was like working off my frustrations. Of course, she wasn't the only one but she happened to get pregnant. I felt bad about that. Went to see her the day the boy was born but they wouldn't let me in. So I went off and got pissed with some friends. Next day I hocked some records and bought her some flowers. She was amazed." He gazed blankly up at the high stage where we could see only the tops of the artists' heads. "We called the boy Julian Mark," he added unnecessarily.

"The first child was a boy as well, wasn't it?"

"So they tell me. I wasn't allowed to see it before they got it adopted. Then when I was twenty-one Linda had one. Linda Lawrence. We called that one Julian, too. I lived with her, tried to knuckle down to the husband and father bit. It lasted just six months. June to Christmas 1964. After that I've tried to be careful. Now I just like to go to bed for a cuddle really. Like you and me last night. Just a cuddle."

Usually, such talk would have embarrassed me. This time it

didn't. Perhaps I was growing up a bit, letting myself face my emotions. I said to Brian, "D'you think you're bisexual? Or homo-sexual?"

He shrugged as if he didn't consider the question important. "I was touched up once at school by an older boy. It was in the shower after a rugby match. It was a bit of a violent assault and it might have had some subconscious effect on me. Maybe it made me go around laying as many girls as I could just to prove I wasn't gay. But now I don't think it matters. All I know is that I don't like sleeping alone and I don't see much difference sleeping with a boy or a girl. Both can be cuddly."

None of the photographers who had been snapping away at us during this intimate conversation had interrupted us. Then Jimi Hendrix came up and Brian introduced us.

Jimi was very striking in looks and dress—six feet tall with wild black hair and brown eyes. He was wearing a frilled orange shirt and red satin trousers that were so tight they even showed his religion, and as he sat down I wondered if they were going to split. Jimi's first hit, "Hey Joe," had reached number seven in the British charts, followed by two more hits—"Purple Haze" and "The Wind Cries Mary."

Jimi told us about his twenty-five-city tour of Great Britain. "Me, Cat Stevens, and Englebert Humperdinck were the supporting acts," Jimi said. "It was the Walker Brothers' show. It boosted my career but it was the worst in-fighting I've ever seen. A brawl." It was known that the Walker Brothers were going to split up after the tour. With their reputation as sex idols, the Walkers attracted mostly girls. Chas, Jimi's manager, seeing a perfect opportunity to capture the Walkers' fans on the tour, decided to work up a sexy routine for Jimi. This act, designed to upstage the Walkers, caused a lot of hard feelings. "For instance," Jimi said, "there was deliberate interference with the lighting and sound systems during my act—in retaliation."

We moved up to the side of the stage as the Who went through their performance. We had seats stage right—Brian was going on imminently to introduce Jimi. The Who gave a riotous performance. "My Generation" concluded with Pete Townshend crunching his guitar to bits, Roger Daltrey hitting the cymbals with his microphone and smoke bombs exploding all around them.

The Grateful Dead came on as a buffer act between the wild ones—the Who and Jimi. The Dead calmed the audience while keeping up their high spirits by telling them to dance on their chairs or with each other, which they did.

I looked at Jimi Hendrix, sitting next to me. He was nervous. Jimi was a sensitive man; he was earnestly telling Brian how hurt he had been by the bad feeling on the tour. "And tonight," he said, "there was a big argument about whether the Who or me would go on first. That upset me a lot." Tonight was to be the first performance of the Jimi Hendrix Experience in America—a debut before 100,000 people. No wonder he was nervous. Most of them had never heard of him.

At last it was time. Brian stood up, dressed in his cloak and his jewels. The American audience greeted him with a great roar. Brian had difficulty in quelling the demonstration. Warmly, he introduced his friend, thereby giving Jimi Hendrix the priceless imprimatur of the Rolling Stones, the kings of black rock.

After the first couple of songs, Brian said, "A mild response. I hope it picks up." It did. When Jimi played "Like a Rolling Stone," the audience went mad and started screaming for Brian, knowing that the song had been written for Brian by Bob Dylan.

A girl stood near me at the side of the stage. More attractive than pretty in the usual sense, she certainly caught my eye. She looked like a gypsy queen. Like Brian, she was a mass of colors from head to toe, aflow with silks and satins. She must have been about twenty-three. Suddenly she lifted a bottle of Southern Comfort whiskey to her lips, took a long swig, lowered the bottle and looked out over the sea of faces below. She turned to me and said in a husky voice something to the effect that 200,000 flowers had been distributed. "Flowers are the symbol of love," she said. Then she took another long swig from the bottle.

Meanwhile, Jimi launched into "Wild Thing." The title was appropriate. He seemed to go berserk. At various stages he played his guitar with his teeth, behind his back and between his legs. After kicking one of the amplifiers and launching an attack on a microphone, he finished by kneeling astride his instrument, throwing gasoline onto it and setting it alight. Then he stood up and waved the blazing guitar above his head; it was a symbolic sacrifice to Monterey and to Flower Power, and it was greeted with hysteria.

At the side of the stage he collapsed into Brian's arms in tears of gratitude while everyone congratulated him.

There was one more act to come, but the cheers and screams went on and on. All the same, Dave Crosby came up and told us to hold on for the last act, as it featured an incredible singer called Janis Joplin. Then, as the applause began to die down, the emcee announced Janis Joplin and Big Brother and the Holding Company. At hearing this, the girl I had been watching upended her bottle, emptied it, and went confidently over to take the microphone. She was Janis.

Dave told us now, as we stood back behind the Big Brother band, "I'll give anyone a thousand to one this is her big break, and brother, she's really earned it. Janis is totally unknown outside of San Francisco."

"I'm transfixed," Brian said as Janis plunged into "Big Mama." "She's something new—a stalking tigress," Brian observed. Her voice went out sharp and challenging over the vast throng, as if she were a hooker and proud of the fact. She needed to put no effort into being sexual. Every movement suggested the abandon attainable usually only in the final moments before orgasm. Her voice went to funky extremes heretofore unheard. The audience roared in encouragement at her brutal defiance. There was something reminiscent of Edith Piaf about her. But she was more savage . . . something of Shirley Bassey, but Janis was less restrained . . . something of Judy Garland, but this one was *never* sentimental. My God, here was a great star coming into being in front of our eyes.

Janis had worked the audience into a frenzy. Ignoring them totally, she pounced into her second song, "Ball and Chain." The fans worshiped her and showered her with flowers.

The last thing I remember before my LSD blackout was leaving the concert with Brian and Jimi. Nodding his head in wonder, Jimi said, "We just witnessed, in Janis Joplin's act, the birth of a legend."

The LSD of the previous day must have overtaken me—and in a unique fashion. Forty-eight hours later I woke up, alone, in the San Francisco Hilton. At the desk downstairs I was advised that everything had been paid for by Brian Jones and that Brian had returned to L.A.

Back in London everyone was talking about the Beatles' latest single, "All You Need Is Love," which was to become the universal anthem for the year 1967. Mick Jagger and Marianne Faithfull joined the Beatles in a historic live performance of the simple chorus of "All You Need Is Love" on TV.

There was no news back in London of Brian, so I assumed he must have stayed on in the States. No one answered when I phoned.

The musical papers were full of stories of the Monkees' forthcoming tour of the States due to begin on June 7. Jimi Hendrix, surprisingly I thought, was going to be a supporting act with them.

I knew that the Monkees had fallen in love with Jimi Hendrix at Monterey. All the same, it seemed to me an odd combination. The Monkees' appeal was mainly to twelve-and fourteen-year-old girls, whereas Jimi's was to more mature people.

It occurred to me that Brian might stay over in the U.S. to see the opening of the tour in Jacksonville.

The trial of Mick Jagger, Keith Richard and the art dealer Robert Fraser took place from June 27–29. Mick was charged with possession of four tablets of amphetamine sulphate and other illegal substances. Mick's defense was that he had been prescribed the tablets by a doctor in Italy and had brought some home with him.

Keith Richard was charged with allowing his home to be used for the smoking of cannabis, Fraser with possession of heroin and amphetamine tablets. All but Fraser pleaded not guilty. The shock of the trial came not so much from their being pronounced guilty by the jury, but from the monstrous sentences imposed by the implacable Judge Block. All were sent to jail—Richard for a year, Jagger for three months, Fraser for six months.

Now the full might of the British press, which had formerly been leveled against the anarchic Stones, turned full circle onto Judge Block and his Draconian punishments.

Block even refused bail pending appeals. Two days later, the two Stones were released on bail after application had been made to a judge in chambers at the Court of Appeal.

The effect of the trial on Brian, now back from Monterey and in his Courtfield Road apartment with Suki Potier as his companion, was traumatic. Suki said, "I'm very concerned about Brian's health, mental *and* physical." On July 6, Brian was delivered to a Roehampton clinic called the Priory Nursing Home. This seemed to do him more harm than good, and after a stormy spell there he returned to his apartment with Suki. For a while he seemed content to spend his time with her and was kept apparently calm by pre-scribed pills.

Jagger's and Richard's appeals were brought forward, after orders had apparently come from high places, to July 31. Keith's conviction was quashed, and Mick's prison sentence was set aside and substituted with a twelve-month conditional discharge. The Lord Chief Justice, Lord Parker, warned Mick of his responsibilities in being a pop idol. Fraser's appeal on both conviction and sentence was dismissed.

As if in celebration, the Stones rushed into Olympic Sound to record a new single, "We Love You." Brian was not looking phys-ically well, but he made another sparkling contribution to the mu-sic, playing Mellotron to almost devilish effect. Paul McCartney sat in on this session and sang in some of the choruses. The record was a weird one on which slamming doors and echoing footsteps played a prominent part. This couldn't have improved Brian's nerves—he was still awaiting the fall of the ax in *his* court case.

With all free publicity of the drug trials, Brian expected "We Love You" to shoot to the top of the charts. The anticipated ava-lanche of sales did not materialize. The record reached at best number seven.

Throughout the Rolling Stones' drug crisis Andrew Oldham was conspicuous in the rarity of his court appearances. Allen Klein did everything he could to help them.

Brian had a bitter irony to swallow. Now that Andrew was fading from the scene, he was at last beginning to come around to Brian's way of thinking about the musical direction the Rolling Stones ought to take.

As Brian put it one evening when I'd been invited to the studio to watch rehearsals, "Andrew's not so keen now on the stuff Mick and Keith are writing. Now, after he's dragged us out of the Crawdaddy, where we were playing my kind of music, and re-shaped us, he's decided he no longer likes the look of us, so he's dropping us."

"He's leaving?"

"I'd bet my life on it."

On the weekend of August 25–27, Jimi, Brian and I were trying to decide what to do on Saturday night. "The Maharishi Mahesh Yogi is staying in Bangor, North Wales," Brian said, laughing. "Want to go up there? Mick and Marianne and all four Beatles and their wives and girlfriends are there." As there was no response from Jimi and me, we all set out for the Pink Flamingo Club.

Eric Burdon and the "New" Animals were playing the Flamingo Club, which had caught the Flower Power fever and had a ceiling ablaze in psychedelia.

Eric dedicated his version of the Hendrix hit, "Are You Experienced?" to Jimi, then launched into his interpretation of "Paint It Black," in which an electric violin played the part that Brian played on sitar. "I like it," Brian pronounced. "I think I'll use it on my next recording."

That Sunday Jimi was due to play two concerts at the Saville on Shaftesbury Avenue. We were all surprised and worried backstage when we realized that Brian Epstein, who was promoting the show, was not going to arrive by showtime. There was no sign of Brian Jones, either.

Jimi was on a roll. His second single, "Purple Haze," and his album, *Are You Experienced?*, had both entered the U.S. *Billboard* Top 100 two days ago. And his Saville performance that night was brilliant. The audience was on its feet, shouting for more. It was as good as Monterey—if not better.

Backstage, I searched for Brian. I found him amid a group of people who all seemed to be in total shock. Brian was sitting on a stool, his elbows on his knees, staring into space, his face ghostly white. I asked someone in the hushed room what had happened.

"It's Brian Epstein. He's dead."

Brian Epstein had been found dead in his house on Chapel Street, Belgravia, about two o'clock that afternoon.

It was an incalculable blow not only to Brian Jones, but to the whole world of pop music. Epstein, who had built up the Beatles into possibly the greatest phenomenon in British entertainment and was a great friend of Brian Jones and half the rock world, had died at the youthful age of thirty-two.

Later that night, after the second show had been canceled, Jimi, Brian, myself and a few others huddled around a bar in a key-club drinking den, saying very little, but thinking a lot.

At one stage Brian said, "First Tara, now Brian. Who's next?"

There was no reply.

In the days after Epstein's death it came to be the view around rock music circles in London that Brian's demise was emblematic. If Monterey represented the zenith of twentieth-century pop music, it was also the beginning of its decline. Brian Epstein's death was a landmark on the downward slope. Brian Jones felt that it was ominous that the Beatles had lost their manager just as the Stones were about to lose theirs.

The inquest on September 8 found that Epstein had died of an overdose of Carbitrol, a bromide-based drug which he had been taking to help him sleep. The coroner recorded a verdict of accidental death.

Brian Epstein had once said, "The only woman I would really consider marrying today has already been found—by Mick Jagger. I am very, very fond of Marianne Faithfull. She's a lovely girl. A girl like her could alter my entire life."

On August 30, 1967, the Stones and Andrew Loog Oldham broke up. This still left a formidable organization at the helm of one of the world's richest acts. The Rolling Stones had Allen Klein as their business manager, Tito Burns of Harold Davison Ltd. as their European agent, and Les Perrin, a particular favorite of Brian's, as their publicist.

Les, who had been hired by Oldham back in September of 1966, was a former Fleet Street man, middle-aged, conventional, and excellent at his job. He was proving to be more than just a publicist. He was a friend, troubleshooter and father confessor. Brian said he was sure Les manipulated things behind the scenes so well that he could get the tabloids to dance to his tune. It was thanks to Les' influence, Brian believed, that *The Times* took up the cudgels on behalf of the Stones and had editor William Rees-Mogg write his memorable lead article, WHO BREAKS A BUTTERFLY ON A WHEEL?

On October 30, 1967, Brian appeared before the Inner London Sessions Court. I stood outside, unable to get into the small public galleries, which had been overflowing with young girls as soon as the doors had been opened. There was a large crowd outside, mostly youngsters, surly with resentment. The strong contingent of police kept them clear of the court entrance.

Brian drove up in his silver Rolls-Royce and parked nearby. There were shouts of "Brian, Brian," and he waved calmly as he went in to surrender to his bail. Les Perrin was with him, fussing like a father figure. Brian was dressed conservatively in a conventional suit and tie.

News of the trial trickled out to those of us waiting outside. Brian was taking full responsibility for possessing cannabis and allowing his home to be used for smoking it. The other charges—including possession of cocaine—were dropped after Brian agreed to plead guilty to the cannabis offenses. Brian's psychiatrist, Dr. Leonard Henry, gave evidence to the effect that any custodial sentence could wreck the balance of Brian's mind.

There was an adjournment, and it was a long, cold wait for Brian's friends outside. Finally, the crowd that had been inside came surging out into the street, screaming and crying and shouting "Brian, Brian." It was then that I learned he had been sentenced to nine months imprisonment. Bail pending appeal had been denied.

My heart bled for Brian. Although it was almost inevitable that the lawyers would get bail for him at a higher court, the tortures Brian would suffer during just one night, alone, behind bars, would leave an indelible scar on his mind. He might even try to kill himself. For all the law cared, he might as well.

That night, as I drove home along the King's Road, I saw one or two posters proclaiming JUSTICE FOR THE STONES and RELEASE BRIAN JONES. A scuffle was taking place near Royal Avenue between police and hippies.

Brian was freed on bail the next day after a judge in chambers granted bail in the sum of $750 with two sureties of $500 each.

A friend who was in the know phoned me at Cheyne Court and tipped me that Brian intended to be picked up at the prison in his Rolls at 7 P.M. that night and be taken to the White Horse Public House near Heathrow Airport.

Brian had said in court the previous day, "I hope this case will be an example to all young people who attempt to take drugs. It never did anything positive for me but brought me trouble and interrupted my career."

Something made me want to go over and see him—find out if he'd really meant that or if he'd been trying to bullshit the judge. Or had someone put the words into his mouth and carefully rehearsed him? That sounded likely.

Driving out to the airport, I thought about an article I had read that day by C. A. Joyce in the *Evening News*. He had written:

> The sentence of nine months on a young man of 24 was a matter that must give rise to concern in the minds of all thinking people. What do we know of this man? He is described as a musician and composer of great ability whose IQ is reported as being exceptionally high . . . By nature he is described as being sensitive (imagine that this description had been applied to someone to whom you are related or whom you know well and the picture will become clearer than it is if you read it impersonally—it always does!)

Mr. C. A. Joyce had been made a member of the Order of the British Empire for his work among young offenders during forty years in the government prison service. His article went on to describe the indignities of what happens to a young man admitted for the first time to a prison; the surrender of personal clothing for the dress common to all prisoners; the handing over of personal property; the supervised bath and the medical inspection.

All this, I thought, would happen to Brian should the appeal fail.

When I got to the pub, Brian hadn't yet arrived. When he did— apparently after there had been a call at a doctor's office—we had time only to greet each other and exchange a few words about his bit of stomach trouble before the place filled with reporters and photographers hot on his heels. Suki and the chauffeur managed to protect him a little. He looked weak and ill. He leaned on the bar and stated affably but firmly, "All I want now is peace and quiet." And after downing three large rum and Cokes, he and the chauffeur managed to heave their way back to the car. Suki shouted at one of the reporters that Brian was going to stay somewhere quiet in the country. The Rolls swept away like a silent rocket into the night.

Now there was a period of miserable suspense until Brian's Appeal Court appearance on December 12. Wherever he and Suki were hiding they managed to keep it a pretty tight secret. Rumors in London had them in Morocco, Los Angeles, and Australia, but nobody really seemed to know. A few days after Brian's bail, most papers reported a press release from Les Perrin: "The Stones will go on, there's no doubt about that." The implication was clear—they would go on with or without Brian Jones.

On December 12, 1967, Brian appeared at the Court of Appeal. This time I had managed, by coming early, to get inside the courtroom. Brian looked confident and calm. He was wearing a knee-length shaggy fur coat over his conventional suit. Brian sat impassively listening to an independent psychiatrist, Walter Neustatter, deliver an assessment of his character. The assessment went on forever and I felt sorry for Lord Parker, who had to attend to such arcane jargon as "Mr. Jones' thought processes do reveal some weakening of his reality ties as a result of intense free-floating anxiety—that is, he experiences very intense anxiety surrounding phallic and sadistic sexuality because of the implicit aggressive strivings."

Only three parts of the long report made any sense to me. One said in effect that he was intelligent; he had an IQ of 133. Another said that he felt very threatened by the world about him. And the third seemed to imply that he felt his mother had rejected him in favor of his sister.

Two other psychiatrists, including Brian's own, Dr. Green, gave similarly jargonistic testimony. Mick Jagger stood with a look of intense concentration on his face, trying to make sense of it all.

What they were all really saying was that if Brian faced nine months—or even a few days—in prison, the experience would probably make him lose his sanity.

Mr. James Comyn, Queen's Counsel, said that Jones had spoken out strongly against drugs, a factor deserving to be taken into account in his favor.

At last, when all the droning was over, Lord Parker substituted a $2500 fine for the prison sentence. He also placed Brian on probation and made a condition that he continue to receive treatment by Dr. Green.

There were a few cheers, and a lot of excited babbling from the gallery as the full impact of what had happened became apparent. Crowds outside cheered as Mick and Brian were whisked away, accompanied by police.

Two days later, Brian collapsed during the night and was taken to St. George's Hospital. He had been at home with a Spanish girl, Carmen, who had called the ambulance. Brian almost immediately discharged himself from the hospital. A doctor assured reporters that there was no serious trouble. He was just tired, suffering from strain, and had had some teeth pulled.

On December 12, the LP *Their Satanic Majesties Request* was released. Brian predicted it would be a disaster and at first it was, though it was destined to live on and achieve full status as a rock classic. There was one song by Bill Wyman, but again, all the others were by Jagger and Richard. This was the first Stones record to be made without the benefit of Oldham's production. Mick produced it himself.

The international notoriety surrounding the Stones' busts and trials aroused enormous anticipation for *Satanic Majesties*. There were advance orders for the U.S. alone worth two million dollars. No other record had ever been more anxiously awaited, nor greeted by such bitter disappointment.

Although Brian had all along opposed the psychedelic approach for the Stones, it was his percussion, his performance on the Moroccan drums, his eerie Mellotron intrusions into the electronic jangling that added a measure of distinction, of mysticism to the tracks. The best track was generally agreed to be "2000 Light Years from Home," and without Brian's Mellotron effects, this track would have been merely a clangorous din. As well as the new stereo noises now becoming the vogue, the record incorporated, thanks to Brian again, such atypical rock instruments as the sitar and violins.

One of the most outstanding features of the record must surely have been its sleeve. On the front, against a gaudy blue and white background, was a very weird scene indeed. It looked as if it had been meant to be a three-dimensional trick picture that had seriously gone wrong. The four Stones, dressed in Eastern clothes, with Mick in a witch's cap, were arranged in a line in front of a Himalayan backdrop. The picture stood raised above the actual cover, and by moving it around it was possible to produce the illusion that heads were turning—all except Mick's. The photograph had been taken by Michael Cooper, and the total cost of the cover had been something like $25,000.

Satanic Majesties was by no means the sensation it had been intended to be. Many pop critics compared it unfavorably with the Beatles' *Sergeant Pepper's Lonely Hearts Club Band*.

At the end of 1967 the Stones were still without a real record producer. Brian now accepted Mick as the leader, gave up any hope of composing for the group, and even contributed to the cramping of his style as a musician. Brian's helpless final slide to destruction began in early 1968 under the weight of those defeats. After that,

Brian made spasmodic efforts to save himself. His fading from the scene toward the final eclipse was painful, lingering and desultory.

Brian was now frequently at my apartment in Chelsea. There were long, morose chats, and sometimes we would get drunk together. One night we were loaded when Brian said, "The whole LP *Their Satanic Majesties Request* was a cock-up from start to finish. It was a travesty of what Mick was trying to do—produce a rival to the Beatles' *Sergeant Pepper's Lonely Hearts Club Band*."

Brian was being roughed up in the recording studios. One time Jagger offered to let Brian play a song he had written. The group might be able to use it on a single or an LP. Brian picked up a guitar and started to play the new song. Mick stopped him almost immediately, saying it was no good. Brian, who was quite drunk, tried another tune. Mick stopped him again. No good, he said. Brian was taking large doses of Bacardi between each rejection. Finally Brian ended up on the floor, drunk, wailing into his harmonica, unaware that everyone in the studio was laughing at him.

Brian held the slimmest hope that the failure of *Their Satanic Majesties Request* would convince Mick to change direction and listen to him.

We had discovered a quiet back-street pub where we could hide away and talk. Brian said, "I know he'd really like me to get out so he'd have everything to himself. At the same time, he's not sure whether the group can go on without me. He's not sure. Not yet. But I know I've gone to pieces. It's impossible to explain what that drug bust did to me last year. I've often wondered what hell would be like, if there was any such place. It would be different for everyone, wouldn't it? I mean, I saw other prisoners and screws laughing and joking that day as if they were just as happy in there as out. But for me, Christ! It was worse than I could ever have imagined hell could be. D'you think they ever take that sort of thing into account, Nicholas?"

"I don't think I know what you're getting at." I had been studying his face, bloated, his eyes circled with black, his hair now lank and with none of the old bounce in it.

"About punishment," he said. He sounded slightly exasperated.

"Don't some of them take into account the kind of guy they're dealing with? I mean, I'm not the type to go beating old ladies over the head. If I was insensitive enough to do that, I'd be insensitive enough to be locked up in a prison. But because I need something to calm me down, they say lock him up for nine months. Christ! Nine months."

"Seems crazy," I agreed. "You're not using anything now, are you?"

He shook his head. "Only the things off the doctor. And this." He held up his glass. "Well, now and then I have a joint if I'm somewhere safe. I don't think they do any harm. But I hate to think any kid would get on hard stuff because of me. I'm dead against hard stuff."

A few days later, back at our hideaway, Brian said, "People think I'm finished, you know that? Mick called a press conference after that lousy recording. It was supposed to boost sales, but he was putting around that I was a washed-up drunkard and a junkie. But we'll see. With or without them, I'll be back. I'll be back better than ever."

I wanted to believe him. I was still as much in love with Brian as ever. But I could not escape the fact that prospects looked bleak for him in his present state.

On March 16, 1968, Brian's life took yet another dramatic turn. Linda Keith, who had once been Keith Richard's girlfriend, attempted suicide after Brian had put her up. Linda recovered in the hospital and was quoted by a girlfriend as saying she was very much in love with Brian Jones. She had had the idea Brian had gotten another girlfriend and gone off, leaving her.

On Saturday, May 11, Brian called me to say that on Sunday the Stones were to make an unscheduled appearance at the Empire Pool, Wembley, in the *New Musical Express* Poll-Winners' Concert. Reporter Norrie Drummond, who worked for the *NME*, and I sat in the front row a few seats away from Marianne Faithfull. She looked excited and happy.

It was the Stones' first public appearance for nearly two years, and they were all brilliant, including Brian. Marianne, who was wearing an odd-looking blouse with razor-blade patterns on it, sat back and started tossing red tulips at Mick onstage.

Brian had come back to life with a vengeance. Here was the old Brian, full of vigor.

At the end of the concert, Marianne, who had been invited onto the stage before "Satisfaction," took Brian's arm—not Mick's. Maybe, I thought, this was Marianne's way of saying thanks for the way he had pulled himself together and helped make this a memorable and restorative night.

Afterward, Brian was lively and bright as a puppy as we drank in a small key club we used as a hangout off the Charing Cross Road.

"That'll show 'em whether I'm a washed up junkie," he said. "Really gave them the answer the Stones don't want to hear."

Later, sitting in the dimly lit cocktail lounge, I asked Brian why recently he had been changing addresses so often.

"The cops," he said. "There's a crooked cop on my tail. Keeps coming and saying he'll bust me if I don't get money for him."

This seemed unbelievable to me, and I suggested he was getting paranoid fantasies.

"Grow up," he said. "If you want to know about corrupted cops, you ask Tony Sanchez. He'll make your hair stand on end."

"Why don't you do something about it? Report it to the high-ups in the police?"

"Yeah," he laughed. "Who's going to believe me? I've got a conviction for it. Tony says I have to pay up and look happy." He looked thoughtful for a moment. Then he said, "Never mind, I *am* happy. One day soon I'm going to move out to the country. Different cops, more honest. Let's have some more booze."

The police busted Brian for dope again on May 21, 1968, while he was in his apartment in Royal Avenue House in Chelsea. Four policemen carried out the raid. I was appalled, watching the news on TV, to see the dejected, devastated figure of my friend leaving Great Marlborough Street Magistrates' Court. He was charged under the Dangerous Drugs Act with being in unauthorized possession of a quantity of cannabis.

Detective Sergeant Robin Constable applied to the bench for a remand so that the seized drugs could be formally analyzed. Brian was remanded until June 11 on bail of $2500 on his own surety and $2500 in the surety of his accountant, Frederick Trowbridge. In replying to a question by Mr. Clive Nicholls for the defense, Detective Sergeant Constable said that it was correct that Mr. Jones had denied the charge throughout.

The Stones had been scheduled to begin shooting their first film, a documentary by Jean-Luc Godard, but now it would have to be postponed because of the court case.

Unlike the Beatles, the Stones were luckless in their attempts to become film stars. For over four years there had been plans afoot for the Rolling Stones as a group to make films. The rights had been obtained for them in Anthony Burgess' book *A Clockwork Orange*, but legal advisers predicted trouble with British censorship, and the property went to Stanley Kubrick, who created a film classic with Malcolm McDowell. Godard's film, a study of the relationship between pop culture and violence in the Sixties, was to be called *Sympathy for the Devil*.

Brian was so enthusiastic about it that he returned to his old love, playing bottleneck country guitar, the blues guitar, and had already recorded his brilliant contributions to several of the tracks for the album that would eventually become *Beggars Banquet*. It was Godard's idea to film the making of one of the tracks—from its inception until it was a finished and saleable pop release. Now, if Brian should become incapable of working with his full vigor, this latest film attempt would fail as well.

Brian went to the London Hilton under the care of Allen Klein's nephew, Ronnie Schneider. I asked Brian, "What happened? Did you refuse to pay up or something?"

"No, it was a genuine bust. They found the stuff in a ball of wool in the apartment. Wool. What the hell would I be doing with a ball of wool? Do I knit now? Christ, I'd only taken the place over about two or three weeks ago and I'd only used it two or three times."

"So it must have belonged to someone else?" I said. "The wool, I mean."

"Yeah. And the cannabis. I might be stupid but I'd hardly leave the bloody stuff ready for that other bastard to find, would I?"

"You mean the crooked cop?"

"Of course. Anyway, I've kicked the stuff. Only booze now and what the quacks give me. So you can understand what the bust has done to me. It's like another kick in the guts just when I was getting up from the last one. Nicholas, I'm going to Sussex for a while and look around for a place in the country. But I'll be seeing you around."

"What about the film?" I said.

"Oh," he said, without interest. "They'll get on with it."

That sounded ominous. Brian was disenchanted with the Stones and with the making of their film, which went on, spasmodically, until September 26, 1968.

On May 24, the Rolling Stones' fourteenth British single, "Jumpin' Jack Flash" b/w "Child of the Moon" was released. Jimmy Miller was now the producer. The group seemed to be returning to their R & B roots but with greater polish. This disk easily surpassed anything so far released. Some critics consider it one of the greatest pop disks ever. While it took the Stones back to their primitive origins, it also added something new, something spooky and mystic. In the Stones' TV performance of it, the intention seemed to be to initiate an androgynous, or unisex, cult, calculated to further scare the hell out of the older generation. "Jumpin' Jack Flash" truly caused a stir and brought the Stones back with an explosion.

On June 11, Brian elected at Great Marlborough Street Magistrates' Court to be tried by jury on the charge, now amended to possession of Indian hemp. His counsel, Mr. Michael Havers, applied for unrestricted bail so that Brian could travel abroad, and this was granted. Police did not object, and bail was renewed as before. The date of the Inner London Sessions was set for September 26.

Godard continued making his film, though with increasing difficulty due to Brian's frequent delinquency. Brian would telephone with reports of ailments while the whole cast at the studio at Olympic, including the other four Stones, stood around and cursed their prima donna partner.

In August Brian told me that he was sure they were going to send him to prison and that the thought of it was occupying the whole of his being with fear. He couldn't concentrate on anything else. He said that the other Stones were planning a tour without him, that he had read reports that Mick was trying to get Eric Clapton to join the Stones. Eric was being propositioned by other people as well when the disbandment of his group Cream came about in December.

"People are being very good to me," Brian said. "Everybody seems to love me—except the right ones. Les Perrin's been marvelous." He went on about others who had been helping in trying to keep up his spirits—Les' wife, Janey, and Shirley Arnold, the secretary of the Stones' fan club.

"But they can't come with me if I get locked up, can they? I ought to have the guts to face up to it, Nicholas, but right now I haven't. Listen, I'm going off to Tangier again for a while. That place seems to relax me. And that music up in the villages, I can work on that. It'll maybe concentrate the mind, as they say. Maybe I'll end up with a record."

"I hope so," I said. And as things turned out, he did. But he never lived to see it produced. The other Stones, as a kind of tribute to him after his death, released *Brian Jones Presents the Pipes of Pan at Joujouka*. Brion Gysin and George Chkiantz helped tape the tracks in Tangier.

"Street Fighting Man" was barred by some American radio stations on the grounds that it could cause further riots in Chicago. All stations serving that city feared the recurrence of the violence that rocked Chicago during the Democratic National Convention. Originally "Street Fighting Man" and the flip side, "No Expectations," were to have been part of the LP *Beggar's Banquet*, but the release of the album was delayed after Decca in England and London Records in the U.S. agreed that the artwork on the cover—a photo of a graffiti-covered wall—was offensive.

On September 26, 1968, Brian, looking small and woebegone,

came up against the great majesty of the English legal system at the Inner London Sessions. Through his counsel, he pleaded not guilty to possession of 144 grains of cannabis resin. Suki, Keith and Mick sat near me in the public gallery.

Prosecuting counsel took the police witnesses through their evidence. They said they had waited for ten minutes before Mr. Jones had answered the door.

As Brian took the oath, I noticed that Keith and Mick were gazing down at him with genuine emotion—and Suki had a handkerchief to one side of her face. Other young girls were sobbing.

Brian gave evidence in a subdued and matter-of-fact voice. Outwardly he was calm, though overawed. Inwardly, I knew he must be almost sick with fear. He was dressed like a businessman in a suit, shirt and quiet tie. He did not agree that he had taken ten minutes to answer his door, but said that there would have been time enough for him to dispose of anything, had he wished to do so. The wool was not his and to his knowledge he had not seen it before. He did not knit; he did not darn socks and did not have a girlfriend who darned socks.

Cross-examined, he said he had been too frightened to take cannabis since his last court case. He said, "The Lord Chief Justice made it clear what would happen to me if I did."

In his summing up, the judge did not sound impressed by the evidence of the prosecution, pointing out that if Brian had known the cannabis to have been there it would have been simple for him to have flushed it down the toilet while the police were trying to gain entry. He also said there was no evidence that Brian had been using the drug. While he also made noises against the defense evidence, as was his duty, he implied that the only evidence against Brian was circumstantial.

As the jury left to consider their verdict, the general opinion in the gallery was that Brian would walk out innocent in about five minutes, after the jury had had a smoke.

Looking around the court, I was surprised not to see Brian's parents, whom I'd met in September of 1966 backstage after a concert. I had never met his sister Barbara, but had seen her in photographs, and she didn't seem to be there either. I was sure if I'd been in trouble my family would have backed me up.

The evidence of Professor Neustatter at the Appeal Court came to mind—or at least the substance of some of it—that Brian felt his mother had rejected him in favor of his sister. Brian had never spoken of his sister to me.

Forty-five minutes later, the jury returned. When they pronounced a verdict of guilty, even the judge and the lawyers looked stunned. In the gallery there were gasps and sobs and tears. The girls cried, "Oh no!" Suki broke down.

Brian stood frozen, stooping a little as if expecting a blow on the head.

Judge Seaton reset his face into a look of stern disapproval and intoned, "Mr. Jones, you have been found guilty. I am going to treat you as I would any other young man before this court. I am going to fine you according to your means. You will pay a $150 fine and $325 in costs. You will have one week to pay."

He added, "But you must keep clear of this stuff. At the moment you are on probation from this court and you really must watch your step. For goodness sake, don't get into trouble again. If you do, there will be some real trouble."

Again the atmosphere changed—this time to one of relief. Given the chance, all the girls in the audience would have awarded the judge a big kiss.

Outside the court, Brian posed happily with Mick and Keith. He climbed into his Rolls beside Suki Potier, probably, I thought, on his way to Keith's home, Redlands. It was a good base to continue his search for a country home of his own, out of reach of the Chelsea Drugs Squad.

Before Mick and Keith were driven away by Tony Sanchez, Mick said to reporters, "We're very happy Brian doesn't have to go to prison." He really seemed to mean it.

Brian told me later about Redlands, Keith's home, where the now notorious drug raid had taken place. Keith had bought the moated, thatched house in West Wittering, Sussex, for $50,000 in 1966.

While Brian was there he seemed to pick up quite a bit mentally. He told me he was now completely drug-free.

"I feel now as if I can face the future without drugs, the Stones or Anita," he said.

On November 13 he told me that he and Suki had found the ideal house where they could live in peace, A. A. Milne's Cotchford Farm. "It has an outdoor, heated swimming pool," he said. "First again, you see? The first Stone to have a pool. Of course, that's if you can still count me one of the Stones."

I knew what he meant. Recently, he had been agonizing about whether to leave and whether the others really knew if they wanted him to leave or not. Temperamentally, it was acknowledged by them all that he was out on his own. The dilemma now was, could they do without him?

Beggars Banquet was an immediate success. Roy Carr of the *New Musical Express* wrote, "*Beggars Banquet* is as much a reflection of the time in which it was recorded as it is of the Stones themselves." The Summer of Love respite was over. Once more there was panic in the streets.

Brian had invited me to the *Beggars Banquet* party at the Elizabethan Room of the Gore Hotel in Kensington, but I was unable to attend. He told me later, "You missed a riot. It was a lunchtime do, and it got slightly out of hand. After the meal they brought in boxes of those custard pie things they use in the theater; you know, for splatting in people's faces. Lord Harlech was there and he caught some, even." Lord Harlech was the father of the Ormsby-Gore girls and a former escort of Jackie Kennedy. "It was the first time Mick and I had met for a month or two. Anyway, he was greeting people at the door, and he told everyone who came in they had to get drunk. When he said it to me, I said, 'Get stuffed.' And I got him in the face with a pie later. Serves the bastard right."

This did not seem very propitious for the Stones' reuniting. Maybe it was all over at last.

From December 10–12 the great Rock and Roll Circus Extravaganza was being filmed at the former "RSG" Studios in Wembley. Nobody knew it would never be seen by the general public, though live audiences were allowed in to watch the recording. Brian wandered around in a spotted top hat with horns. The show presented the great rock and roll bands in a circus ring; the set was designed to give the impression that the action was taking place under a big top. Among the acts participating were the Stones, Marianne Faithfull, John Lennon, Yoko Ono, Eric Clapton, Mitch Mitchell, Jethro Tull, Taj Mahal, Donyale Luna and the Who. The production was a joint effort by Michael Lindsay-Hogg and Mick Jagger.

As well as all these international stars, real circus acts were to be included in this extraordinary production.

Brian and I were sitting beside the stage amid all the chaos of rehearsals when he said, "I'll be bloody glad when this lot comes to an end. It's getting more and more out of hand. Mick seems to be going around the twist. Besides everything else, he's now going to see the wizard. He and Marianne, Keith and Anita, are going off after this to learn about magic, so they say. Going to Rio to see a man who specializes in black and white magic. They're quite serious about it. They can't pronounce the guy's name, so they call him Banana. Strikes me the whole bloody lot of them are going bananas. For instance, d'you know Mick and Michael turned down Led Zeppelin for this circus? Glyn Johns recommended them but he and Michael thought they were a bit heavy, overemphasized the guitar too much. It's a bloody shame really. Led Zeppelin haven't had a chance to appear yet on TV."

At the circus the audience was part of the act as well. They had to put on colorful ponchos as they were admitted to the studios.

Yoko Ono and John Lennon were sitting together on a plank. Yoko had the most fascinating Oriental face, olive-skinned and serene. Brian saw me looking at her. "You like?" he said.

"Yes. They seem to have something our girls don't have, those Eastern girls."

Brian looked thoughtful for a moment, then he said, "John gave me some advice. I don't know whether I've got the guts to take it, though."

I waited for him to go on. He was just gazing down at the bare concrete floor.

"I was bellyaching, you know the way I do, about Mick and Keith. It was after I'd played sax for him on a Beatles track. He told me it was no good blaming Jagger for pushing me out. He said it was my own fault for not being tough enough. Anyway, he said if I was really dissatisfied, I should get out and do my own thing. He reckons I'm still the star and I can still knock the shit out of the kids. So maybe I will. Get out and start again—and this time be tough and stay on top of my own sodding group."

There were trapeze acts, midgets, horses and kangaroos milling around as well as musicians tuning up unlikely instruments. Someone said that Anita Pallenberg was going to play a bearded lady.

The next time I visited the set, Brian was dressed in tight golf trousers and a long-haired fur coat. Mick wore a black bearskin. Both watched Marianne—looking nervous but sexy in a wine-colored satin evening dress—rehearse the song, "Something Better," written by Goffin and King. Nearby a fire-eater was rehearsing. It was like something out of a psychedelic dream.

On December 18, Brian flew to Ceylon with Suki Potier. On the same day, Mick, Keith, Marianne and Anita took a ship for Rio. They went by boat because Anita was now pregnant and didn't want to fly.

Brian returned for his Appeal Court hearing. He came to my apartment on Cheyne Walk for a drink. Brian looked really well, full of stories about Ceylon and the people he'd met. He had got into a fight over Suki when two other guys had made a pass at her. He had visited Arthur C. Clarke, the science fiction writer. "Very intelligent," he said. "Wouldn't it be nice to be good at doing something like that, where you don't need anyone else? You're just a one-man show."

"You'd miss the limelight," I said.

He thought for a moment, then shrugged. "Maybe. But as soon as this bloody appeal is over, I'm getting away from the limelight and going to Cotchford. Maybe there I'll be able to sort myself out."

The appeal was dismissed on January 13, 1969. Brian's second conviction for a drugs offense was now a scar on his character.

In the spring of 1969, after Brian moved into Cotchford Farm with Suki Potier, he told me the bitterness between him and the other Stones had "opened up a chasm" between them. He had grown even closer to Suki. He seemed happier, less moody.

It was all over the London pop world that Brian had been recording anonymously with the Beatles. He had been featured extensively on the album *Sergeant Pepper's Lonely Hearts Club Band*, which was still selling. Just as Brian was breaking away from the Stones, so was the Lennon and McCartney partnership beginning to disintegrate. Brian was actually credited with playing soprano saxophone on "Baby, You're a Rich Man", the flip side of "All You Need Is Love." Later he was also credited for playing tenor saxophone on "You Know My Name," the flip side of "Let It Be," which was released in March of 1970.

On my first visit to Brian at Cotchford I quizzed him about all this. He had shown me around the beautiful house and gardens. A happy and contented Suki had given us lunch, and we had adjourned—just Brian and I—to the Hay Waggon pub in Hartfield.

Sitting on a bar stool, he said, looking inscrutable, "Towards the end of last year, Nicholas, four musicians made a trial recording for Apple, the Beatles' label. They played under the group name of Balls." He grinned. "One of them was John Lennon and one of them was me. The other two swore me to secrecy, so I can't tell you about them, except to say one was a lead guitar and the other a drummer. We recorded one track called 'Go to the Mountains.'"

"So there is some truth in the rumor," I said. "Is there any hope of forming a group with Lennon?" The idea sounded marvelous.

He gave his usual evasive shrug. "It's early days," he said. "And there are others interested. Bob Dylan asked me once to join his backup group. Then again, I could team up with Jimi Hendrix. Trouble is, after losing that drugs bust appeal, I'm going to be lucky to be allowed into the States again. And you know how much I love the States."

I said, "I heard once that you and John Lennon didn't hit it off very well."

"Once we didn't. He reckoned he couldn't put up with my moods. But at the Rock and Roll Circus we got on fine. I admire him as a composer and he says he likes the way I play." There was a pause. "I hear Eric Clapton has decided not to join the Stones."

"I heard that was because he respects you too much."

He gave a dismissive grin and said, "Nice to know somebody loves me. Maybe he and I could get together."

"*Somebody?*" I said. "I've never known anyone who's been loved by as many people as you. Suki's obviously potty about you."

"Yeah, she's a nice kid. And this place suits us both." He paused. "Well, mostly. Sometimes I think that old split personality really is me now. I mean, when I'm down here I'm the rich country gentleman, going for walks on my estate, lounging by my pool, having the occasional binge. Up there in town, according to the press and the cops, I'm a tearaway pop singer, a junkie, a criminal. And I don't know what I want to be—one or the other. Or neither."

Whatever he was, I thought, as we strolled back up the lane to Cotchford, where the new leaves and buds gave a green haze to the hedgerows, he had changed since he'd come down here. Although he was calm and loose, there were lines now on that once-young face—premature lines of care brought on by those earlier excesses. He admitted that he sometimes drank too much beer, wine and even brandy, but insisted he had himself under control.

After that visit all seemed to be going well with him. I paid several other visits and found him in the same frame of mind, still indecisive about his future, but not too uptight. And then he telephoned me on May 5, 1969. He sounded nervous and jumpy.

"Hey, you know we were talking about me forming a new group?"

"Yes."

"Yeah, well, don't discuss it, please. Have you said anything to anyone about it?"

"I don't think so. Why?"

Now he was irritable. "Have you or not?"

"No, I'm sure I haven't."

"Please don't then. I never thought of it before, but Alexis [Korner] pointed out it could be dangerous. There's so much money involved, he says. I think he might be right. If certain people believed John and I were thinking of teaming up, they might get jittery. It could be a threat to both the Stones and the Beatles. And that, as he said, could cost a lot of people a lot of loot."

"I see his point."

"Alexis and I were talking about me going on a German tour with him and his new band, New Church, when he brought the subject up. He said that in many countries it was still Brian Jones and the Rolling Stones instead of Mick Jagger—as it once was John Lennon and the Beatles instead of Paul McCartney. He said a band with John Lennon and Brian Jones together could be bigger than either."

"I'm sure it would be."

"Yeah, but on top of that, add the name of Jimi Hendrix. In the same outfit."

"Jimi?"

"That's right. He's falling out with Noel Redding and Mitch Mitchell—his bass guitarist and his drummer. He doesn't want to carry on with the old stuff; wants to play something new. So it could be all three groups could fall apart and a new one be born. John, Jimi and me."

"God. That *would* be something."

"Yes, but I rang to warn you. Don't say anything. Alexis reckons it could be very dangerous."

On June 9, the *Daily Sketch* reported:

BRIAN JONES QUITS THE STONES AS
GROUP CLASH OVER SONGS

Rolling Stone Brian Jones last night quit the group after a clash with Mick Jagger and the three other Stones. Jones said at his Sussex home: "I no longer see eye to eye with the discs we are cutting." An unknown guitarist is to replace him. He is Mick Taylor, twenty-year-old lead guitarist with the John Mayall group.

The next twenty-two days at Cotchford were chaotic. Many telephone calls came from Brian; then one from Suki, asking me to go down and saying that she had left him at the beginning of the month because of frequent drinking bouts and rows.

I was at Cotchford on Thursday, June 12, when the telephone rang. As Brian was resting upstairs, I answered it. It was Anita Pallenberg and she sounded distressed. She asked urgently for Brian. Brian picked up an extension, and so I put down my receiver. Later I asked him what the phone call was about; he became abusive, so I left him. It was my penultimate visit to Cotchford Farm.

On June 17, Brian phoned and told me he had a new girlfriend living in. She was called Anna Wohlin. He was quite drunk. He was having one of his fantasies about being watched, being guarded, being spied upon. Or *was* it a fantasy?

On July 1, Mitch Mitchell and Noel Redding told a reporter on the *Evening Standard* they were quitting the Jimi Hendrix Experience. So that was it, I thought. Any time now John Lennon would leave the Beatles and the greatest group ever would begin to emerge.

And then came that last call from Suki Potier.

12

*B*RIAN STARTED TO WALK as far as the car with us, and the next
time I looked at the pool the two men had vanished as if into
the ground. Just as we came in sight of the drive, Brian suddenly
gave Richard and me a big shove toward some trees; I lost my
balance and toppled to the grass. Brian himself crouched behind a
bush.

Just before the shove, I had caught a glimpse of another
blonde—or perhaps the same one—approaching the garages at the
side of the house.

Brian apologized and said she was Thorogood's girlfriend, Janet
Lawson, and that he hadn't wanted her to see us. Thorogood was
one of the several men working at Cotchford Farm. Another was
Tom Keylock, now Brian's chauffeur/bodyguard.

Then he said, "I've told him she can't stay here. They'll have to
stay in the town. I'll have to tell him again tonight."

The drive to Haywards Heath took about twenty-five minutes; it
was then 7:40 P.M. We parked near the station and asked a woman
the way to the Hayworth Hotel. Having found it quite nearby, we
searched the bars and the restaurant for a lone Spanish-looking
young lady. There was no one remotely resembling one. The clientele was mostly middle-aged and there were no unaccompanied
females. We asked at the reception desk. The man said he had been
on duty since 4 P.M. and had seen no young ladies looking lost.

Quite annoyed at this apparent wild-goose chase we'd been sent on, I decided we should stay for a drink or two. About an hour later we left and went back to the station. We asked the ticket collector if he had seen a girl looking for the Hayworth, and after a bit of head-scratching he said he hadn't, but perhaps we should try across the road at a pub called the Burrell Arms. There was no sign of her there either, but we had another drink. After a while I noticed a girl sitting alone at a table. She didn't look very Spanish but I went over to her all the same, taking Brian's note out of my pocket.

Reading from it, I said, "Excuse me, are you Luciana Martinez Delarosa?"

In a sneering cockney accent she said, "Yeah, that's right, love. And you're the King of Siam, I s'pose."

"What's your trouble, cock?" said a voice behind me. Turning, I found a great brute of a man glowering down at me from a height of about six feet three. He was carrying two drinks in his hands, which was probably fortunate. I beat a hasty retreat with Richard back to the car, undecided what to do and a bit unnerved by the encounter with the giant.

In the car Richard said, "You look like you need a smoke. D'you want a joint?"

"You've got some?" I said.

"Yeah, I've got about an ounce hidden about the car."

My need overcame my annoyance that he should carry cannabis about in my car. I should have given him hell, especially since Brian was neurotic about having illegal drugs found on his property again. But feeling weak and inexplicably depressed, I said nothing and puffed contentedly at the joint Richard handed me. He lit another for himself, and we sat in the car for a while unwinding.

"Where the hell can that girl have gone?" I said.

Richard said, "Perhaps there wasn't any girl. Maybe he just wanted us out of the way for a bit."

"I don't think Brian's as devious as that," I said, "If he'd wanted a bit of tail he would have said so."

After the smoke we went back to the Hayworth to take another look. There was still no sign of anyone who might be Luciana.

Again I felt tense, annoyed and uneasy, and we stayed on for more drinks. We sat at the bar.

"What did you think of Cotchford?" I asked Richard. Although he had met Brian a few times before, he had never been to the farm.

"I found it creepy, somehow," he said. "Impressive but creepy. Eerie."

"Really? Why d'you say that?"

"I don't know. I've got a weird sort of intuition, or imagination, if you like. All houses have atmospheres, vibrations. Well, to me they do. And the vibes there were creepy."

"With all that lovely garden and Winnie-the-Pooh? Creepy?" I knew Richard had some peculiar fancies, but this really surprised me.

"Yes," he said thoughtfully. "It's partly because of that. I felt that the statues and the innocent monuments to childhood resented the presence of the people who are there now. Some of the people at least."

I laughed at him. "What d'you think of Brian?"

"Oh, he's all right but he's a bit odd, isn't he? While you were asleep he kept asking me if you and I slept together."

"What!" I yelled. "Christ, what did you tell him?"

"I said of course not. I thought that would be best. But he didn't seem to believe me."

"You're right," I said. "He is odd."

After a time I decided to ring Brian and ask whether the girl had turned up there or had rung again. Using the telephone in the foyer I dialed the number.

A girl's voice said, "Hello?"

I asked to speak to Brian. There was no answer. In the background I could hear a lot of noise and loud music, as if a party was going on. This struck me as odd. Brian hadn't mentioned any party and there had hardly been anyone about when we had left. Could Luciana have arrived with a bunch of friends?

I said, "Hello?" There was still no reply, only the sound of revelry. After no one had answered about three minutes later, someone put the phone down at the other end. What the hell was going on? I hadn't recognized the girl's voice on the telephone. It hadn't sounded foreign. Why had she refused to answer after that first hello? Had someone taken the handset from her? Perhaps Thorogood, or one of the other employees—Keylock? I looked at my watch. It was five to ten.

Going back to join Richard at the bar, I began to feel a rather vague sort of alarm and nervousness.

"There's something wrong, Richard," I said. "They won't let me talk to Brian, and there's a party going on. I heard the music, and people talking and laughing."

"Maybe he's started mixing drugs with booze again. Maybe he's stoned. Couldn't be bothered to take the call."

"Oh no, those days are over, I hope. He won't let anyone bring drugs onto the premises. He's too scared of being busted. Anyway, he told me the only drugs he's on now are prescribed by his doctor."

"D'you think we'd better get back and see what's happening?"

"I don't know," I said drowsily. "Let's have one more while we're thinking about it."

It was almost 11:15 P.M. when Richard pulled the car around to the right, off Maresfield Road and onto Cotchford Lane, off which the drive to the house ran. And then it all began—the terror that I was to relive over and over in nightmares for the rest of my life.

The lane ran through thick hedges. As we came into it, we were blinded. Two powerful headlights on high beam were glaring into our windshield from a fixed position. We stopped, and Richard swore.

Brave with anger, we set off toward the headlights. Fifty yards away, blocking the drive to the house, was a foreign car, left-hand drive. The driver's door was open. By the interior light we could tell that the car was empty. I walked around the back of it and into the opening of the drive. I saw lights from the house dancing in the leaves of the trees. There was silence.

Richard hung back. "Not that way," he called in an urgent whisper. "There's something going on. Let's go through the trees."

We went back to my car where there was a gap in the hedge leading into Bluebell Wood. We clumsily groped through the trees. At first, in almost total darkness, we tripped on brambles, stumbled on dead branches. What was I doing? What was happening? Would we get lost in the woods? But no. We got glimpses of light through the leaves. We emerged behind the beamed stone wall of the summer house in shadow, where we heard muffled voices. We skirted the summer house, came around to its side and saw the full glare of the lights now over the pool and in the windows of the house. We were in a kind of twilight here at the corner of the summer house. We had a clear view of the pool and of what was going on there. And what the hell *was* going on?

At the far right-hand corner of the swimming pool three men were standing. They were dressed in sweaters and jeans. Their clothes gave the impression they were workmen. The power of the spotlights blotted out their features and made their faces look like white blobs. The moment I became aware of them, the middle one dropped to his knees, reached into the water and pushed down on the top of a head that looked white.

At the opposite corner of the pool—far left—stood two other people, a man and a woman, gazing down into the pool where the kneeling man was pushing down on the head, keeping it under. The man to the right of the kneeling man said something. It sounded like a command and I caught the words ". . . do something." At that, the third man on that side jumped into the water the way an animal might jump, arms outstretched, knees bent. He landed on the back of the struggling swimmer. The man who snapped out the command seemed to be preparing himself also to jump in. Breathless, unbelieving, paralyzed, I looked at the man and woman. She was standing a little in his shadow and I couldn't see her face. But why didn't they move? Do something? They looked like extras on a film set, waiting to play their parts. Somebody had got to do something. Could Richard and I. . . ?

Out of the bushes right next to us stepped a burly man wearing glasses. He pushed Richard out of the way. He grabbed my shoulder. His other hand made a fist, which he put in my face menacingly.

"Get the hell out of here, Fitzgerald, or you'll be the next," he growled. It was a cockney accent. I was terrified. He meant it. There was no way I could do battle with him. He turned me around and pushed me hard in the back into the woods. I almost fell, but went stumbling blindly into the darkness under the trees. Ahead of me I heard the rustle and the swish as Cadbury went struggling away. I followed this sound, briars grasping my ankles like the claws of a cat, twigs and leaves brushing my face. I fell and hit a tree with my head. Some kind of creeper tried to entwine itself around my chest and waist. I broke free. Were there sounds behind me? *Please, God, no.*

And now I saw the lights of the parked car. I saw Cadbury climbing into mine. I got in beside him and I couldn't breathe. Asthma. I grabbed my inhaler and puffed too many times. My heart was pounding. Why wasn't the bloody car moving? Were those people out there searching for us with lights?

"Richard," I said. I looked at him. He was slumped over the steering wheel, groaning.

"What the hell's the matter?" I was almost shrieking. Shock, I told myself. I was in shock. "Get this bloody thing out of here!"

His hand trembled uncontrollably, but the engine revved up and we were flying backward, straight into the main road, the tires screaming for mercy, then forward with a roar that should have woken the whole village. We were going the wrong way, on the road to Uckfield instead of London. But we were away from that damned place, away from those damned people.

The effect of the shock that night was to numb my mind, to blot out all the horror of what I had seen. Once we were on the open road my mind became quite clear, but the episode at Cotchford was locked away in a sealed compartment of my brain. Neither Richard nor I spoke until, after we had traveled about a mile and a half, the car began to splutter, the engine cut out and the car came to rest away from the curb.

"Out of gas," he said in a dull, toneless voice.

I switched on the light inside the car. There was blood both on my hands and streaming down Richard's face from a cut on his forehead. He looked like a man hypnotized as I wiped his face with my handkerchief.

"I saw a place back there," he said. "About half a mile. I'll try and knock them up." He left, walking like a man in a trance, into the darkness. It was the last time I ever saw him.

I wiped the blood off my hands, found a roach and rolled a joint. I sat there smoking it, my mind going blank, refusing to look back. I dozed a little, then smoked another joint. I didn't notice time passing, didn't care. And then two glaring headlights were coming toward me. It was a huge truck, and its horn blasted and its lights flashed. It went past slowly, then stopped a little way down the road. I roused myself as a face came to the driver's window. He was a middle-aged man with stubble on his face.

"You all right, son?" he said.

"I think so." I didn't seem to have much control over what I was saying. "Broken down. Friend gone for help."

"Well, we better get you off the road and switch them lights off." he said.

We pushed the car up onto a grass shoulder.

"What's the matter with it?"

"It's out of gas."

"Gas? Oh well, I can't help you there. Let's hope your mate finds some."

"You going to London?" I said.

He was and he agreed to take me. We would pick Richard up along the way, I thought. The next thing I remember was the truck driver shaking me awake. He was wearing a red check shirt and blue jeans. At first I couldn't think who he was.

"You said you live at Cheyne Court, didn't you?" he said, regarding me with an odd expression. "This is as close as I go. Battersea Bridge."

I got out and thanked him, wondering where Richard Cadbury had gone. Then, hardly knowing where I was, where I had been, I staggered back to my apartment building. I took the elevator to the third floor, let myself in and thanked God for sanctuary. The memory of Cotchford was still safely locked away. To make sure it remained so I took a lot of Valium tablets and collapsed on the bed, taking the receiver off the bedside phone. Sara, my girlfriend, was already sound asleep. Now I was safe from the mad world out there, and that locked away memory would be released when I woke as a bad, bad dream.

Waking at 12:20 P.M. on Thursday, July 3rd, my mind did begin to gnaw vaguely at the problem. But I was only half-awake. Turning on the radio, I listened to the music until the news came on at twelve-thirty. The first item said that Brian Jones, the former Rolling Stone, was dead. He had been found dead in his swimming pool. They said it was believed he may have died as the result of an asthma attack while swimming.

I smiled and shook my head. No, I thought, this is still a part of that half-recalled dream I'd been having. Brian dead—it was absurd. *"Get the hell out of here, Fitzgerald, or you'll be the next."* That had been part of the dream, hadn't it? I took a couple of Sodium Amytal tablets and fell asleep again, determined that the dream must end.

Then Sara was shaking me and shouting, "Nicholas, Nicholas!" I opened my eyes and saw her blearily. I smiled.

"Nicholas, have you heard what happened? Have you seen the papers?" She thrust the London *Evening News* and the evening edition of the *Standard* in front of me. Her face was swollen and there were tears dropping on the bed.

"He's dead, Nicholas. Brian's dead!"

Slowly I sat up. Though my eyesight was blurred by the effect of drugs, I couldn't miss the identical banner headlines on both front pages: BRIAN JONES DEAD IN POOL TRAGEDY.

So now the time had come to face the truth. But what truth? That I had seen him being murdered? Time to open up that locked compartment in my mind? But the headlines served only to bring about a relapse into shock.

Sara was babbling on, asking me questions.

"Did you go down yesterday?" I heard her say.

"Er, yes. Yes, we went down. Got there about lunchtime."

"They're talking about his asthma. Was his asthma bad, Nicholas?"

I wanted her to go away.

"I don't think so. Anyway, he had his inhaler with him. He always had that. Like me."

I started trying to read the papers—read what they were saying about his death but she kept talking, asking questions.

"But what time did you leave him?"

"Er, oh, about a quarter past seven. Look, Sara, this is a hell of a shock to me, d'you mind . . ."

Then the telephone rang. She must have replaced the receiver. It was Richard Cadbury, and his voice was very shaky.

"Nicholas. God, I'm scared. I'm getting out. I've moved all my stuff out of the studio. The car's downstairs, I've left the keys . . ." The phone went dead. The dial tone came on. He hadn't, as he usually did, used a pay phone. He hadn't a telephone at his studio. That was the last I ever heard from Richard Cadbury.

Sara at last took in the fact that I was upset and wanted to be alone, and she left the room.

The newspaper article said nothing about the three men who had been beside the pool when Brian was drowning. They said he had been alone and had been found by Frank Thorogood, Janet Lawson, and Anna Wohlin lying on the bottom of the pool.

Well, perhaps it had all been in my imagination. Or this was still a part of the dream. I took more Sodium Amytal tablets and yet again drifted into sleep.

Sara had the good sense and kindness to leave me in peace the rest of that day and night, answering all the telephone calls from my friends and relatives, and generally seeing that I wasn't disturbed.

The next morning I woke feeling refreshed, at least in body, though extremely distressed, nervous and anxious. It still didn't seem possible that Brian could be dead. He had become so much a part of my life it was impossible to imagine a future without him.

When Sara next came in she brought two of the day's papers with her before going off to get me some coffee and toast. It seemed there was to be a postmortem and an inquest into Brian's death. I had only a vague idea what an inquest was. I thought there would be plenty of witnesses, assuming that all the people I heard making a noise when I telephoned must have been at the house when Brian died. But were they? Did they see anything?

Anna Wohlin was quoted in the *Daily Mail*: "He was a wonderful person. It's sad, so very sad." Mention was made that Frank Thorogood, having discovered Brian lying on the bottom of the pool, had called Anna from the house and together they pulled Brian out and tried to revive him. All this, the paper said, happened just after 11:00 P.M. Ambulance men arrived at 11:40 P.M. Well, I was there at 11:15 P.M., and I had seen three other men there. Could it be that they had been trying to rescue Brian?

In the *Daily Express* Mick was quoted as saying, "I think the only help we can give Brian is by going ahead with the concert"— (tomorrow's free concert in Hyde Park)—"and by so doing to give all the love that was supposed to be . . . and give it to Brian. I am just so unhappy." Bloody pompous, I thought.

Both papers gave the probable cause of death as an asthmatic attack while swimming. I just couldn't believe it. There was no mention of the three men. The inquest was to be held on Monday, they said, but it would probably be adjourned for further tests.

When Sara came back, I said, "What goes on at an inquest?"

"Honestly, you're so unworldly," she said, not for the first time. "It's to investigate how a person died. The cause of death, Why?" I hesitated, not sure whether to tell her the whole story.

"Oh, it just says here there'll be an inquest on Brian. Monday."

"D'you think you ought to go?"

"Why?"

"Well, you were with him earlier. They might want to know if he was suffering from asthma."

"Oh, there were plenty of people with him after that. No, it's nothing to do with me. I can't help."

In the afternoon, when Sara was out having her hair done for that night's party, I tried to think logically about the whole thing, though the effect of the pills and my depression over Brian's death made it difficult.

If those three men had really been trying to rescue Brian, why had the man with the glasses given me that warning ". . . or you'll be the next?" It sounded pretty unambiguous. And if it was a rescue attempt, why was the kneeling man pressing down instead of pulling, and why did the other one dive onto his back? Just clumsiness? Or had I allowed my imagination to run away with me? No, nothing made any sense except that Brian was being murdered and I had witnessed it. Then, shouldn't I go to the police? Oh God, what a fuss that would make in the family. Were the police likely to believe me? Maybe they could find Cadbury and he would back me up. How dangerous was it likely to be if I did go to the police? The man who had warned me off knew my name.

The phone kept interrupting my thoughts, now that Sara had gone. My mother called and said she was sorry to hear of the death of my "musical friend." Numerous friends phoned to commiserate. Oddly, there was no call from Suki Potier.

I was shocked and horrified when one of my friends told me that the Stones had gone ahead with their appearance the previous night live on "Top of the Pops." They had been plugging their latest record, "Honky Tonk Women." Surely they could have called that off on the day their founder and their most talented member had been declared dead? *My God*, I thought, *what a callous business it all was*. Brian had arranged the number—but I believe it was re-recorded without him.

After Sara had left for Prince Rupert Loewenstein's party that evening, I decided to call a man called D, a shady character who hung out on the fringes of the "in" crowd and was able to put them in touch with drug pushers, procurers, moneylenders, bodyguards and bullyboys, to ask his advice on going to the police. But just as I went to the phone, it rang again.

It was Carolyn Benson, a friend of Sara's, asking whether she had left for the party. I told her she had.

She told me that Mick and Marianne had already arrived and that Keith and Anita were coming.

Sickened, I said, "I would have thought they'd let Brian's body get cold before they started party-going. I suppose Mick's dressed in white, as arranged?"

"Oh yes, a kind of white tunic."

"God," I said. "How's Marianne taking it?"

"She looks really upset. She's the only one in black. I don't think she really wanted to come. You know, everyone was supposed to be dressed in white."

"Yes," I mumbled. "I suppose you know the Stones went on 'Top of the Pops' last night?"

"Oh yes," she said brightly. "Weren't they good? They'll soon be back at the top of the charts. They deserve to be."

Not without Brian they won't, I thought. I slammed the phone down in disgust.

Then I rang D, told him what I had seen and asked what I should do.

"Keep out of it, son," he said quietly, in that husky voice with the cockney accent, so familiar among the rich youngsters of London.

"You don't think I ought to go to the police? It looks as if he was murdered."

"All the more reason not to go, old son. It's been in the cards a long time, anyway. He's been gettin' too much of a pain in too many people's asses."

"How d'you mean?" I said, bewildered.

"Oh well, if you don't know, I can't tell you."

"Couldn't I go to the police and get protection—or get some bodyguards from you?"

"Yeah," he said, with a little chuckle. "Listen, son, if the orders go out to get you, you'll be got. Don't make no mistakes about that. They got the two Kennedys, didn't they? If they can get them when they're in the middle of a bleedin' army of bodyguards you got no chance, my son. Just keep yer 'ead down and yer mouth shut, that's my advice. It's a more dangerous world than you seem to reckon on."

For a long time I sat and thought about Brian and considered D's advice. Then I took some Valium and got into bed. *Keep my head down*, I thought, *and keep my mouth shut*. Brian was dead. Nothing would bring him back.

Hyde Park, London, July 5, 1969

Mick Jagger glanced nervously to his right as he fumbled with a small book containing sheets of tear-stained paper on which Marianne Faithfull had copied stanzas 39 and 53 of Shelley's *Adonais*. One of the two huge, blown-up color photographs of Brian Jones stared defiantly back at him.

Mick Taylor, Brian's replacement, stood well back in line with the other three Stones. Brian Jones, Jagger's only contender for leadership and magnetism, was gone.

Mick's eyes fell from the photograph and rested for a moment on Marianne's face—a face that had once been a mirror image of Brian's, but which now was swollen and contorted with grief. She sat opposite me, nursing and clutching at her young son, Nicholas. She was utterly devastated.

It was being estimated that a quarter of a million people were out there on the grass facing their idol. I had been permitted to perch myself on the edge of the high platform constructed of scaffold and boards.

Jagger said into the microphone, "Now listen, cool it for a while. I really would like to say something about Brian, and about how we feel about him going when we didn't expect it."

Mick was nervous, broken up.

As the vast audience that filled about a quarter of the park began to hush, their eardrums were assaulted by the master of ceremonies, Sam Cutler, bawling into another microphone again to announce that the Stones wanted everyone to observe a minute's silence in Brian's memory.

Amazingly the multitudinous voices ceased, and the silence was such that the traffic around the park became audible. The Hell's Angels—the self-appointed police at all outdoor pop concerts—patrolled the crowd, wearing Nazi helmets and insignia. It was a hot day, and many of the youngsters were half-naked. Among the upturned sea of faces were many wet with tears.

On the stage, Mick Jagger glanced over at Marsha Hunt, a star in the musical *Hair* and a future girlfriend of Mick's, who was standing behind me. She looked as if she had come direct from Prince Rupert's party, dressed in white buckskin. She nodded at him, as if in encouragement. Now that he was undisputed king of the Stones, he looked lonely. He looked vulnerable.

Charlie, Bill and Keith all had their eyes turned downward, as if in thought or prayer. Mick Taylor was edgy and nervous, as if the ghost of Brian was haunting him.

As for me, I didn't really know why I was there. I was so full of Valium I almost rattled when I moved. I gazed at the giant poster of the man who had been my friend; then I turned to Jagger. Our eyes met for an instant, and his were hostile. Then he lifted his head and raised the paper to his eyes.

> "Peace, peace! He is not dead, he doth not sleep—
> He hath awakened from the dream of life—
> 'Tis we, who lost in stormy visions, keep
> With phantoms an unprofitable strife . . ."

It was ridiculous, ludicrous, I thought. The least they could have done was bring on someone who could have read these inspiring lines with conviction. Somone like Richard Burton. Or at worst some trendy priest or out-of-work Shakespearean ham. Instead, there was Mick Jagger, wearing a white, bow-buttoned blouse that was almost like a minidress over tight white pants, and with a gold-studded dog collar around his neck, piping away like somebody reading a weather forecast.

Looking at Brian's giant image again, I half expected him to be smiling wickedly or winking at me. Turning away with a lump in my throat, I longed for that familiar, playful pat on the shoulder. I could almost hear him saying, "Hey, what's all this about? Jagger going into poetry now?"

Yet out there, where the sea of faces stretched as far as I could see, there were tears enough to raise the level of the Serpentine Lake.

"Life, like a dome of many-colored glass,
Stains the white radiance of Eternity
Until Death tramples it to fragments—Die,
If thou wouldst be that which thou dost seek."

Vaguely, I was aware that the sham of a recital was now over. Road managers and other helpers were lifting cardboard boxes and opening them, shaking them. A few white butterflies flew out and a lot of dead ones fell to the floor. The butterflies, which had been intended to fly off in a white cloud to symbolize the soul of Brian ascending, had been kept enclosed too long in the heat, and even the survivors flew drowsily down into the spectators.

I heard a voice behind me saying something like, "That was a bloody stupid idea, wasn't it?" The last time I had heard that voice it had said, "Get out of here, Fitzgerald, or you'll be the next."

Panic-stricken, I turned and saw a man in a red cardigan and white trousers. He had his back to me. He was burly. I climbed quickly from the stage and made my way around the edge of the crowd.

Already Keith was playing the opening bars of "Lemon Squeezer." Already the fans were drying their eyes and beginning to squeal and scream in delight.

But as I slipped for the last time from the company of the privileged "in" crowd around the Stones, accompanied only by my chauffeur, I recalled those words I had read of John Lennon talking to Brian Epstein: "The Rolling Stones will break up over Brian Jones' dead body." Now Epstein was dead as well, so he would never see it. And neither would I, because without Brian Jones, to me, the Stones had already become a phenomenon of the past. I tore up my blue and red backstage passes and handed them to a bemused "Guardian Angel."

In the New York Post about that time, Al Aronowitz wrote an article, concluding: "It was only several weeks ago that Brian announced he was leaving the Stones and Mick Jagger announced that a guitarist named Mick Taylor would replace Brian. Replace Brian? Over his dead body."

Cheltenham, Thursday, July 10, 1969

The chauffeur steered the Bentley swiftly and silently around Oxford and began the gentle climb into the Cotswold Hills. Sara was at my side in the rear. I didn't know much about funerals. The papers had said it was to be a private one and hadn't mentioned where it was to be, though all the "in" crowd soon found out. I considered that Brian's parents would not mind my turning up. It had also been rumored among the "in" crowd that the police had requested the more famous among Brian's friends to stay away, as it would be difficult for them to control the crowd of fans that even a private funeral would attract.

I was dazed and numbed with drugs. Sara and I said little during the journey. What was going on in my mind over and over were the events of the past eight days.

The sensational and speculative stories in the Sunday papers had shocked and sickened me almost as much as the death itself. It seemed that the platitude "life must go on" had been followed to the ultimate degree. Everyone—or almost everyone—who had even brushed shoulders with Brian Jones had some earth-shattering, flesh-creeping scandal to relate about him, which the worst of the rags gleefully embellished and regurgitated onto their front pages.

The *News of the World* ran on an inside page an article by Edward Trevor under the heading THE TRUTH ABOUT BRIAN JONES. It was a travesty and almost made me vomit.

The People used the front page banner headline THE SHOCKING TRUTH ABOUT BRIAN JONES over an exclusive, sordid story by an ex-chauffeur, Brian Palastanga.

The *Sunday Mirror* carried an article by Dick Hattrell, who claimed he had been a "brother" to Brian over the past fifteen years. He said that Brian had been on the downward path. I wondered what kind of "brother" he had been. Long-lost, maybe. Certainly I had never met him over the past four years, when Brian could have done with a brother, though I had heard Brian occasionally mention someone called Dick.

The French newspapers were saying that Brian Jones had died of a heroin overdose. But he had never taken heroin, the killer drug. If he had, with his insatiable appetites he would have overdosed long before.

Then on Monday the inquest was held at East Grinstead. In the papers on Tuesday it was reported that a verdict of misadventure had been recorded—that he had drowned while under the influence of alchohol and drugs. It was reported that Anna Wohlin said in evidence that she left Brian "to answer the telephone."

Janet Lawson was quoted as saying she had known Jones for about a year and had decided to spend a few days at his farm. She had been worried about Brian swimming in his state of intoxication, and felt she should keep an eye on him and Frank Thorogood, who had also been drinking. According to the report I read, she went on, "Finally, [Brian] flopped into the pool and managed to make some strokes, but they were rather sluggish. I left him swimming for a few minutes and when I returned I saw him lying face down at the bottom of the pool. Frank had gone into the house to fetch a towel." *Perhaps a cigarette as well,* I thought. I wished I could recall what the man and woman I'd seen at the left of the pool had been wearing. But it was gone from my mind completely.

Then last night I was told by telephone that Marianne Faithfull had taken a massive overdose of tablets at the Chevron Hotel in Sydney, Australia, where she had flown with Mick on Sunday for the shooting of the film *Ned Kelly,* and that she was now in the intensive care unit at St. Vincent's Hospital in a coma.

It was all pressing in on me. I asked the driver to pull up at a hotel. He told me that the pubs weren't open, but Sara said she would fix that. We stopped at a small hotel in the next village. Sara went to the side door and before long emerged by way of the front door followed by a clearly impressed landlord who, gazing at the gleaming Bentley, ushered us in. We ordered two large drinks and sat on stools at the bar.

After a while Sara looked nervously at me as I gazed vacantly ahead. "You're going to miss him a lot, aren't you?" she said.

I nodded.

Encouraged that this time I had actually acknowledged one of her questions, she said, "You've heard the rumors, I suppose, about Anita's baby?"

"Yes," I said. Anita's baby was expected next month.

"Whose do you think it is?"

For a moment I didn't answer, and she probably thought I was going back into the silent gloom that had enveloped me for more than a week now. But I was thinking about that telephone call from Anita to Brian at Cotchford five weeks ago. I thought about the call this morning from Pat Andrews, who had had Brian's child. Pat had intended to come with us to the funeral but had been too ill to go. And I thought about Brian's other lovers: Linda Lawrence, Linda Keith, Suki Potier . . . and Anita Pallenberg. If Brian had lived, would he and Anita have gotten together again?

At last I said, "I don't really like gossip of that sort. Now that Brian's gone it would be better for everyone if it's accepted as Keith's baby."

I cursed myself as I noticed that the landlord was listening to every word. He could see we were dressed for a funeral. If he was only reasonably bright it wouldn't take him long to put two and two together and make a few hundred.

The last time Brian Jones had upset the genteel and respectable image of The Royal Borough of Cheltenham Spa was in 1958, when he had impregnated a fourteen-year-old schoolgirl. That story had made the national press. After the baby was born it was adopted, and the outraged town simmered down to its slow and easy pace again. Brian soon disappeared from the scene. When he later became famous not many of the natives even knew that he was a son of Cheltenham.

Today, for the second time, Brian stunned the Royal Borough— this time as the most celebrated corpse to be carried into the portals of its parish church for many a long year; and to bring with him what to Cheltenham was a "bunch of long-haired scruffs" from all over Europe and the U.K. It seemed that half the population of the Borough was out in the streets and in the churchyard. Also, he brought along for good measure press and TV cameras from all over the world. And this was what they called a private funeral? It would have been more private in the middle of Trafalgar Square on May Day. The small contingent of police was hopelessly inadequate to control the crowd beseiging the church, but as the magnificent coffin was taken from the hearse and along the path to the church entrance, the people respectfully parted. This was at least in part due to the skill and dignity of the undertakers, who were always used by the Royal Family. A policeman stood on either side of the church porch, presumably to ensure that no undesirables were admitted, but as they were dealing with pop music people, it must have been difficult to know who was undesirable and who was famous. Anyway, Sara and I were admitted without trouble, possibly because we had had to bring our wreaths from London—Cheltenham's fourteen florists were unable to cope with the demand. We handed them to the undertaker's assistant and followed the mourners through the gothic entrance of the ancient church. Asked who we were by an usher inside, we were found a place to the rear on the left-hand side of the aisle.

Over to our right were Keith Richard, Anita Pallenberg, Mick Taylor and Spanish Tony. Further back were Tom Keylock, Frank Thorogood, Bill Wyman and his girlfriend Astrid Lundstrom, Charlie and Shirley Watts, Michael and Ginger Cooper, Les Perrin, Don Short, Linda Lawrence and Shirley Arnold, among many others.

Mick, of course, was not there. He had no alternative about going to Australia. All the schedules for the shooting of the film *Ned Kelly* had been set up a long time ago, and he would have had to break his contract to attend the funeral.

Looking around, I was surprised I couldn't see Alexis Korner anywhere, nor Andrew Oldham, nor Allen Klein. Also, I had heard that George Harrison and Bob Dylan were planning to come, but there was no sign of either. Maybe they had decided to assist the police by staying away. I was particularly interested to see if Anna Wohlin was there, and though I looked all around like a curious boy she seemed to be conspicuous by her absence.

A lot of the women appeared deeply distressed. All the Jones family—including a large contingent from Wales—were, of course, at the front of the church, maintaining a stoic dignity. Keith Richard looked near to a breakdown. Keylock and Thorogood just appeared very serious. Suki was up front with the family. Anita looked devastated and drained of life.

I was dazed and followed very little of the service as my eyes wandered about this great cave of a church and the voice of Canon Hopkins boomed around the walls and bounced down on us from the beamed roofs and lofts. Explaining his decision to allow a church service, the Canon read a telegram Brian had sent to his parents on that day back in May 1967 when he had been arrested and charged with unlawful possession of Indian hemp. The message was simple: "'Please don't worry. Don't jump to hasty conclusions and please don't judge me too harshly. All my love, Brian.' Here I believe Brian speaks to us, not only for himself but also for all his generation . . ." My mind was unable to take in any more. I vaguely heard him tell the story of the Prodigal Son and offer a brief prayer for the recovery of "the girl in Australia—Marianne."

When it was over and the family and friends followed the bronze coffin outside, I decided to stay in the church until all the circus out there was over. Sara and I would wait somewhere then for the end of the masquerade that was bound to take place at Priory Road Cemetery in Prestbury, where the body was to be interred. A couple of hours would do it, I thought. Maybe we would have some lunch and a drink.

Just as we prepared to leave the church, I saw that Keith and Anita were still sitting in their pews, stunned and miserable, as if they hardly had the will to live, let alone get up and go.

As things turned out, we were wise to wait before going on to the cemetery. I learned later what a sacrilegious pantomime had been enacted with the press and TV cameramen brawling at the gravesite to take pictures as the coffin was lowered in.

Later I gazed across a sea of flowers that stretched around the grave for a quarter of an acre. They were beautiful. Beyond were the gently rolling hills of the Cotswolds, where the fields are edged by dry-stone walls. The cemetery church was near the grave—a typically English medieval church with a slim spire rising above the spruce trees that were dotted about between the graves.

Many people were still hovering about, some on their knees in prayer, many of them reading the messages on the flowers.

At last Brian had attained peace in this haven on the edge of Cheltenham. I found my own wreath—of yellow roses—and saw my last tribute to him elegantly inscribed:

SLAN LEIBH GRADH—GOODBYE MY FRIEND